William Blake 1757–1827

P_g Canto 29 & 30

TATE GALLERY COLLECTIONS: VOLUME FIVE

William Blake
1757 - 1827

Martin Butlin

THE TATE GALLERY

LONDON

in association with

UNIVERSITY OF WASHINGTON PRESS

SEATTLE

frontispiece
Beatrice addressing Dante from the Car 1824–7
(detail)

ISBN 1 85437 014 6
Published by order of the Trustees 1990
Copyright © 1990 The Tate Gallery All rights reserved
Designed and published by Tate Gallery Publications,
Millbank, London SW1P 4RG
Phototypeset by Keyspools Limited, Golborne, Lancs
Printed in Great Britain by Balding + Mansell UK Limited

ISBN 0 295 96952 0
Published in North America by
University of Washington Press
P.O. Box 50096, Seattle, WA 98145

CONTENTS

PREFACE

7

ACKNOWLEDGEMENTS

9

THE FORMATION OF THE COLLECTION

11

THE ART OF WILLIAM BLAKE

17

CHRONOLOGY

27

EXHIBITIONS

32

LITERATURE

34

CONCORDANCE

38

CATALOGUE NOTE

41

93.50

CATALOGUE ENTRIES

42

Early Works *c.*1779–*c.*1793 [42]   Miscellaneous Illuminated Books 1789–1795 [71]

The Large Colour Prints *c.*1795–1805 [82]   Tempera Paintings *c.*1799–1800 [106]

Illustrations to the Bible 1800–1805 [118]   Blake's Exhibition 1809 [145]

Visionary Heads *c.*1819–1825 [153]   Late Works 1820–1827 [165]

The Book of Job *c.*1821–1826 [185]   Dante's Divine Comedy 1824–1827 [202]

Attributed to Robert Blake 1767–1787 [242]   Formerly Attributed to William Blake [247]

APPENDIX

249

PREFACE

This is the third edition of the catalogue of the works by William Blake in the Tate Gallery first published in 1957 in celebration of the Blake bicentenary year; a second, completely revised edition was published in 1971. Two essays that appeared in the earlier editions have reluctantly been omitted: that on 'The Formation of the Collection' by John Rothenstein, and that on 'The Art of William Blake' by Anthony Blunt. No amount of up-dating could disguise the fact that these essays are now over thirty years old. However, part of John Rothenstein's first-hand account of the acquisition of works by William Blake during his Directorship has been incorporated in the new article on 'The Formation of the Collection' contributed by Krzysztof Cieszkowski, Assistant Librarian at the Tate Gallery, and Anthony Blunt's important contribution to Blake studies can be found in his book *The Art of William Blake* published in 1959.

The scope of the catalogue itself has been considerably enlarged by giving fuller treatment to all the engravings by Blake in the collection. These engravings are not unique works and have been fully dealt with in other publications; the treatment is therefore not as full as in the case of the unique works already catalogued in the two previous editions. It was thought, however, that they should be included and treated in rather more than list form to give a more complete picture of the collection and William Blake's work as a whole. In addition a number of works have been acquired since the edition of 1971, including two important paintings in tempera. A colour print by W. Graham Robertson in which he sought to reproduce Blake's unique technique, acquired for the Tate Gallery archive in 1976, is included as an Appendix. After this catalogue went to press the Tate acquired from Mr David C. Preston, through Christie's, 'A Vision: The Inspiration of the Poet'; it was purchased through the great generosity of Mr Edwin Cohen and the General Atlantic Partners Foundation. Full details of this work which is associated with the 'Visionary Heads' (catalogue numbers 61–67) are found on page 251 after the Appendix. It has been catalogued by Robin Hamlyn.

All the earlier entries on Blake's paintings, watercolours and drawings have been fully revised on the basis of the entries in the author's more general catalogue of *The Paintings and Drawings of William Blake*, published for the Paul Mellon Centre for Studies in British Art by Yale University Press in 1981, the publication of which was initiated by the William Blake Trust and made possible by gifts from Mr Paul Mellon and the Yale Center for British Art. Revision to the material published in 1981 has been confined largely to an up-dating of the literature and exhibitions. However, the discovery late in 1981 that some of the large colour prints, though dated 1795 by Blake himself, are on paper watermarked 1804 has meant a considerable rethinking of the section on this group of works. An important reassessment of Blake's illustrations to Dante's *Divine Comedy*, published by David Fuller in 1988, has also been taken into account, as has the appearance of a second

Blake-Varley sketchbook containing examples of Blake's 'Visionary Heads'.

This edition is more fully illustrated than before, with more works being reproduced in colour. It takes its place as one in a continuing series of detailed catalogues of works in the Tate Gallery. Most of these deal with complete periods, such as that by Elizabeth Einberg and Judy Egerton on *The Age of Hogarth: British Painters Born 1675–1709,* published 1988. Other individual artists have however been treated, John Constable in Leslie Parris's *The Tate Gallery Constable Collection,* 1981, and the Tate Gallery's oil paintings by Turner, together with those in other collections, in Martin Butlin and Evelyn Joll, *The Paintings of J.M.W. Turner,* 1977, second revised edition 1984. Future acquisitions of works by Blake, as in the case of other artists, will be catalogued in the Tate Gallery's biennial publication, the *Illustrated Catalogue of Acquisitions,* and, in the case of Blake and artists close to him, acquisitions will also be reported in the periodical *Blake, an Illustrated Quarterly.*

The Blake collection at the Tate Gallery owes much to the scholarship and insights of Martin Butlin, Keeper of the Historic British Collection since 1967. I thank him most warmly for the care and dedication which he has brought to Blake studies over this long period.

Nicholas Serota *Director*

ACKNOWLEDGEMENTS

Much of the material for the original 1957 edition of this catalogue came from two sources. In the first place, for works acquired before 1942, I was able to use information on previous owners, exhibitions and reproductions prepared and kindly presented to the Tate Gallery by Ruthven Todd. Similarly, such information about works in the collection of W. Graham Robertson was based on entries in *The Blake Collection of W. Graham Robertson*, edited by Kerrison Preston, published by Faber & Faber in 1952. I was also greatly helped by advice and further information from Anthony Blunt, Sir Geoffrey Keynes and Kerrison Preston. For the second edition of 1971 I continued to benefit from the advice of Blake scholars, too many to have mentioned individually by name. However, in addition to those mentioned above I received particular benefit from conversations and correspondence with Professor G.E. Bentley, Jr., Professor David Bindman and Professor David Erdman, and I also received assistance from Robert N. Essick, John E. Grant, Ruth E. Fine, Morton D. Paley, Charles Ryskamp, Michael J. Tolley, Robert R. Wark and Edwin Wolf 2nd. My work on the large catalogue of *The Paintings and Drawings of William Blake* of 1981 was largely financed by the William Blake Trust under its Chairman Sir Geoffrey Keynes and I am greatly indebted to them as also to John Nicoll at the Yale University Press who subsequently took over the publication. For this publication I was indebted, as before, to those listed above with in addition, among others, Gabriel Austin and Nicholas Draffin and my colleagues at the Tate Gallery, particularly Leslie Parris and Judy Egerton; the full list of my indebtedness is given in the Acknowledgements in that book. My latest revisions are, yet again, dependent on both published and unpublished contributions by Blake scholars including, as well as those mentioned above, Eleanor Garvey, Jenijoy La Belle and, among others in the Tate Gallery Conservation Department, Anna Southall and Kasia Szeleynski; John Mills of the National Gallery has kindly analysed the medium of 'Moses Indignant at the Golden Calf'. Finally I must thank the four Directors of the Tate Gallery who have presided over and encouraged the publication of successive editions of this catalogue, Sir John Rothenstein, Sir Norman Reid, Sir Alan Bowness and Nicholas Serota.

Martin Butlin
July 1989

THE FORMATION OF THE COLLECTION

A combination of opportunity and availability, individual generosity and financial possibility, has determined the nature and composition of the Tate Gallery's Blake collection – the same factors as have operated on the accumulation of the Gallery's collections as a whole. At no point was a formal decision taken to bring together a discrete collection of works by Blake, but the opening of the Tate Gallery in 1897 coincided with a widespread if belated recognition of Blake's stature as one of England's supreme painters as well as poets, and the works that were acquired by the Tate, uniquely diverse in their medium and format, necessarily assumed the aspect of a separate collection.

Almost a century had to pass following Blake's death before he received official, institutional recognition. In the nineteenth century Blake had been accorded only grudging mention or none at all by Redgrave and Palgrave in their respective anthological compilations, and his work had been dismissed as eccentric or inept, esoteric or insane. Since then, however, both scholarly and popular interest in Blake's work has intensified, and his supreme stature is now established. This interest has been both reflected and promoted by the Tate Gallery in the ninety years of its existence: a fortuitous combination of judicious pursuit and generous donation has resulted in the Tate's now possessing one of the richest and most comprehensive collections of Blake's paintings and watercolours in the world, and this collection and its concomitant exhibitions have done much to establish Blake's stature in the public mind.

The Tate acquired its first two works by Blake in 1909 (nos.41 and 71) by transfer from the National Gallery, to which they had been presented in 1878 by George Thomas Saul. Two further works, nos.59 and 39, were transferred from the National Gallery in 1931 and 1934 – ironically, the latter work had belonged to Palgrave, who had presented it to the National Gallery in 1884. Alfred de Pass presented a watercolour drawing to the Tate in 1910 (no.5), and two paintings in tempera were acquired in 1914 – no.58 by purchase and no.36 through the National Art-Collections Fund.

While there has been a sporadic influx of works up to the present time, two occasions in particular have enriched the collection and established its unique composition – the acquisition of works from the Linnell sale of 1918, and the W. Graham Robertson gift 1939 (together with his subsequent bequest of 1948).

John Linnell, Blake's young disciple as well as patron, had been instrumental in commissioning most of the works of the last six years of Blake's life, and these remained in the possession of his family until they were put up for sale at Christie's by his grandson, Herbert Linnell (d.1937), on 15 March 1918. This was by far the greatest collection of Blake's works ever to appear on the open market, and its chief treasure was lot 148, the unfinished series of 102 illustrations to Dante's *Divine Comedy* which Blake had drawn in the last years of his life.

This should have been a unique opportunity for the Tate (then still the National Gallery of British Art, dependent by statute on the National Gallery), but unfortunately its Director, Charles Aitken (1869–1936), had no purchase grant at his disposal. Wartime circumstances had removed most of his potential sources of funding, and the imminent implementation of the 1915 Curzon Report's recommendations on the administrative separation of the Tate from the National Gallery had resulted in a period of financial uncertainty. An added problem arose when Herbert Linnell turned down Aitken's request that the Dante drawings be auctioned individually rather than as one lot, apparently on the grounds that this would have created problems for the auctioneers.

Unable to bid for the entire series on behalf of the Tate, Aitken was obliged to devise a strategy for sharing out the cost of the series among a number of interested parties. Within the space of a few days he appealed to the Gallery's benefactors for donations in connection with the purchase, ascertained the wishes and intentions of a number of other public institutions and private individuals, and successfully acquired the Dante illustrations on behalf of an unofficial consortium for the sum of 7,500 guineas (£7,665), heading off a rumoured American attempt to purchase the entire series.

The subsequent division of the series may appear regrettable in hindsight, but was unavoidable given the financial circumstances at the time. The procedure of division was undertaken according to an elaborate codified system devised by Aitken and supervised by Charles Ricketts, Laurence Binyon of the British Museum and Charles Holmes of the National Gallery. In accordance with this system, the 102 works were separated into four categories of presumed desirability and apportioned among the participating institutions and individuals in proportion to the amount of money they were able to contribute to the consortium. The twelve drawings that were presumed to be the least important or attractive were put aside as the 'debris' (Ricketts's phrase) of the series, and the remaining ninety were divided into three categories; each contribution of £250 entitled the participant to one share, consisting of three works, one from each category. Furthermore, the order in which participants selected works in each category was scrupulously regulated by Aitken.

The National Art-Collections Fund acted as banker for the consortium, 'thus enabling several public galleries which wished to acquire some of the drawings, but lacked funds to buy the whole collection, to combine in a joint purchase' (*16th Annual Report*, 1919); the Fund raised the sum of £9,022.13.0 specifically for the purchase of the Dante illustrations and some other works included in the sale.

As a result, the Tate Gallery acquired twenty of the Dante drawings (nos. 131–150), among them some of the finest in the series; the money for this purchase, the most significant since the foundation of the Gallery twenty-one years earlier, came from its parent-body the National Gallery (£581 from the Clarke Fund), the National Art-Collections Fund, and a number of individual benefactors, including Lord Duveen (who contributed £2,000), Lady Wernher and Sir Edward Marsh.

The rest of the watercolours in the series went to the National Gallery of Victoria, Melbourne (36 works – Robert Ross [1869–1918], Oscar Wilde's friend and literary executor, had strongly urged the purchase in his capacity as London

Adviser to the Felton Bequest), the British Museum (13), the City Art Gallery, Birmingham (6), the Ashmolean Museum (3) and the Truro Museum (1 work, presented by Alfred de Pass, who in 1910 had given a Blake watercolour, no. 5, to the Tate). Charles Ricketts himself acquired four works, which in 1943 entered the Fogg Art Museum at Harvard University, as did a further nineteen works which had passed through various American private collections. Thus the unfinished series of watercolour drawings dating from the last three years of Blake's life, the 'great book (folio)' in which the bedridden Blake was drawing when the young Samuel Palmer saw him for the first time in October 1824, is currently divided between seven public and university museum collections in England, Australia and the United States.

The elaborate process of division seems to have been concluded to the satisfaction of all of its beneficiaries: Ricketts complimented Aitken on the result – 'I feel you worked heroically in this matter which was badly started', and C.F. Bell, of the Ashmolean Museum, wrote 'I feel that we have been treated most nobly and have every reason to be gratified and grateful'.

However, mistakes had been made and not everybody was satisfied: the Curator and Chairman of the Whitworth Art Gallery, Manchester, Robert Bateman and Walter Butterworth, complained that 'we have not been well treated' – the Whitworth had been among the institutions originally offering to participate in the consortium, but a misunderstanding seems to have resulted in its offer being mislaid. As a result the Whitworth was excluded from the share-out of the works in the series, and only belatedly was it offered what 'can justly be described as almost the dregs of the collection', which it turned down. James L. Caw, of the National Gallery of Scotland, likewise did not feel justified in recommending purchase of the works his gallery was offered in the post-auction share-out, considering them inferior and of little actual merit.

Among the other letters of congratulations, however, Aitken received the following from a schoolmaster in Bristol, George H. Leonard, who had lectured on Blake to the troops in France (but had been prevented from using lantern-slides of Blake's work, on grounds of security). On 7 April 1918 he wrote to Aitken:

> I wanted to write as a private person, to thank you for what you have done in getting these things for the Nation – and Empire. There are public thanks, I know, of a sort – but I thought I should like to say that there are private people who care very much indeed to know that these treasures will now be available for all, and who feel they must add their private thanks to you and others.

(Unless otherwise stated, all letters quoted selectively or in their entirety in this essay are in the Public Records of the Tate Gallery kept in the Archive Department.)

In addition to its share of the Dante illustrations, the Tate also acquired a set of the seven completed engravings made from the Dante illustrations (nos. 152–8), a full set of twenty-two engravings for *The Book of Job* (nos. 109–130), and two separate colour-printed pages from *Visions of the Daughters of Albion* (nos. 21–2).

A tempera panel (no. 70) was presented to the Tate in 1918 by Miss M.H. Dodge, and a painting in tempera and other media (no. 60) was bought in 1920. In 1922 a watercolour (no. 55) and a portfolio of drawings (nos. 2, 7, 9–10, 23, 43, 50, 53–4, 107, 151,), together with fragments from the illuminated books (nos. 15–20) and drawings by Blake's younger brother Robert (nos.166–9), were presented to the Tate by Mrs John Richmond – these had belonged to Frederick Tatham, Blake's self-appointed executor, and subsequently to his brother-in-law George Richmond. In 1924 Herbert Linnell presented the Gallery with a set of wood engravings for Thornton's *Virgil*, printed by John Linnell from the blocks cut by Blake in 1821 (nos.73–89).

The next fifteen years saw no further additions to the Tate's Blake collection, and the lack of an independent purchase-fund meant that in the 1920s and 1930s a number of important opportunities were missed. It was the outbreak of the Second World War, however, that was the direct occasion of the Tate's acquiring some of the finest works in its Blake collection, namely the large colour prints which had belonged to Blake's friend and patron Thomas Butts (nos.25–33). These had come into the possession of the painter and theatrical 'angel' W. Graham Robertson (1866–1948), who in 1931 had written that his Blake collection represented 'one of my few excuses for existence'.

On 3 September 1939 Robertson wrote to John (later Sir John) Rothenstein, Director of the Tate since 1938, offering to hand over the works in his collection that he planned to leave to the Tate, in order to protect them from the anticipated dangers the War would bring:

> I am looking round to find a place of safety for my London pictures and it has occurred to me that, as some of them are dedicated to the Tate Gallery in my will, you might care to take charge of them. For instance, the set of 9 large colour-printed designs by William Blake which you admired much in my house ... – Blake's most important pictures and the very flower of his work. I am rising 74 and pretty shaky, and the return of peace is not likely to find me here so – if you cared to find a harbour of refuge for these pictures – I could present them to the Tate at once.

As well as the Blakes, the collection included works by Rossetti, Whistler and Sargent. Robertson elsewhere commented that, at this time, the Director of the Tate Gallery 'had a magnificent Blake gallery without a single first-rate Blake in it', disliking as he did most of the Dante illustrations, which he regarded as 'the work of a sick man at the end of his powers' (*Time Was: Reminiscences*, 1945).

There was no time for the Trustees (who at this time included Augustus John and Sir Edward Marsh) to meet to consider this offer, and instead they immediately approved acceptance of the bequest by post. Robertson's gift greatly enriched the Tate's Blake collection, although the works rested only briefly in the Gallery before being evacuated from London along with the entire collection of the Tate Gallery – as Rothenstein wrote at the end of September 1939, in a letter to Robertson, 'Even leaning against the wall in a dimly lit passage during their brief sojourn here they made a brilliant show'.

Happily longevity prevailed, and Robertson lived to see the restoration of peace; following his death in 1948, nine years to the day after the Tate had received his offer, four more Blakes from his collection were bequeathed to the Tate (nos.34, 52, 64, 69), and a further eight were presented to the Gallery by his executors through the National Art-Collections Fund (nos.14, 37–8, 44, 47–9, 51).

A further major bequest of works by Blake occurred in 1940, when Miss Alice

Carthew bequeathed a quantity of drawings and watercolours, including several of the Visionary Heads executed for the benefit of John Varley, which she had bought at the Linnell sale in 1918 (nos. 1, 4, 6, 8, 40, 56, 63, 65–7; also five copies after Blake, nos. 24, 42, 45–6, 72).

In 1941 the novelist Sir Hugh Walpole (1884–1941) bequeathed a drawing to the Tate (no.57). A watercolour of 'Los and Orc', no.13, which had belonged to Apsley Cherry-Garrard (who had been a member of Scott's ill-fated expedition to the South Pole in 1910–12 and in 1922 had published the definitive account of the expedition), was bequeathed to the Gallery by Mrs Jane Samuel in 1962. In 1969 the drawing 'An Allegory of the Bible', no.3, was bequeathed to the Tate by Miss Rachel Dyer, granddaughter of Alexander Macmillan, the original publisher of Gilchrist's *Life of William Blake*.

More recent acquisitions have included modern impressions from Blake's engraved plates for the Dante illustrations (nos. 159–65), presented in 1975 by Lessing J. Rosenwald, and from his wood engravings for the illustrations for Thornton's *Virgil* (nos. 90–106), presented in 1977 by British Museum Publications. A sheet with two drawings dating from 1821–3 (no.108) was presented to the Gallery by the Friends of the Tate Gallery in 1981. Three recent acquisitions are the tempera works 'Winter' (no.68), originally painted for the Reverend John Johnson in the 1820s and bought from a family sale in 1979, 'Moses Indignant at the Golden Calf' (no. 35), bequeathed to the Gallery in 1986 by Ian L. Phillips, and 'A Vision: The Inspiration of the Poet' purchased 1989.

The Tate Gallery's Blake collection can be regarded as representing all the phases of Blake's work in tempera and watercolour; although there are fine examples of his Virgil, Job and Dante engravings in the collection, as well as individual pages from the illuminated books, the major national collections of his engraved work are those in the British Museum and the Victoria and Albert Museum. Some areas of Blake's artistic activity, notably the watercolour illustrations to Milton and the large-scale tempera paintings, are more fully represented in the Blake collections of the Fitzwilliam Museum in Cambridge (particularly since its recent acquisition by bequest of the magnificent collection of the late Sir Geoffrey Keynes, 1887–1982), the Whitworth Art Gallery in Manchester, the Fogg Art Museum at Harvard University (Cambridge, Massachusetts), the Museum of Fine Arts in Boston, the Pierpont Morgan Library in New York, and the Henry E. Huntington Library and Art Gallery in San Marino, California.

In addition to displaying its collection and publishing documentary and scholarly material on the works in its possession, the Tate Gallery has also been instrumental in bringing together major exhibitions of Blake's work, augmenting its own collection with loans from other public and private collections. In October-December 1913 it staged the first exhibition of Blake's work to be held in a public gallery in this country (a reduced version of the exhibition subsequently visited Manchester, Nottingham and Edinburgh). After the Second World War, when bombing had reduced much of the building to a roofless shell, an exhibition of Blake's works in the Tate Gallery's collection was one of several Tate exhibitions which the British Council toured round a number of European capitals in 1947. Most recently, in March-May 1978 the largest and most comprehensive exhibition of Blake's work ever was mounted at the Tate Gallery, with the entire range of his work represented for the first time in an exhibition.

If in the 1860s Palgrave and Redgrave were able effectively to ignore Blake, their present-day successors have no justification for doing so: a century of scholarship, exegesis and debate has served to confirm the opinion of such early enthusiasts as Alexander Gilchrist, Dante Gabriel and William Michael Rossetti, Swinburne and Yeats, and although the multitude of controversies regarding interpretation of Blake's work continues to proliferate, Blake's presence now exerts an assured and abiding influence on English cultural life, and refuses to be ignored.

Krzysztof Cieszkowski

THE ART OF WILLIAM BLAKE

The Blake collection at the Tate Gallery is the most representative collection of his work readily available to the public. It comprises all phases of his career, from works of his early twenties when he was completing his long period of training to examples from his great series of watercolour illustrations to Dante which was left unfinished at his death. In addition the collection includes every kind of subject and ranges from rough sketches to finished works in all the main techniques employed by Blake. However, it does not include any of what were perhaps his most personal works, the illuminated books in which he printed and illustrated his own texts, in a special technique developed by himself, but even these books are represented by individual designs that he issued separately. More important, it must be remembered that Blake's work in the visual arts was only half of his achievement, his poetry being one of the glories of English literature.

Full details of Blake's life and career, so far as they are known, are given in the Chronology on p.27. In addition, the various sections into which this catalogue is divided, and the introductory notes to each section, provide a broad survey of the development of Blake's art. However, it is important to stress the length and thoroughness of his training as an engraver, and the paucity if not complete absence of any training as a painter. The very technique of engraving would have encouraged his interest in experimentation, and both his watercolours and the works in his own particular form of tempera stand out in technique from those of his contemporaries. The development of his illuminated books, and their culmination in the large colour prints of 1795, is the most striking example of how experiments in technique went hand in hand with the development of his thought.

Indeed, Blake's art is exceptionally dependent upon his thought and there is a particularly close relationship between his writings and his designs. Not that the latter are merely illustrations to his writings; rather, both writings and designs were regarded by Blake as the expression of a single Poetic or Prophetic Genius. Only through this genius could eternal truths be apprehended by the artist and passed on to his fellow men, and this alone was the justification of art.

Blake's art was based on a fully thought out philosophy, but during his life this underwent considerable changes. In particular the revolutionary ideas of his early years, when he was associated with such political radicals as Joseph Johnson, Thomas Paine, Joseph Priestley, Mary Wollstonecraft and William Godwin, were checked and forced underground in the 1790s by the outcome of the French Revolution and the repressive policies of William Pitt's government. This may in part account for the obscurity of most of Blake's later writings and may also have encouraged him to express a greater proportion of his most deeply-felt beliefs in pictorial form. The end of all hopes of political reform in Britain and the distortion of the ideals of the French Revolution may also have helped to produce the feeling of despairing nihilism that marks Blake's works of the mid-1790s, a development epitomised in the difference between the *Songs of Innocence* of 1789 and the *Songs of Experience* that Blake added to them in 1794. Blake never actually abandoned a basic form of Christianity but at this period it approached the heresy of Manicheism, which represented Satan as an equal force to Christ with the Jehovah of the Old Testament as a negative force. From about 1800, particularly during the only three years that Blake spent outside London, at Felpham in Sussex, he began to reconcile the presence of evil and material existence with a renewed faith, though his Christianity was always anything but orthodox. In eternity, so Blake told Crabb Robinson in 1825, 'We are all coexistent with God – Members of the Divine Body – all partakers of the divine nature'; Christ 'is the only God...and so am I and so are you'.

Blake's thought, as well as his literary style, was fundamentally based on the three English classics, the Bible in the King James translation, Shakespeare and Milton. However, his thought also includes elements from a much wider range of sources, both Christian and non-Christian, including the Apocrypha, Paracelsus, Emmanuel Swedenborg, Jakob Böhme, and Neo-Platonism as introduced into this country by Thomas Taylor. Blake saw man's predicament in the material world of the Earth as a division between the various elements that in eternity ideally complement each other; in division however they fall to warring against each other. He saw the biblical Fall in this light, as merely one of a series of fallings into division. The Creation itself was another, giving over-emphasis to the material aspect of man; the terrifying 'Elohim Creating Adam' (no.25) expresses this negative view. However, the Creation was also a stage towards redemption: any act of giving form to error, any definition of error, was a stage in understanding it and therefore in being able to overcome it. Locke and Newton were examples of scientists who, by defining error, made it recognizable and therefore more vulnerable; Blake's colour print of 'Newton' (no.29) is both a condemnation and a stage in redemption. However, the prime agent in overcoming error was not the intellect or reason but the imagination. Indeed, although the reason ranked equally with the imagination, the emotions and the natural senses as the four main elements into which the fallen man has been divided, Blake was particularly suspicious of the faculty of reason, equating it with the supression of the imagination that resulted from the unenlightened exercise of any authority, in particular religious or political. Further divisions, such as the creation of woman and the propagation of children, represented further stages of the Fall.

After a few tentative intimations in his early lyrical poems and the satirical *An Island in the Moon*, Blake's philosophy found written expression in a series of epic Prophetic Books, written and produced in his own particular technique in the first half of the 1790s. In these he evolved what may be called his own mythology, his concepts acquiring personal identities and names rather like the protagonists in Wagner's *Ring* though without their background in northern mythology; a possible source of the general idea and structure of Blake's myth may have been the so-called writings of Ossian, not then fully recognized as the fabrications of Macpherson (in fact Blake, in his annotations of 1826 to Wordsworth's poems, wrote, 'I believe both Macpherson & Chatterton, that what they say is Ancient, Is so'). Personages with names such as Urizen, Los, Enitharmon and Orc struggle in a primaeval world of frozen depths, tormenting fires and globules of blood. They stand for the successive subdivision of the original, innocent man into the individual elements that make up his unified being, but the exact meaning given to these figures by Blake is constantly changing and developing; any attempt to identify them in too systematic a manner is misleading.

However, the most important of his personifications, akin to the four humours, are Los, the imagination and eventual source of redemption; Urizen, the reason and also the vengeful Jehovah of the Old Testament as opposed to the merciful Christ of the New; Tharmas, the senses; and Luvah, the emotions. These, of whom the first two are the most important, are the four Zoas, the Greek name for the four beasts of the Book of Revelation (a typical example of the cultural cross-references in Blake's thought). Each of them can exist in a fallen or a redeemed state, and they often acquire different names according to which state they are in (for instance Urthona is Los in his spiritual state).

In addition, each of these four main figures has an emanation, a female off-shoot who not only represents a further stage of division but also makes things worse by attempting to dominate her male counterpart. The most important of these is Los's emanation, Enitharmon, who also represents Pity, for Blake an impure and destructive emotion (see no. 30). Yet another stage of division occurs when Los and Enitharmon give birth to Orc, the spirit of energy, another important force in the achievement of salvation but one which alarms not only Urizen, the embodiment of reason and authority, but also Los himself, partly out of jealousy for Enitharmon's love for her son; thus even love can become an impure emotion.

The Prophetic Books, particularly *Urizen*, *Vala or the Four Zoas*, and *Jerusalem*, deal with the conflict between these personifications of man's divided self. An apocalyptic Last Judgement and the end of the world, expressed in terms closely paralleling the Book of Revelation, herald man's final salvation.

Blake's mythological figures, and the awesome situations in which they find themselves, are most clearly described in Blake's writings and the illustrations to these writings in his illuminated books. However, even his seemingly direct illustrations to the Bible, Shakespeare, Milton and Dante reflect his own philosophical ideas and their expression in his writings, and his imagery in these works parallels that in his writings. But one cannot read Blake's pictures as if they were his poems, translating each image into purely verbal terms. Blake, because of the very fact that he was equally proficient in both media, must have realised the differences between them and consciously used them as differing modes of expression.

Nevertheless, visual identifications can be made in Blake's paintings with the figures in his mythology, for instance Orc, a child or young man amidst flames, the Apollo-like Los, and Urizen, the horrific bearded old man. The equation of Urizen with the vengeful, oppressive Jehovah of the Old Testament is as much a visual identification with the figure as he appears in the book *Urizen* and as he appears in Blake's illustrations to the Bible as it is a written one. But not every old man with a beard is Urizen, urizenic or even negative. Context is vital, and a simple equation of type with type makes for gross over-simplification. This is true the other way round as well. Blake's condemnation of unenlightened reasons finds one of its greatest expressions in the colour print 'Newton' (no. 29). However, Newton is not shown in the guise of Blake's old man, Urizen type at all (though there are close links with another depiction of the Creation, 'The Ancient of Days', the frontispiece to *Europe* in which it is Blake's Urizen-Jehovah who wields the same pair of compasses, or 'dividers', a pun that may well be deliberate).

In Blake's most successful works the general message is conveyed through visual means; one's identification of Blake's personifications merely confirms what is visually apparent. The best of the large colour prints of 1795 are typical. 'Newton', despite showing a physically-ideal, handsome young man, is obviously condemnatory of his slavish drawing of an abstract diagram with his compasses. 'Elohim Creating Adam' (no.25) is clearly an extremely negative view of the biblical Creation. 'God Judging Adam' (no.26) is a scene of horror and oppression, with the condemned Adam being shown in the negative guise of Blake's Urizen-like Jehovah. In other cases, content and visual impact seem to be mismatched as a result of Blake's failure to find a suitable image.

Blake's personal philosophy was not a complete retreat from everyday reality, despite the political disillusionment that came in the 1790s. Nor did the distinctive and overpowering visionary quality of his best works mean that he was completely other-worldly, despite repeated suggestions even during his lifetime that he was insane. The visionary quality of Blake's art has sometimes been claimed as something different in kind from that of other artists, not just in degree. Indeed, in part because of the intensity of his visual experience combined with a vocabulary coloured by the great religious writings of English literature, Blake often expressed himself in terms that implied specific visionary experiences, and these were seized upon by his early biographers. According to Gilchrist, Blake, 'as he will in after years relate', had his first vision on Peckham Rye at the age of eight or ten; it was of 'a tree filled with angels'. Gilchrist also relates how, while working as an apprentice in Westminster Abbey, Blake saw a vision of Christ and the Apostles. It was Blake himself, in a now untraced letter to his friend and patron Thomas Butts, who described how he had seen a great procession of monks, priests, choristers and incense-bearers, accompanied by organ music. According to J. T. Smith, Blake saw a vision of 'The Ancient of Days' at the top of his staircase at Hercules Building, Lambeth, though the composition it allegedly inspired, the frontispiece to *Europe*, has been shown to derive from visual and verbal prototypes; indeed, he used preliminary sketches and underdrawing just like any other artist. Blake clearly believed his inspiration to be a form of vision; after his creative difficulties at Felpham he would say 'the visions were angry with me at Felpham'. When sitting for his portrait by Thomas Phillips they got into a discussion about the relative merits of Raphael and Michelangelo. When Phillips challenged Blake's claim to have actually seen a work by Michelangelo Blake quoted the authority of the Archangel Gabriel. He claimed that Joseph, the sacred carpenter, had told him the secret of Italian tempera painting, and that his dead brother Robert had revealed to him the technique of stereotype printing.

However, a clue to the actual nature of Blake's visions is given in a letter he wrote to Hayley on 6 May 1800 about his brother. 'Thirteen years ago I lost a brother & with his spirit I converse daily & hourly in the Spirit, & See him in my remembrance in the regions of my Imagination'. When asked by Mrs Aders where he had seen a vision of a field full of lambs which turned into sculpture he replied '*here*, madam', touching his forehead. As Frederick Tatham said, 'these visions of

Blake seem to have been more like peopled imaginations, & personified thoughts'. The Visionary Heads, Blake's drawings of historical or imaginary personages purportedly conjured up in vision, are a special case (see nos.61–7). Produced for the credulous John Varley, they seem to be different in kind from Blake's other visionary experiences, and to have been to a considerable extent the result of Blake's determination to oblige his friend. This is supported by the fact that this particular form of image only seems to have appeared to Blake over a limited period, largely confined to the autumn of 1819.

Both types of vision have been explained as possibly a result of the physiological phenomena known as eidetic images, which are characterised by sharpness of definition, optical reality and involuntary appearance, often under conditions of nervous excitement producing a form of auto-suggestion. This ties in with Blake's own insistence that visions are not 'a cloudy vapour or a nothing: they are organized and minutely articulated beyond all that the mortal and perishing nature can produce'. However, a particularly strongly developed creative imagination coupled with an exceptional visual memory may well be sufficient explanation.

It is no discredit to Blake's achievement to treat it as a normal if exceptionally developed example of artistic creativity, nor to place it in its historical context. His images, despite his claims to visionary inspiration, were firmly based on a long tradition of figurative art, in which the human figure was used for emotional and moral effect. The tradition of figure painting was relatively unestablished in Britain: landscape seems to have been a more natural mode of expression, in which Blake's two rather younger contemporaries Turner and Constable achieved their greatness. Figure painting was mainly confined to portraiture. What native figurative tradition there was stemmed largely from Hogarth, small-scale figures used to point a moral rather than to elevate the spirit, illustrations to novels or plays such as Highmore's *Pamela* series or Hayman's Shakespearian subjects, and genre paintings, leading on to the great flood of nineteenth-century genre painting; all this shaded into the small-scale portrait group or conversation picture.

But Blake, both through inclination and through the luck of the particular artistic circumstances of his time, partook of the mainstream of European, or more specifically Italian, figurative art, in which subjects of high import were treated in a suitably elevated style. This style had characterised the art of Antiquity, the High Renaissance and much of seventeenth-century art, and was revived again in the mid eighteenth century by theorists such as Winckelmann and by a group of artists working in Rome in the 1760s, in particular the Scot Gavin Hamilton and the American-born Benjamin West. This development coincided with the creation of exhibiting institutions in Britain, first the Society of Artists in 1760, then (and pre-eminently) the Royal Academy which held its first annual exhibition in 1769. Blake's earliest exhibits must be seen in the light of this Neo-Classical style based on antique reliefs and the compositions of Raphael and Poussin. It was a style based on figures inter-related by gesture, deployed across the surface of the picture and confined to a relatively narrow stage in the foreground, any landscape or architectural setting acting merely as a foil to the main action.

A slightly later manifestation of the style, also associated with Rome but with a group of artists who worked there mainly in the 1770s, was the strangely

SAINT PETER'S COLLEGE LIBRARY
JERSEY CITY, NEW JERSEY 0730/

imaginative, almost mannerist development associated at its most extreme with Fuseli but also practised in England by Mortimer, Barry and Romney. These artists added an emotional *frisson* to the style and, while seeking inspiration in the same basic schools of art in the past, concentrated on rather different works, the Laocoön rather than the Apollo Belvedere, the works of Michelanglo rather than those of Raphael.

More important than individual sources of motifs or poses, though these have been amply demonstrated in Blake's work, was the common vocabulary established by this long tradition of figurative art, a vocabulary that the connoisseur could recognise intellectually and even the non-expert would perceive emotionally and sensuously because of the expressive effect of the forms. The Apollo Belvedere evoked, for the cognoscenti, the whole intellectual significance of this god of light, the epitome of reason, the arts and intellectual achievement; and for those who did not understand the significance of the subject's background, the classical poise, elegant form and smooth modelling would express the same general idea. Equally, the agony of the Laocoön was sufficiently expressive even if one did not know the story of the protagonist's tragic fate at the hands of the ancient gods. The vocabulary established by these models was as much a question of 'pathos formulae' conveyed by the entire body as of facial expression. Today, it is difficult to appreciate this vocabulary to the full, largely because the discipline of classical academic art collapsed in the nineteenth century; whatever this may have meant in the increased freedom of art to express a wider and stronger scale of emotion, it destroyed the assumptions on which all artists, whether conformist or rebel, could rely in the late eighteenth century. Blake came from the last generation that could assume a knowledge of this vocabulary. A number of artists of the time, although their roots were in the academic tradition, were in fact instrumental in breaking it down, including Stubbs, Blake himself, and Turner.

Blake's achievement as an artist is enlarged, not diminished, by this context. Using this common vocabulary, his revolt was all the greater and the uses to which he put it all the more revolutionary. But, in part to achieve his particular aims, he limited an already limited style still further. Partly through his training as an engraver, partly through his inclinations which led him to reject much of the discipline of the Royal Academy Schools, particularly as regards copying from life or sculptural casts, Blake minimised the three-dimensional elements of the style both in the figure itself and in its spatial setting. His figure compositions moved away from the narrative to the emblematic.

In some ways this development paralleled the increasing abstraction of much Neo-Classical art, but Blake's simplifications were never at the expense of the concrete or the specific. By the time he reached the age of about fifty he was able to equate this development with his role as visionary prophet. Visionary experience, far from being most suitably expressed in vague, suggestive forms, necessitated the sharpest clarity, avoiding the 'obscuring demons' of three-dimensional modelling through light and shade and all complex spatial connotations. In his later works, though he returned to a more three-dimensional modelling of the individual figure, this is no way represented a return to everday reality.

Neither Blake's aesthetic theories nor his style were fully formed from the beginning. His theories were formulated only gradually, just as he only gradually achieved a truly personal independence from the formulae of contemporary Neo-Classicism. In fact the development of his mature aesthetic principles took considerably longer than the maturing of his style. From 1789, with *Songs of Innocence*, Blake's individuality as an artist is unmistakable, and with the large colour prints of 1795 he had reached a position which marks him off completely from such imaginative and forceful contemporaries as Fuseli and Barry. In 1799 however he was still flattering himself of being capable of painting cabinet pictures not 'unworthy of a Scholar of Rembrandt & Teniers' and it was not until the *Descriptive Catalogue* of his own exhibition of 1809 and writings contemporary with this that his own personal aesthetic theories were fully developed. Indeed, these theories were only reconcilable with his actual artistic practice because of a further development in his style, away from the forcefulness of the mid 1790s. Much damage is done to the appreciation of Blake's earlier art by seeing his whole output as a monolithic creation moulded by the theories he expounded in his later years. Blake himself may have helped this process, by reading back into his own account of his early days the views of his maturity. For instance, his work in Westminster Abbey as an apprentice to James Basire was neither as revolutionary nor as profound an influence on his early work as in 1805 he led his first biographer Benjamin Heath Malkin to suppose.

Blake's fully developed aesthetic theories are found in his annotations to Reynolds' *Discourses*, largely made *c.*1805–8, the *Descriptive Catalogue* of 1809, his description of his picture of 'The Last Judgment', drafted in 1810, and certain later writings such as the inscriptions on the 'Laocoön' print of *c.*1820. Putting it simply he can be said to have moved from the general Neo-Classical position which looked back to the art of antiquity as the ideal, to considering the great works of antiquity merely as a reflection of far greater but now vanished Hebrew works of art, themselves only indirectly known from the biblical description of the cherubim in the holy of holies in the Temple of Solomon (I Kings VI, 23–8). True art was thus indivisibly linked with true religion. Not only 'Grecian' but also 'Hindoo' and Egyptian art reflected lost originals. Blake derived certain elements, such as the form of the halo of 'The Spiritual Form of Pitt' (no.59), from engravings of Buddhist art; similarly plates 46 and 53 of *Jerusalem* derived motifs from oriental art.

For Blake, as for the Neo-Classicists, the classical tradition and the Gothic were united in their basic principles. In his mature writings Blake made a very clear distinction between linear and painterly art, and, as he claimed both Raphael and Michelangelo had done before him, he 'contemned and rejected' painterly art 'with the utmost disdain'. He set the Florentine school against the Venetian, the early Flemish primitives against Rubens and Rembrandt, and the technique of tempera or fresco (which he tended to muddle together) against that of painting in oils. As he said of his own paintings 'The Spiritual Form of Nelson' and 'The Spiritual Form of Pit' (nos.58 and 59), 'Clearness and precision have been the chief objects in painting these Pictures. Clear colours unmudded by oil, and firm and determinate lineaments unbroken by shadows, which ought to display and not to hide form, as is the practice of the latter Schools of Italy and Flanders.' 'Colouring does not depend on where the Colours are put, but on where the lights and darks are put, and all depends on Form or Outline. On where that is put; where that is wrong, the Colouring never can be right; and it is always wrong in Titian and Correggio, Rubens and Rembrandt. Till we get rid of Titian and Correggio, Rubens and Rembrandt, We never shall equal Rafael and Albert Durer, Michael Angelo, and Julio Romano.' Interestingly. Blake makes absolutely no allowance for Rembrandt's deep insight as a religious painter, nor for his position as a rebel, misunderstood by his materialistic contemporaries: in these respects style, not content or context, was the sole criterion.

Blake's attitude to Reynolds was more complex. Despite opening his annotations to Reynolds's *Discourses* with 'This Man was Hired to Depress Art', Blake agreed with much that Reynolds said, particularly over such things as the superiority of history painting over all other genres and the praiseworthiness of Raphael and Michelangelo. What he attacked were Reynolds's deviations from strict academic doctrine and what he regarded as jibes at the imaginative qualities of Mortimer, Barry and Fuseli (perhaps significantly, Benjamin West, whose Neo-Classical subject pictures lie behind many of Blake's earliest works, but who succeeded Reynolds as President of the Royal Academy, was only once mentioned by Blake and then because of his equivocation over the respective merits of the engravings of Woollett and the more linear Basire). Blake's most profound difference from Reynolds was over how one should apprehend the ideal forms that both agreed were the fundamental basis of art. Both advocated copying the best masters; 'to learn the Language of Art Copy for Ever is my Rule', said Blake. However, rather than advocating that the artist should seek perfection through studying the details of nature, which were of necessity imperfect, and gradually refining from these the more perfect whole unknown in nature, Blake held that the artist could apprehend ideal beauty without reference to nature at all. 'Knowledge of Ideal Beauty is Not to be Acquired. It is Born with us. Innate Ideas are in Every Man Born with him; they are truly Himself. The man who says that we have No Innate Ideas must be a Fool & Knave, Having no Con-Science or Innate Science.' This Platonic rather than Aristotelian concept was closer to High-Renaissance and Mannerist theory than to what was common in the seventeenth and eighteenth centuries.

For Blake colour was subservient to form. At its best however his colouring is, like his imagery and formal composition, of the greatest beauty. Again, he developed from the conventional colouring of the Neo-Classicists to something much more personal. Neo-Classical colouring is basically representational though without any attempt to imitate through brushwork and subtle relations of tone the exact semblance of shade and texture. Blake moved steadily away from even this qualified reality to create a largely non-representational, expressive or hieratic style of colouring. Often, particularly from about 1803, when his compositions became more symmetrical, the colouring of the figures supports this symmetry or acts as a counterpoint to it. Sometimes colour may be used symbolically, for instance for the robes of Dante and Virgil in the illustrations to Dante (see nos.131–150). At its best Blake's colouring is capable of every gradation from extreme delicacy, as in some of the biblical watercolours and the Dante illustrations (for example nos.52 and 149), to the sonorous oppressive tones of other of the biblical watercolours, the tempera paintings and above all the large colour prints of 1795. This end of the scale called for new textures and even new techniques. The first half of the 1790s saw, in his books and therefore in direct relationship with the development of his writings, the creation of a unique form of colour printing that led first to independent works in this medium and then to his own particular form of tempera. Later however this particular line of development was abandoned, in parallel with the evolution of his aesthetic theories.

Blake made a number of attempts to appeal to the general public, for instance through individual exhibits at the Royal Academy between 1780 and 1808 and with his own one-man exhibition at the house of his brother in 1809–10 (see nos. 58–60), but with very little success. In fact his life was a continual struggle against misunderstanding and poverty. The field of engraving, in which he had been trained, was more profitable, particularly when after the work of others, than his own independent work, but he was constantly passed over or involved in schemes that for one reason or another disappointed his expectations, such as the illustrations to *The Grave* (see no. 57). What work he did get was largely through his friends, Fuseli, Flaxman and George Cumberland, and even such relationships as these often soured. His dealings with possible patrons for his original works were equally hazardous as can be seen from his correspondence with the Rev. Dr Trusler, who expected to dictate the actual composition of the works he had commisioned, and the patronage of William Hayley who tried to direct Blake into more economically viable projects at the expense of his own imaginative work. Three patrons stand out for their faith in Blake: the minor civil servant Thomas Butts, for whom Blake executed from *c*.1799 onwards a series of illustrations to the Bible (see nos. 35–52), the Book of Job and the poems of John Milton; the Rev. Joseph Thomas who commissioned the first sets of most of Blake's illustrations to Milton; and John Linnell, the young painter who, in Blake's last years, commissioned a second set of Job watercolours and the engravings (nos. 109–130), the Dante illustrations (nos. 131–165) and much else besides.

Linnell was also the agent through whom a group of young admirers, many of them artists, gathered round Blake in his last years, in particular Palmer, Calvert and Richmond, whose early works owe much to Blake. But what Palmer and his friends took from Blake was only a very small part of the full significance of his art. Palmer and Calvert drew particularly from the exquisite but untypical woodcut landscapes illustrating Thornton's *Virgil* (nos. 73–89). Moreover Palmer, far from sharing Blake's deeper beliefs, was a High Church Anglican who campaigned against the Reform Bill of 1832, while Calvert reverted in later life to what his friends termed 'paganism'. Richmond at least drew his early inspiration from Blake's figure style but later concentrated on portraying his eminent contemporaries. A deeper kinship with Blake was perhaps felt by Dante Gabriel Rossetti, like him both poet and painter, inspired by Dante and, though in a very different way from Blake, both visionary and mystic. He and his brother William helped in the publication of the first full biography of William Blake, that by Alexander Gilchrist, after Gilchrist's death, and participated in the revival of interest in Blake's works in the second half of the nineteenth century. The influence of the Virgil woodcuts persisted, by way of Palmer and Calvert, into the twentieth century in the early works of such artists as Paul Nash and Graham Sutherland and the tradition of the visionary poet-painter reappears, with affinities of style, in the work of David Jones. It is therefore a happy accident that, as a result of historical circumstances, the Tate Gallery's collection of works by William Blake not only takes its place in a sequence of British painting from the sixteenth century to the present day, but also shares a home with the national collection of modern art.

(Parts of this introduction are taken from that to the catalogue of the exhibition of William Blake held at the Tate Gallery in 1978.)

CHRONOLOGY

The information on which this chronology is based can be largely found in Blake's letters and G.E. Bentley Jr's *Blake Records*, 1969. Information dependent on hearsay is identified by the name of the source being given in brackets, e.g. Malkin, Gilchrist; such sources, which were at least in part based on first-hand accounts, are themselves listed in this chronology.

1757
28 November. Born at his parents' home, 28 Broad Street (now 74 Broadwick Street), Golden Square, Soho, London, the son of a hosier; baptised in St James's Church, Piccadilly, 11 December.

1767
4 August. Probably birthdate of favourite brother Robert (see p.242)

1767–8
Entered Henry Pars' drawing school in the Strand at the age of ten, copying from Antique casts (Malkin).

1769
Blake's father may have joined the Baptist Church, Grafton Street. Blake himself, his parents and his brother Robert were all to be buried in Bunhill Fields, the dissenters' burial ground.

1769–70
Aged twelve Blake began writing the poems included in *Poetical Sketches* (published 1783) which contained writings of up to his twentieth year, 1777–8.

1772
Bound as apprentice for seven years to James Basire (1730–1802), the engraver, of 31 Great Queen Street, Lincoln's Inn Fields, and probably went to live in his home.

1773
Probable date of first known engraving, that after Michelangelo entitled on a later state 'Joseph and Arimathea among the Rocks of Albion' and then dated '1773'.

1774
First securely datable drawings attributed to Blake, those of 'The Body of Edward I in his Coffin' (Society of Antiquaries of London).

1775
Dated drawings of monuments in Westminster Abbey attributed to Blake (Society of Antiquaries).

1779
8 October. Admitted to the Royal Academy Schools as an engraver (though engraving was not apparently taught at this time). Though entitled to use the drawing facilities for six years he probably dropped out after a few months. Fellow students included his friends John Flaxman (1756–1826) and Thomas Stothard (1755–1834).

1780
May. First exhibit at the Royal Academy, 'Death of Earl Goodwin', sending in from 28 Broad Street. George Cumberland, in *The Morning Chronicle and London Advertiser* for 27 May, mentioned the work, 'in which, though there is nothing to be said of the colouring, may be discovered a good design, and much character'.

6 June. Borne along by the mob that liberated Newgate Prison in the Gordon Riots (Gilchrist).

About this time, on a sketching trip by boat up the Medway, with Stothard and James Parker (1750–1805, a fellow apprentice under Basire) arrested as French spies but released on assurances from members of the Royal Academy (Stothard's daughter-in-law, in an account of *c.*1850).

Begin doing commercial engraving for the radical publisher Joseph Johnson.

1781–2
Fell in love, in his twenty-fourth year, with Polly Wood but was refused (Tatham).

1782
2 April. Robert Blake, presumably William's youngest and favourite brother, admitted to the Royal Academy Schools as an engraver (see nos.166–9).

18 August. Married Catherine Butcher (or Boucher, born 25 April 1762), and moved to 23 Green Street, Leicester Fields (now Irving Street).

1783
Flaxman and the Rev. A.S. Matthew, husband of the bluestocking Mrs Harriet Matthew, financed the publication of Blake's *Poetical Sketches*. Flaxman also secured Blake a commission for a drawing from John Hawkins, 'a Cornish Gentleman', on about 18 June.

1784
First met J.T. Smith at Harriet Matthew's.

26 April. Flaxman wrote to William Hayley that he was sending him a copy of Blake's *Poetical Sketches* and reported that John Hawkins had not only commissioned several drawings from Blake but 'is so convinced of his uncommon talents that he is now endeavouring to raise a subscription to

send him to finish his studies in Rome'; this never took place. Flaxman also reported that 'M.r Romney thinks his [Blake's] historical drawings rank with those of M.l Angelo'.

May. Two works at the Royal Academy, 'A Breach in a City, the Morning after a Battle' and 'War unchained by an Angel, Fire, Pestilence, and Famine following', sent in from 23 Green Street.

4 July. Blake's father James buried, probably leaving him a small sum of money, enough to enable him to set up a print shop with James Parker at 27 Broad Street, next door to his birthplace, now occupied by his eldest brother James. Blake and Parker published two prints on 17 December, the only documented works of this partnership.

Autumn. Probable date of satirical manuscript *An Island in the Moon*, based on the literary circle of Harriet Matthew.

1785

May. Four works at the Royal Academy, three of the story of Joseph and 'The Bard, from Gray' (untraced; see no.60).

By Christmas had moved to 28 Poland Street, Soho, leaving the Parkers at 27 Broad Street.

1787

February. Death of favourite brother Robert, buried 11 February.

1787–8

First got to known Henry Fuseli (1741–1825), and through him and Joseph Johnson the circle of radicals that included William Godwin, Mary Wollstonecraft, Joseph Priestley, Richard Price, Thomas Paine and Thomas Holcroft, secretary of the London Corresponding Society (Gilchrist).

1788

'W Blakes Original Stereotype was 1788' (inscription on *The Ghost of Abel*, 1822). This reference to Blake's personal form of relief etching probably refers to *There is No Natural Religion* and *All Religions are One*, which seem to be Blake's first books of this kind.

1789

13 April. One of those signing a declaration that they believed in the doctrines of Emmanuel Swedenborg at the first session of the New Church, but unlike Flaxman never actually joined the New Church and attacked Swedenborg in *The Marriage of Heaven and Hell*, 1790–93.

Tiriel usually dated to this year (see no.9). *Songs of Innocence* (see nos.15–19) and *The Book of Thel*.

Listed in two dictionaries of engravers published in Paris (review of Bentley 1969 by David Bindman, *Burlington Magazine*, CXIII, 1971, p.219) and Leipzig.

1790

Autumn. Moved to 13 Hercules Buildings, Lambeth. Began *The Marriage of Heaven and Hell*.

1791

The French Revolution, to be published by Johnson as an ordinary book, got no further than page-proofs. His illustrations to Mary Wollstonecraft's *Original Stories from Real Life* published by Johnson. Began engravings for John Gabriel Stedman's *Narrative, of a Five Year's Expedition, against the Revolted Negroes of Surinam*, completed 1793 but not published by Johnson until 1796.

1792

About 7 September. Death of Blake's mother Catherine.

About 12 September. Blake said to have warned Tom Paine to escape from England (Tatham and Gilchrist) but this is probably highly exaggerated; however, it reflects his continuing contacts with radicals, now under pressure from Pitt's government as it reacted to events in France.

1793

The Marriage of Heaven and Hell (begun 1790), *Visions of the Daughters of Albion* (see nos.21–2), *America* and *For Children: The Gates of Paradise* (first version).

1794

Songs of Experience, Europe (see no.20) and *The [First] Book of Urizen* (see nos.23–4).

1795

The Song of Los, The Book of Ahania and *The Book of Los*.

Commissioned by Richard Edwards to illustrate Young's *Night Thoughts*, published 1797.

1796

Illustrated G.A. Bürger's *Leonora* (engraved by Perry). Publication of George Cumberland's *Thoughts on Outline* with eight plates engraved by Blake.

Probably began work on unfinished manuscript 'Vala or the Four Zoas', not abandoned until *c.* 1807 (British Library).

1797

Commissioned by John Flaxman to illustrate Gray's *Poems* for his wife Ann, commonly known as Nancy.

1798

Annotated Bishop Richard Watson's *An Apology for The Bible in a Series of Letters addressed to Thomas Paine*. Also annotated Francis Bacon's *Essays* about this time.

1799

May. Exhibited small tempera painting of 'The Last Supper' at the Royal Academy.

August. First mention of the patronage of Thomas Butts (see p.106) and the would-be patronage of the Rev. Dr. Trusler.

7 October. Gift of a copy of *America* to C.H. Tatham, the father of Blake's later friend and *de facto* executor Frederick Tatham.

1800

May. Tempera of 'The Loaves and Fishes' at the Royal Academy.

June. Publication of William Hayley's *Essay on Sculpture* with three engravings by Blake after Flaxman.

18 September. Moved to Felpham, near Chichester, under Hayley's patronage (see no. 55). During his three years there he probably got to know the third Earl and Countess of Egremont at Petworth nearby.

5 October. Publication of Hayley's *Little Tom the Sailor* with engravings by Blake.

Annotations to Boyd's translation of Dante's *Inferno*, 1785, about this time.

1801

31 July. Flaxman passed on to Blake the Rev. J. Thomas's commission for illustrations to Milton's *Comus* and Shakespeare.

One engraving after Fuseli in Fuseli's *Lectures on Paintings*.

1802

First edition of *Ballads* by Hayley with illustrations by Blake.

1803

First two volumes of Hayley's *Life of William Cowper*, with four plates engraved by Blake, one after his own design; volume III, with two further engravings by Blake after others, published 1804. Hayley's *Triumphs of Temper*, with six plates engraved by Blake after Maria Flaxman. Working on plates for Hayley's *Life of George Romney*, published 1809.

12 August. Blake ejected a soldier named John Scolfield from his garden, leading to a charge of sedition.

19 September. Returned to London, at first to his brother's house, 28 Broad Street, but by 26 October had settled at 17 South Molton Street.

1804

11 January. Acquitted on charge of sedition at Chichester. Greatly impressed by the Truchsessian Gallery of Pictures, a speculative collection of Old Masters particularly notable for its 'Gothic' pictures by or after fifteenth-century Flemish and German artists, but also containing works attributed to the artists Blake particulaly singled out for praise or blame in succeeding years.

Date on title-pages of *Milton*, not actually finished until 1808 or later, and *Jerusalem*, not finally completed until 1820.

1805

Second edition of Hayley's *Ballads* with illustrations by Blake.

Commissioned by Robert Hartley Cromek to illustrate Blair's *Grave* (see no. 57).

1806

Benjamin Heath Malkin's *A Father's Memoirs of his Child* published with frontispiece engraved by Cromek after Blake and with a biographical account of Blake in Malkin's introductory letter.

1807

May. Thomas Phillips's portrait of Blake (National Portrait Gallery) exhibited at the Royal Academy.

1808

May. Two watercolours at the Royal Academy: 'Jacob's Dream' and 'Christ in the Sepulchre, guarded by Angels'.

The Grave published with Blake's designs engraved by Luigi Schiavonetti and a frontispiece after Phillips's portrait. Robert Hunt, in the *Examiner* for 7 August, attacked Blake's designs, as did the *Antijacobin Review* for November in a long article of some ten pages. However, the *Monthly Magazine* for 1 December said of the designs, 'there is considerable correctness and knowledge of form in the drawing of the various figures; the grouping is frequently pleasing, and the composition well arranged; some of them have even an air of ancient art, which would not have disgraced the Roman school. In the *ideal* part . . . there is a wildness of fancy and eccentricity, that leave the poet at a very considerable distance.'

Annotated Reynolds's *Discourses* about this time.

1809

May. Opening of Blake's exhibition of his own work, with his *Descriptive Catalogue*, at his brother's house, 28 Broad Street. Robert Hunt wrote a hostile review in the *Examiner* for 17 September. Though due to close on 29 September it was still open well into 1810 (see p. 145 and nos. 14, 58, 59 and 60).

1809–10

Seymour Kirkup (1788–1880) met Blake through Butts and, according to his account in 1865, was 'much with him from 1810 to 1816', when he settled in Italy.

1810

Blake's engraving after his painting of 'Chaucer's Canterbury Pilgrims' (Pollok House, Glasgow). Stothard's rival picture (Tate Gallery) was the cause of the two friends falling out.

28 April. Henry Crabb Robinson visited Blake's exhibition, and took Charles Lamb there on 11 June.

1811

January. Henry Crabb Robinson's essay on 'William Blake, Künstler, Dichter, und Religiöser Schwärmer' ('Artist, Poet and Religious Mystic') published in the first issue of *Vaterländisches Museum*, Hamburg.

July. The poet Robert Southey visited Blake.

1812

Blake exhibited four works, as a member, with the Associated Painters in Water Colour: 'The Canterbury Pilgrims', 'The Spiritual Form of Nelson, 'The Spiritual Form of Pitt' (see nos.58 and 59), and 'Detatched Specimens of an original illustrated Poem, entitled *Jerusalem*, *The Emanation of the Giant Albion*'.

1813

11 April. George Cumberland, on his Spring visit to London from his home in Bristol, visited Blake.

1814

3 June. Cumberland again visited Blake, 'still poor still Dirty' (but he described Stothard as 'still more dirty than Blake'). Flaxman and Fuseli remained his friends throughout these relatively undocumented years (Gilchrist).

1815

20 April. Cumberland's two sons, George and Sydney, visited Blake and found 'him & his wife drinking Tea, durtyer than ever . . .'. Blake showed them 'his large drawing in Water Colors of the last Judgement; he has been labouring at it till it is nearly as black as your Hat'. 'His time is now intirely taken up with Etching & Engraving.'

Spring. Probably date of Blake's visit to the Royal Academy to copy the cast of the Laocoön for Rees's *Cyclopedia*.

Summer and Autumn. Blake engraving outlines of Wedgwood-ware for their salesmen's pattern-books.

1816

Included in *A Bibliographical Dictionary of the Living Authors of Great Britain and Ireland*.

Probably got to know Charles Augustus Tulk, a friend of Flaxman and Coleridge, about this time.

1817

John Gibson, the young sculptor from Liverpool (1790–1866), called on Flaxman, Fuseli and, among others, Blake on his way to Rome.

The critic William Paulet Carey, writing about Benjamin West, praised Blake's illustrations to *The Grave*, described Blake as 'one of those highly gifted men, who owe the vantage ground of their fame solely to their own powers', regretted his lack of success, and reported that there had been some doubt as to whether he was still alive.

1818

20 January, or 20 June 1820. Blake at a dinner party given by Lady Caroline Lamb and also attended by Sir Thomas Lawrence 1769–1830), who later commissioned two watercolours by Blake (see no.72).

6 February. Coleridge, given a copy of *Songs of Innocence and of Experience* by C.A. Tulk, wrote to H.F. Cary that Blake 'is a man of Genius – and I apprehend, a Swedenborgian [this was probably a bit of wishful thinking by Tulk, who was] – certainly, a mystic *emphatically*.' On 12 (?) February

Coleridge wrote to Tulk, assessing the various *Songs* in five orders of excellence.

June (?). John Linnell (1792–1882) introduced to Blake by Cumberland's son George. On 12 September (if not earlier) Linnell introduced John Varley (1778–1842; see p.153) and John Constable (1776–1837) to Blake; on 19 September, Dr R.J. Thornton. Linnell regularly visited art collections with Blake, and tried to interest other possible patrons in his work, as well as buying most of his output himself until Blake's death.

For the Sexes: The Gates of Paradise, a revised version of *For Children: The Gates of Paradise* of 1793, probably from about this time.

1819

14 October. First dated example of the Visionary Heads, drawn by Blake for Varley (see nos.61–67).

1820

8 August. Letter in *London Magazine* from Fuseli's pupil T.G. Wainewright (1794–1847), the painter, author and poisoner, advertising that 'my learned friend Dr.Tobias Ruddicombe M.D. [Blake] is casting a tremendous piece of ordnance . . . "Jerusalem the Emanation of the Giant Albion".'

October (?). At a meal with the collector Charles Aders, Lawrence, James Ward, Linnell and others defend Blake's Virgil woodcuts against Thornton's plan to have them recut (see nos.73–106).

The single plate of *On Homer's Poetry* and *On Virgil* probably etched about this time.

1821

Publication of Dr Thornton's *The Pastorals of Virgil* with Blake's woodcuts (nos.73–106).

Blake moved to his last home on the first floor of 3 Fountain Court, off the Strand.

Sold his collection of prints to Colnaghi's at this time.

1822

28 June. The Royal Academy Council resolved to pay Blake, 'an able Designer & Engraver laboring under great distress', twenty-five pounds.

The Ghost of Abel.

1823

1 August. Had his life-mask taken by James S. Deville (Fitzwilliam Museum), as 'representative of the imaginative faculty' (so Richmond told Mrs Gilchrist).

1824

6 March. Linnell moved to Hampstead where Blake continued to visit him.

May. Visted the Royal Academy with Samuel Palmer (1805–1881), they having first met while Blake was working on the Job engravings. On 9 October Linnell took Palmer (later his son-in-law) to see Blake while he was bedridden and working on the Dante drawings (see nos.131–150).

12 June. Date of inscription on copy of Blake's *Descriptive Catalogue* given by Blake to Frederick Tatham (1805–1878), later his executor and biographer.

December (?). Blake's horoscope published in the periodical *Urania*, with a note on his works, particularly the Visionary Heads.

1825

George Richmond (1809–1896) first met Blake 'as a lad of sixteen' (Gilchrist) at the home of C.H. Tatham, later Richmond's father-in-law. Blake met other members of this circle of young artists and enthusiasts about this time: Edward Calvert (1799–1883), Francis Oliver Finch (1802–62), Palmer's cousin John Giles and Henry Walter.

Summer (?). Went with Palmer and Calvert to Palmer's grandfather's home at Shoreham, Kent.

10 December. Crabb Robinson's long account of Blake's conversation at a party at the Aders'. On 17 December Robinson visited Blake at home, finding him at work on the Dante illustrations 'of which I have nothing to say but that they evince a power of grouping & of throwing grace & interest over conceptions most monstrous & disgusting which I should not have anticipated'. On a further visit on 24 December Robinson read Blake 'Wordsworth's incomparable Ode [*Intimations of Immorality*] which he heartily enjoyed'. Either on this occasion or sometime in 1826 Robinson lent Blake a copy of Wordsworth's poem which Blake annotated.

1826

18 February. Blake gave Robinson his own manuscript copy of Wordsworth's *The Excursion*, again with annotations. The next day Robinson sent Dorothy Wordsworth a summary of his conversations with Blake about Wordsworth, and reported that Coleridge had visited Blake, apparently taken by Tulk to see 'The Last Judgment' (James Spilling in *New Church Magazine*, 1887).

William Hazlitt, in *The Plain Speaker*, included Blake in a list of 'profound mystics' of his day together with Flaxman, de Loutherbourg, Cosway, Varley, etc.

1827

2 February. Robinson took the young German painter Jacob Götzenberger to see Blake; he 'seemed highly gratified' by the Dante illustrations.

12 August. Blake died at 3 Fountain Court. Obituaries appeared in the *Literary Gazette* for 18 August, the *Literary Chronicle* for 1 September, the *Monthly Magazine* for October, the *Gentleman's Magazine* for November, etc.

11 September. Catherine Blake went to live with Linnell at Cirencester Place (now Street) as his housekeeper.

1828

March or June. Catherine left Linnell and moved to 20 Lisson Grove, where she lived as Frederick Tatham's housekeeper.

J.T. Smith included a long section on Blake in the second volume of his *Nollekens and his Times*; Blake was singled out in reviews in the *Athenaeum* and the *Eclectic Review*.

1830

Allan Cunningham's *Lives of the Most Eminent British Painters, Sculptors, and Architects* included a long section on Blake in the second volume, of which a revised edition appeared the same year. This was in part criticised in an anonymous article, probably by C.A. Tulk, on 'The Inventions of William Blake, Painter and Poet' in the March issue of *London University Magazine*.

1831

Catherine Blake retired to lodgings at 17 Charlton Street, Fitzroy Square, where she died on 18 October.

c.1832

Frederick Tatham's manuscript 'Life of Blake'.

1852

Henry Crabb Robinson's *Reminiscences*, a revised version of his diary, covering his meetings with Blake between 1810 and 1827.

1850s

John Linnell's manuscript autobiography, which breaks off c.1822; further worked on in 1863 and 1864.

1863

First edition of the *Life of William Blake*, 'Pictor Ignotus' by Alexander Gilchrist, who had died in 1861: D.G. Rossetti and his brother William helped Gilchrist's widow to see it through the press.

1892

A.H. Palmer's *The Life and Letters of Samuel Palmer*.

1893

A Memoir of Edward Calvert, Artist, by his third son, Samuel.

1926

The Richmond Papers, edited by A.M.W. Stirling from the papers of George Richmond and his son Sir William Blake Richmond.

EXHIBITIONS

EXHIBITIONS referred to in the Catalogue in abbreviated form are listed below in full, in chronological order; they took place in London unless otherwise stated.

The annual exhibitions of the Royal Academy (RA) are referred to in the Catalogue as 'RA 1780', etc. For those during Blake's lifetime the Summer Exhibition of contemporary art is indicated; for those after his death the Old Master exhibitions held in the Winter. Similarly for the Royal Hibernian Academy (RHA).

1809
Pictures, Poetical and Historical Inventions, Painted by William Blake . . ., 28 Broad Street. May 1809–June (or later) 1810. (See p.145; Blake's catalogue is listed separately under 'Literature'.)

1876
The Works of William Blake, Burlington Fine Arts Club.

1893
Works by Old Masters . . . including a collection of Water Colour Drawings, &c, by William Blake . . ., Royal Academy, Winter.

1902
Pictures by French and British Artists of the 18th Century, Glasgow Art Gallery and Museum. October.

1904
Works of Art, Cartwright Memorial Hall, Bradford.

Works by William Blake, Carfax and Co. January.

1906
Frescoes, Prints and Drawings by William Blake, Carfax and Co. June-July.

1910
Fitzwilliam Museum, Cambridge: loan of works by Blake from the W. Graham Robertson collection. (No catalogue.)

1911
The Century of Art Exhibition, 1810–1910. International Society of Sculptors, Painters and Gravers, Grafton Galleries. June – July.

1913–14
Works by William Blake, Tate Gallery; Whitworth Institute, Manchester; Art Museum, Nottingham Castle; with *David Scott*, National Gallery of Scotland, Edinburgh. October 1913–July 1914. (Separate catalogues, and slightly different contents, at each centre, the first two with detailed entries by Archibald G.B. Russell.)

1920–39
Tate Gallery: loan of works by Blake from the W. Graham Robertson collection at various times between 1920 and 1939.

1927
Blake Centenary Exhibition, Burlington Fine Arts Club.

1929
Exposition rétrospective de peinture anglaise (XVIIIe et XIXe siècles). Musée Moderne, Brussels. October – December.

1934
British Art, c.1000–1860, Royal Academy. January – March. (References are given both to the ordinary catalogue and to the *Commemorative Catalogue* published in 1935.)

The Graham Robertson Collection, Whitechapel Art Gallery. April – May.

1936
Two Centuries of English Art, Stedelijk Museum, Amsterdam. July – October.

1937
Water-Colours by Turner, Works by William Blake, Bibliothèque Nationale, Paris, and Albertina, Vienna. January – April.

1938
English Painting, Eighteenth and Nineteenth Centuries (British Council), Louvre, Paris.

1939
Works of William Blake selected from Collections in the United States, Philadelphia Museum of Art. (Detailed catalogue by Elizabeth Mongan and Edwin Wolf 2nd; introduction by A. Edward Newton.)

1942
The Tate Gallery's Wartime Acquisitions, National Gallery. April – May.

1945
The Tate Gallery's Wartime Acquisitions, Second Exhibition (Council for the Encouragement of Music and the Arts – CEMA), Birmingham, Liverpool, Derby, Wakefield, Newcastle and Norwich. January – August.

Two Centuries of British Drawings from the Tate Gallery (CEMA), Chester, Harrogate, Huddersfield, Luton and Hull. April – November.

1947
William Blake (1757–1827), Galerie René Drouin, Paris; Musée Royal des Beaux Arts, Antwerp; Kunsthaus, Zurich; Tate Gallery (with extra works). March – September.

British Romantic Art (Arts Council), Leeds, Hull, Harrogate, Derby, Cardiff and Bristol. May – November.

1949
Original Works by William Blake from the Graham Robertson Collection, Bournemouth, Southampton and Brighton. April – June.

1949–50
British Painting from Hogarth to Turner (British Council), Kunsthalle, Hamburg; Kunstnernes Hus, Oslo; Nationalmuseum, Stockholm; Statens Museum for Kunst, Copenhagen. October 1949 – April 1950.

1950
William Blake, Lady Lever Art Gallery, Port Sunlight. July – September.

1951
The Tempera Paintings of William Blake, Arts Council Gallery. June – July. (Detailed catalogue by Geoffrey Keynes.)

1955
English Water-Colours (c.1750–1820), Norwich Castle Museum. January – February.

1956–7
Masters of British Painting, 1800–1950, Museum of Modern Art, New York; City Art Museum, St. Louis; California Palace of the Legion of Honour, San Francisco. October 1956 – May 1957.

1957
The Art of William Blake, National Gallery of Art, Washington, D.C. October – December.

1959
The Romantic Movement (Arts Council), Tate Gallery and Arts Council Gallery. July – September.

1969–9
Royal Academy of Arts Bicentenary Exhibition, Royal Academy, December 1968 – March 1969.

1969
William Blake: Poet, Printer, Prophet (William Blake Trust), Whitworth Art Gallery, Manchester. May – June. (An englarged version of the exhibition shown at the Tate Gallery in 1964.)

William Blake, Illuminated Books and Engravings, National Library of Scotland, Edinburgh. August – September.

1972
Le Peinture romantique anglaise et les Préraphaélites (British Council), Petit Palais, Paris. January – April.

1975
William Blake 1757 – 1827 (British Council), Kunsthalle, Hamburg, and Städelschen Kunstinstitut, Frankfurt am Main. March – July. (Detailed catalogue entries by David Bindman, introduction by Werner Hofmann.)

1978
William Blake, Tate Gallery. March – May. (Catalogue by Martin Butlin.)

1982–3
William Blake: His Art and Times, Yale Center for British Art, New Haven, and Art Gallery of Ontario, Toronto. September 1982 – February 1983 (for catalogue by David Bindman see 'Literature').

1983
Blake e Dante, Casa de Dante in Abruzzo, Castello Gizzi, Torre de'Passeri, Pescara. September – October (for catalogue by Corrado Gizzi and others see 'Literature').

LITERATURE

LITERATURE and sources of reproductions referred to in the Catalogue in abbreviated form are listed below in full, in chronological order. Where a publication is relevant to only one section of the Catalogue it may be listed at the end of that section's headnote rather than here. This is not a complete Blake bibliography, nor is full bibliographical information given for the publications included; for this see G.E. Bentley, Jr., *Blake Books*, 1977.

1809
William Blake, *A Descriptive Catalogue of Pictures, Poetical and Historical Inventions, Painted by William Blake, in Water Colours, Being the Ancient Method of Fresco Painting Restored* . . . See p.472; reprinted in Keynes *Writings* 1957, pp.563–86, and Erdman *Poetry and Prose* 1965, pp.520–41.

1828
J.T. Smith, *Nollekens and his Times*, reprinted 1920, ed. W. Whitten, and, the section on Blake only, in Bentley *Blake Records* 1969, pp.455–75.

1830
Allan Cunningham, *Lives of the Most Eminent British Painters, Sculptors and Architects*. The chapter on Blake from the 2nd ed. of vol.II, also published in 1830, is reprinted in Bentley *Blake Records* 1969, pp.476–507.

1863
Alexander Gilchrist, *Life of William Blake*, 2 vols. See also 1880.

William Michael Rossetti, 'Annotated Catalogue of Blake's Pictures and Drawings' in Gilchrist 1863, vol.II. Arranged in three numbered lists: 1, Works in Colour; 2, Uncoloured Works; 3, Works of Unascertained Method. Unless otherwise stated reference is to list 1. See also 1880 and 1907.

1880
Alexander Gilchrist, *Life of William Blake*, new and enlarged edition, 2 vols.

William Michael Rossetti, 'Annotated Catalogue', enlarged, in Gilchrist 1880, vol.II.

1898
Laurence Binyon, *Catalogue of Drawings by British Artists . . . in the British Museum*, vol.I.

1903
William Michael Rossetti, ed., *The Rossetti Papers 1862–1870*.

1904
E.T. Cook and Alexander Wedderburn, eds., *The Works of John Ruskin*, vol. XIV.

1907
Alexander Gilchrist, *Life of William Blake*, ed. W. Graham Robertson.

W. Graham Robertson, 'Supplementary List' (to Rossetti's 'Annotated Catalogue') in Gilchrist 1907.

Arthur Symons, *William Blake*.

1909
E.T. Cook and Alexander Wedderburn, eds., *The Works of John Ruskin*, vol.XXXVI.

1912
Archibald G.B. Russell, *The Engravings of William Blake*.

1921
Geoffrey Keynes, *A Bibliography of William Blake*.

A. Edward Newton, *A Magnificent Farce and Other Diversions of a Book Collector*.

1922
Laurence Binyon, *The Drawings and Engravings of William Blake*.

1924
S. Foster Damon, *William Blake, his Philosophy and Symbols*.

Joseph Wicksteed, *Blake's Vision of the Book of Job*, 2nd edn., revised and enlarged. Originally published 1910.

1925
Darrell Figgis, *The Paintings of William Blake*.

1927
Geoffrey Keynes, *Pencil Drawings of William Blake*.

Mona Wilson, *The Life of William Blake*. See also 1971.

1928
Philippe Soupault, *William Blake*.

1929
Thomas Wright, *The Life of William Blake*, 2 vols.

1935
Laurence Binyon and Geoffrey Keynes, *Illustrations of the Book of Job by William Blake*, 5 vols.

Geoffrey Keynes, *The Notebook of William Blake called the Rossetti Manuscript*.

1936
C.H. Collins Baker, 'William Blake, Painter' in *Huntington Library Bulletin*, vol.X, pp.135–48.

1938
Milton O. Percival, *William Blake's Circle of Destiny*.

1938–9
Anthony Blunt, 'Blake's "Ancient of Days"; The Symbolism of the Compasses' in *Journal of the Warburg Institute*, vol.II, pp.53–63. Reprinted in Essick 1973, pp.71–103.

1940–1
C.H. Collins Baker, 'The Sources of Blake's Pictorial Expression' in *Huntington Library Quarterly*, vol.IV, pp.359–67.

1943
Anthony Blunt, 'Blake's Pictorial Imagination' in *Journal of the Warburg and Courtauld Institutes*, vol.VI, pp.190–212.

1946
Geoffrey Keynes, *Blake* (in *The Faber Gallery* series).

Mark Schorer, *William Blake, the Politics of Vision*.

Ruthven Todd, *Tracks in the Snow*.

1947
J. Bronowski, *William Blake, a Man without a Mask*.

Northrop Frye, *Fearful Symmetry, a Study of William Blake*.

1949
Geoffrey Keynes, *Blake Studies*, See also 1971.

1950
Geoffrey Grigson, 'Painters of the Abyss' in *Architectural Review*, vol.CVIII, pp.215–20.

Geoffrey Keynes, *William Blake's Engravings*.

1952
David V. Erdman, 'Blake's Vision of Slavery' in *Journal of the Warburg and Courtauld Institutes*, vol.XV, pp.242–52.

Kerrison Preston, *The Blake Collection of W. Graham Robertson, Described by the Collector*.

1953
Geoffrey Keynes and Edwin Wolf 2nd, *William Blake's Illuminated Books: A Census*.

Kerrison Preston, ed., *Letters from Graham Robertson*.

Albert S. Roe, *Blake's Illustrations to the Divine Comedy*.

Joseph Wicksteed, *William Blake's Jerusalem*.

1956
Geoffrey Keynes, *Pencil Drawings by William Blake*, 2nd series.

Geoffrey Keynes, *Engravings by William Blake: The Separate Plates*.

1957
C. Wingfield Digby, *Symbol and Image in William Blake*.

Geoffrey Keynes, *William Blake's Illustrations to the Bible*, with an Introduction by George Goyder.

Geoffrey Keynes, ed., *The Complete Writings of William Blake*. The pagination remains the same in subsequent editions, with a supplement on pp.929 onwards. In this catalogue Blake's original punctuation, or lack of it, has usually been restored, quoting from Erdman 1965.

Vivian de Sola Pinto, ed., *The Divine Vision: Studies in the Poetry and Art of William Blake*.

1958
Martin Butlin, 'The Bicentenary of William Blake' in *Burlington Magazine*, vol.C, pp.40–3.

1959
Anthony Blunt, *The Art of William Blake*.

1960
Geoffrey Keynes, 'Blake's Visionary Heads and the Ghost of a Flea' in *Bulletin of the New York Public Library*, vol.LXIV, pp.567–72.

1964
Joseph Burke, 'The Eidetic and the Borrowed Image: An Interpretation of Blake's Theory and Practice of Art' in Frantz Philipp and June Stewart, eds., *In Honour of Daryl Lindsay*, pp.110–27. Reprinted in Essick 1973, pp.253–302.

Jean H. Hagstrum, *William Blake, Poet and Painter*.

W. Moelwyn Merchant, 'Blake's Shakespeare' in *Apollo*, vol.LXXIX, pp.318–24. Reprinted in Essick 1973, pp.233–52.

1965
S. Foster Damon, *A Blake Dictionary*. Second impression, revised, 1967; revised edition with a new foreword and annotated bibliography by Morris Eaves 1988.

David V. Erdman, ed., *The Poetry and Prose of William Blake*. The pagination remains the same in subsequent editions; in the 1982 edition all of Blake's letters, rather than a selection, were included.

Jean H. Hagstrum, '"The Wroth of the Lamb", A Study of William Blake's Conversions' in Frederick W. Hilles and Harold Bloom, eds., *From Sensibility to Romanticism*, pp.311–30.

1967
G.E. Bentley Jr, *William Blake: Tiriel*.

1968
John Beer, *Blake's Humanism*.

Geoffrey Keynes, ed., *Letters of William Blake*. Revised edition of work first published 1956. A further revised and amplified edition was published in 1980.

Kathleen Raine, *Blake and Tradition*, 2 vols.

1968–9
Martin Butlin, letter in *Blake Studies*, vol.I, p.212. Apropos Taylor 1968–9.

John E. Grant, 'You can't write about Blake's Pictures like that' in *Blake Studies*, vol.I, pp.193–202. Apropos Taylor 1968–9.

Clyde R. Taylor, 'Iconographical Themes in William Blake' in *Blake Studies*, vol.I, pp.39–85.

1969
John Beer, *Blake's Visionary Universe*.

G.E. Bentley Jr, *Blake Records*.

Martin Butlin, 'The Evolution of Blake's Large Color Prints of 1795' in Rosenfeld 1969, pp.109–16.

Martin Butlin, *The Blake-Varley Sketchbook of 1819*.

David V. Erdman, *Blake, Prophet against Empire*. Revised edition of work first published 1954. The pagination of this edition was followed in the 3rd edn. of 1977, *q.v.*

John E. Grant, 'Two Flowers in the Garden of Experience' in Rosenfeld 1969, pp.333–67.

Jean H. Hagstrum, '"The Fly"' in Rosenfeld 1969, pp.368–82.

Anne T. Kostelanetz, 'Blake's 1795 Color Prints: An Interpretation' in Rosenfeld 1969, pp.117–30.

Albert S. Roe, '"The Thunder of Egypt"' in Rosenfeld 1969, pp.158–95.

Alvin H. Rosenfeld, ed., *William Blake: Essays for S. Foster Damon*.

Kaethe Wolf-Gumpold, *William Blake, Painter, Poet, Visionary*.

1970
David Bindman, *William Blake: Catalogue of the Collection in the Fitzwilliam Museum, Cambridge*.

David V. Erdman and John E. Grant, eds., *Blake's Visionary Forms Dramatic*.

Geoffrey Keynes, *Drawings of William Blake, 92 Pencil Studies*.

Morton D. Paley, *Energy and Imagination*.

Janet A. Warner, 'Blake's Use of Gesture' in Erdman and Grant 1970, pp.174–95.

1971
John Gage, 'Blake's *Newton*' in Journal of the Warburg and Courtauld Institutes, vol.XXXIV, pp.372–7.

Robert R. Wark, 'Blake's "Satan, Sin and Death"' in *Ten British Pictures* [in the Huntington Library] *1740–1840*, pp.79–91.

Mona Wilson, *The Life of William Blake*. Third edn., ed. Geoffrey Keynes, of work first published 1927.

1971–2
Duncan Macmillan, 'Blake's Exhibition and *Catalogue* Reconsidered: On the Occasion of The Fitzwilliam Museum Exhibition and *Catalogue*, 1971' in *Blake Newsletter*, vol.V, pp.202–6.

1972
Roger R. Easson and Robert N. Essick, *William Blake: Book Illustrator*, vol.I, Plates Designed and Engraved by Blake.

Kathryn R. Kremen, *The Imagination of the Resurrection: The Poetic Continuity of a Religious Motif in Donne, Blake, and Yeats*.

Peter Tomory, *The Life and Art of Henry Fuseli*.

1972–3
Roland A. Duerksen, 'A Crucial Line in *Visions of the Daughters of Albion*' in *Blake Newsletter*, vol.VI, p.72.

Thomas H. Helmstadter, 'Blake and the Age of Reason: Spectres in the *Night Thoughts*' in *Blake Studies*, vol.V, pp.105–39.

Michael J. Tolley, review of 1971 edition of this catalogue, in *Blake Newsletter*, vol.VI, pp.28–30.

1973
David Bindman, 'Blake's "Gothicised Imagination" and the History of England' in Paley and Phillips 1973, pp.29–49.

David V. Erdman and Donald K. Moore, *The Notebook of William Blake*. See also 1977.

Robert N. Essick. 'The Altering Eye: Blake's Vision in the *Tiriel* Drawings' in Paley and Phillips 1973, pp.50–65.

Robert N. Essick, ed., *The Visionary Hand, Essays for the Study of William Blake's Art and Aesthetics*. A collection of essays by different writers, all but one published previously and listed above when appropriate.

Bo Lindberg, *William Blake's Illustrations to the Book of Job*.

Morton D. Paley and Michael Phillips, eds, *William Blake: Essays in Honour of Sir Geoffrey Keynes*.

Gert Schiff, *Johann Heinrich Füssli*, 2 vols.

1974
David V. Erdman, *The Illuminated Blake*. First British edn. 1975.

Anne Kostelanetz Mellor, *Blake's Human Form Divine*.

1974–5
Roland A. Duerksen, 'Bromion's Usurped Power – Its Source, Essence and Effect: A Replication' in *Blake Newsletter*, vol.VIII, pp.95–6.

Mary V. Jackson, 'Additional Lines in *VDA*' in *Blake Newsletter*, vol.VIII, pp.91–3.

E.B. Murray, 'Bound Back to Back in Bromion's Cave' in *Blake Newsletter*, vol.VIII, p.94.

1975
Robert Rosenblum, *Modern Painting and the Northern Romantic Tradition*.

Joseph Anthony Wittreich Jr, *Angel of Apocalypse: Blake's Idea of Milton*.

1976
Andrew Wilton, 'Blake and the Antique' in *British Museum Yearbook*, vol.I, pp.187–218.

1976–7
Irene Tayler, 'Blake's Laocoön' in *Blake Newsletter*, vol.X, pp.72–81.

1977
David Bindman, *Blake as an Artist*.

David V. Erdman, *Blake, Prophet against Empire*. Third edn. of work published in 1954 and, revised, in 1969; the chief additions are in the Appendix and references are otherwise still given in this catalogue to the 1969 edn.

David V. Erdman and Donald K. Moore, *The Notebook of William Blake*. Second edn. of work first published 1973.

Milton Klonsky, *William Blake: The Seer and his Visions*.

1978
John Beer, 'Influence and Independence in Blake' in Michael Phillips, ed., *Interpreting Blake*. pp.196–261.

David Bindman, *The Complete Graphic Works of William Blake*.

Robert N. Essick and Donald Pearce, eds., *Blake in his Time*.

W.J.T. Mitchell, *Blake's Composite Art*.

Morton D. Paley, *William Blake*.

Morton D. Paley, '"Wonderful Originals" – Blake and Ancient Sculpture' in Essick and Pearce 1978, pp.170–97.

1979
Roger R. Easson and Robert N. Essick, *William Blake Book Illustrator*, vol.II, Plates Designed or Engraved by Blake 1774–1796. A vol.III, on plates designed or engraved by Blake after 1796, was planned.

Geoffrey Keynes, *The Complete Portraiture of William and Catherine Blake*.

1979–80
Martin Butlin, 'Thoughts on the 1978 Tate Gallery Exhibition' in *Blake*, vol.XIII, pp.16–23.

1980
Robert N. Essick, *William Blake, Printmaker*.

John E. Grant, Edward J. Rose and Michael J. Tolley, co-ordinating editor David V. Erdman, *William Blake's Designs for Edward Young's 'Night Thoughts'*, 2 vols. Further vols. are planned.

Geoffrey Keynes, ed., *The Letters of William Blake*. Revised and amplified edition of work previously published in 1956 and 1968.

1980–1
Jenijoy LaBelle, 'Michelangelo's Sistine Frescoes and Blake's 1795 Color-Printed Designs', in *Blake*, vol.XIV, pp.66–84.

Bo Ossian Lindberg, review of Jack Lindsay, *William Blake: His Life and Work*, in *Blake*, vol.XIV, pp.166–8.

1981
Martin Butlin, *The Paintings and Drawings of William Blake*, 2 vols.

Christopher Heppner, 'Reading Blake's Designs: *Pity* and *Hecate*', in *Bulletin of Research in the Humanities*, vol.LXXXIV, pp.337–65.

1981–2
Martin Butlin, 'A Newly Discovered Watermark and a Visionary's Way with his Dates' in *Blake*, vol.XV, pp.101–3.

Bo Ossian Lindberg, review of Essick 1980 in *Blake*, vol.XV, pp.140–8.

1982
David Bindman, *William Blake: His Art and Times* (catalogue of exhibition held at New Haven and Toronto 1982–3).

David V. Erdman, ed., *The Complete Poetry and Prose of William Blake*. A newly revised, and now fully complete edition, with all the letters, of the work first published in 1965.

Kathleen Raine, *The Human Face of God: William Blake and the Book of Job*.

1982–3
David Bindman, 'An Afterword on *William Blake: His Art and Times*' in *Blake*, vol.XVI, pp.224–5.

Robert N. Essick, review of Butlin 1981 in *Blake*, vol.XVI, pp.22–65.

1983
Stephen C. Behrendt, *The Moment of Explosion: Blake and the Illustration of Milton*.

Robert N. Essick, *The Separate Plates of William Blake: A Catalogue*.

Corrado Gizzi, ed., *Blake e Dante* (publication to accompany exhibition at Pescara).

Nelson Hilton, *Literal Imagination: Blake's Vision of Words*.

1983–4
Martin Butlin, '*Paintings and Drawings of William Blake*: Some Minor Additions' in *Blake*, vol.XVII, p.159

1984
Janet A. Warner, *Blake and the Language of Art*.

1985
Robert N. Essick, *The Works of William Blake in the Huntington Collection, A Complete Catalogue*.

Terence Allan Hoagwood, *Prophecy and the Philosophy of Mind: Traditions of Blake and Shelley*.

1986
Rodney M. Baine with Mary R. Baine, *The Scattered Portions: William Blake's Biological Symbolism*.

1987
Albert Boime, *Art in an Age of Revolution 1750–1800*, pp.308–70.

CONCORDANCE

OLD TATE GALLERY INVENTORY	NEW TATE GALLERY INVENTORY	1957 CATALOGUE NUMBER	1971 CATALOGUE NUMBER	1988 CATALOGUE NUMBER
1110	N 01110	41	47	59
1164	N 01164	24	28	39
2230	N 02230	27	30	41
2231	N 02231	39	45	71
2686	N 02686	3	4	5
3006	N 03006	40	46	58
3007	N 03007	22	25	36
3340	N 03340	49	55	70
3351	N 03351	50	56	131
3352	N 03352	51	57	132
3353	N 03353	52	58	133
3354	N 03354	53	59	134
3355	N 03355	54	60	135
3356	N 03356	55	61	136
3357	N 03357	56	62	137
3358	N 03358	57	63	138
3359	N 03359	58	64	139
3360	N 03360	59	65	140
3361	N 03361	61	67	141
3362	N 03362	62	68	142
3363	N 03363	63	69	143
3364	N 03364	60	66	150
3365	N 03365	64	70	144
3366	N 03366	65	71	145
3367	N 03367	66	72	146
3368	N 03368	67	73	147
3369	N 03369	68	74	148
3370	N 03370	69	75	149
3371 i/viii	A 00005/11	–	see p.24	152/8
3372 i/xxii	A 00012/32	–	see p.24	109/30
3373	N 03373	7	10	21
3374	N 03374	8	11	22
3551	N 03551	42	48	60
3694 i	A 00033	35	39	50
3694 ii	A 00001	83	87	167
3694 iii	A 00838	82	see p.24	170
3694 iv	A 00034	–	see p.24	20
3694 v	A 00035	–	see p.24	18
3694 va	A 00036	–	see p.24	19
3694 vi	A 00037	–	see p.24	17
3694 vii	A 00038	–	see p.24	15
3694 viii	A 00039	–	see p.24	16

OLD TATE GALLERY INVENTORY	NEW TATE GALLERY INVENTORY	1957 CATALOGUE NUMBER	1971 CATALOGUE NUMBER	1988 CATALOGUE NUMBER
3694 ix	A 00002	85	85	168
3694 x	A 00003	84	84	166
3694 xi	A 00040	70	7	9
3694 xii (3694a)	A 00041	73	79	55
3694 xiii	A 00042	71	78	10
3694 xiv	A 00004	86	86	169
3694 xv	A 00043	75	32	43
3694 xvi	A 00044	72	77	7
3694 xvii	A 00050	–	see p.24	171
3694 xviii	A 00045	81	82	2
3694 xix	A 00046	80	83	107
3694 xx	A 00047	79	76	151
3694 xxi	A 00048	76	43	54
3694 xxii	A 00049	77	42	53
3696	N 03696	9	12	23
3866 i/xvii	A 00111/27	–	see p.24	73/89
5055	N 05055	11	14	25
5056	N 05056	18	20	31
5057	N 05057	16	23	33
5058	N 05058	13	17	29
5059	N 05059	12	16	28
5060	N 05060	20	22	32
5061	N 05061	14	18	27
5062	N 05062	17	19	30
5063	N 05063	15	15	26
5183	N 05183	6	6	8
5184	N 05184	46	49	63
5185	N 05185	43	50	65
5186	N 05186	45	52	67
5187	N 05187	44	51	66
5188	N 05188	74	81	56
5189	N 05189	2	1	1
5190	N 05190	10	13	24
5192	N 05192	19	21	12
5193	N 05193	30	34	45
5194	N 05194	–	see p.24	172
5195	N 05195	26	29	40
5196	N 05196	38	41	72
5197	N 05197	28	31	42
5198	N 05198	4	3	4
5199	N 05199	31	35	46

OLD TATE GALLERY INVENTORY	NEW TATE GALLERY INVENTORY	1957 CATALOGUE NUMBER	1971 CATALOGUE NUMBER	1988 CATALOGUE NUMBER
5200	N 05200	5	5	6
5300	N 05300	78	80	57
5875	N 05875	21	24	34
5887	N 05887	37	41	52
5888	N 05888	48	54	69
5889	N 05889	47	53	64
5892	N 05892	29	33	44
5893	N 05893	23	26	37
5894	N 05894	25	27	38
5895	N 05895	32	36	47
5896	N 05896	33	37	48
5897	N 05897	36	40	51
5898	N 05898	1	9	14
5899	N 05899	34	38	49
T.547	T 00547	–	8	13
T.1128	T 01128	–	2	3
T.1334	T 01334	–	–	61
T.1335	T 01335	–	–	62
T.1801	T 01801	–	see p.24	11
T.1950/6	T 01950/6	–	–	159/65
T.2115/31	T 02115/31	–	–	90/106
T.2387	T 02387	–	–	68
T.3233	T 03233	–	–	108
–	T 04134	–	–	35

OLD TATE GALLERY INVENTORY	NEW TATE GALLERY INVENTORY	1957 CATALOGUE NUMBER	1971 CATALOGUE NUMBER	1988 CATALOGUE NUMBER

NOTE

Measurements are given in millimetres, followed by inches in brackets. Height precedes width.

Inscriptions are presumed to be by Blake unless the contrary is stated or is clear by inference. The position of the inscription is given by the abbreviations t.l. (top left), b.r. (bottom right), b.c. (bottom centre), etc.

All inscriptions are on the recto of the work unless otherwise indicated.

Exhibitions (Exh), literature (Lit) and reproductions (Repr) are usually referred to in abbreviated form; see pp.32–7.

The numbers preceded by a 'B', placed immediately after the inventory numbers preceded by an 'N', 'T' or 'A', refer to the catalogue numbers in Martin Butlin, *The Paintings and Drawings of William Blake*, 1981.

EARLY WORKS *c.*1779–*c.*1793

The early works by Blake in the Tate Gallery cover the period from his time as a student at the Royal Academy Schools to one of the last of his works in a conventional Neo-Classical style, 'The Penance of Jane Shore' (no.14). The first item in the catalogue is also Neo-Classical in style, and a comparison of the two works indicates the development of Blake's abilities in this period. Other examples, of greater or lesser accomplishment, are nos.3, 4, 5 and 6. In these works Blake was following the example established in the Royal Academy exhibitions by Benjamin West.

A more decorative style, influenced by the works of Blake's friend and near contemporary Thomas Stothard (1755–1834), is represented by 'Age teaching Youth' (no.8). Blake's need to earn money through reproductive engravings is reflected in that after Hogarth's 'The Beggar's Opera' (no.11). At the other extreme, 'An Allegory of the Bible' (no.3) seems to show Blake illustrating a more personal subject. The sketches for *Tiriel* (no.9) show him illustrating one of his own poems and 'Los and Orc' (no.13) shows two of the figures from his own personal mythology; like 'The House of Death' (no.12) this is related to the great series of large colour prints discussed in a later section of this catalogue (nos.25–34).

I **Lear and Cordelia in Prison** *c.*1779

N 05189/B 53
Pen and watercolour 123 × 175 ($4\frac{15}{16} × 6\frac{7}{8}$) on paper 132 × 182 ($5\frac{3}{16} × 7\frac{3}{16}$)
Bequeathed by Miss Alice G.E. Carthew 1940

PROVENANCE
Mrs Blake, sold *c.*1828–9 to Mrs Samuel Smith and Miss Julia Smith; by descent to Miss Thena Clough, sold Sotheby's 5–6 March 1934, 2nd day (337, repr.) £30 bt Miss Carthew

EXHIBITED
BFAC 1876 (in 223); *Shakespeare in Art*, Arts Council, April–May 1964 (32)

LITERATURE
Blunt 1959, p.10, pl.8a; Merchant in *Apollo*, LXXIX, 1964, p.359, pl.2 (reprinted in Essick 1973, pp.236–7, pl.64); Bentley *Blake Records* 1969, p.367; Bindman in Paley and Phillipps 1973, pp.34, 41–2, pl.9; Butlin 1981, pp.17–18 no.53, pl.45

On the matt below the drawing is written 'Lear and Cordelia (early manner)' and, on the back, presumably by Mrs Samuel Smith or Miss Julia Smith, 'Bought of Mrs Blake the first or second year after her husband's death. Price for this and "The Grave" was about £8.8.' A further inscription on the back of the matt reads 'Exhibited at Burlington Fine Arts Club 1876 No.223 lent by Miss Julia Smith. It is described as 2 drawings in one frame. The other drawing was offered to me with this by their owner a connection of Miss Smith but I did not care for it'. The other drawing is of 'A Female Figure Crouching in a Cave' (possibly later used for plate 16 of *The Gates of Paradise*), now in the collection of Anthony E. Wolf (Butlin 1981, no.134, pl.150).

This watercolour is similar in style and dimensions to, and probably forms part of, a series of small watercolours of historical subjects that also includes the first version of 'The Penance of Jane Shore' (see no.14). The subject was therefore almost certainly chosen to illustrate an incident from early English history rather than Shakespeare's play, in which this scene does not appear. David Bindman has suggested that, although the incident does occur in Nahum Tate's adaptation of *King Lear* of 1681 (as a stage direction for the third scene of Act V, 'Scene, *A Prison*. Lear asleep, with his head on Cordelia's lap'), a more likely source is Milton's

1

History of Britain, 1670, in which Lear appears as the last in line from the Trojan Brutus, in legend the great-grandson of Æneas and the first king of England; Trojan Brutus's landing in England is the subject of another of this series of watercolours, now in Princeton University Library (Butlin no.51, pl.47).

Blake, in his *Descriptive Catalogue* of 1809, describes what seems to be the first version of 'The Penance of Jane Shore' as having been 'done above Thirty Years ago', and another watercolour from this series, 'The Death of Earl Goodwin' now in the British Museum (Butlin no.60, colour pl.178) was almost certainly exhibited at the Royal Academy in 1780 (315). Blake later planned to publish 'The History of England, a small book of Engravings, Price 3s.', as he announced in his *Prospectus to the Public* of 10 October 1793. No copy of this is known but a list of subjects in Blake's Notebook seems to refer to its contents. The most accurate transcription of this list is in Erdman and Moore 1973, at N116; see also Keynes *Writings* 1957, pp.208–9. A number of these subjects are the same as those of the early series of watercolours and Blake seems to have painted at about this time larger, more accomplished versions of some of them; in view of the fact that these reworkings are close in size to the separate engraving of 'Edward & Elenor' also announced in the 1793 *Prospectus* it may be that when Blake came to look again at his early watercolours he was led, rather than to use them for 'a small book of Engravings', to rework them on a larger scale with an eye to further separate larger prints. No.14

below is an example of one of these larger reworkings. (For the two series of illustrations to English history and related drawings see Butlin 1981, nos. 51–70 and the introductory text on p. 16.)

What may have been a sketch for this composition is the indian ink drawing, said to measure $11\frac{1}{4} \times 15\frac{1}{4}$ in, sold at Puttick's on 21 July 1937 (432) and untraced since. The subject also appears as one of the seven small watercolours, oval in format, now in the Museum of Fine Arts, Boston (Butlin no. 84 4, pl. 84, where dated *c*.1780, but Essick 1982–3 dates them rather later, say *c*.1783).

Blunt, who also dates this work slightly later than the other historical watercolours of *c*.1779, sees the figure of Cordelia as a reflection of a drawing by or after Daniele da Volterra.

2 **Charon, Copy from the Antique?** *c*.1779–80(?) (recto)

Part of a Face, Copy from the Antique? *c*.1779–80(?) (verso)

A 00045 / B 178
Recto: pen approx. 395 × 260 ($15\frac{1}{2} \times 10\frac{1}{4}$);
Verso: pencil approx. 110 × 145 ($4\frac{1}{4} \times 5\frac{3}{4}$); on paper 435 × 338 ($17\frac{1}{8} \times 13\frac{5}{16}$)
Inscribed on recto by Frederick Tatham, 'Charon by William Blake copied from something else not designed by him Fredk Tatham' b.r.
Presented by Mrs John Richmond 1922

PROVENANCE
Mrs Blake; Frederick Tatham; his brother-in-law George Richmond, sold Christie's 29 April 1897 (in 147, with nos. 7, 9, 10, 15–20, 43, 50, 53–5, 107, 151, 166–9, 171 and 172) £2.10.0 bt 'Dr. Cicely' (Dr Richard Sisley); his daughter, Mrs John Richmond

LITERATURE
Keynes *Drawings* 1970, no. 82, recto repr.; Bindman 1977, pp. 19, 228–9 n. 5; Butlin 1981, pp. 67–8 no. 178, pl. 251; Mary Lynn Johnson, 'Observations on Blake's Paintings and Drawings', in *Blake*, XVI, 1982–3, p. 6

Blake did a number of copies after the Antique for engravings (see Russell *Engravings* 1912, pl. 161–2, 166, 180–1) but no antique protypes or dependent engravings have been discovered that relate to the drawings on this sheet. However, Mary Lynn Johnson reports seeing at the gallery of Rafael Valls in London in 1977 a large finished pencil drawing from what seems to have been the same original as that shown on the recto; 'the head, eyes, beard, staff, and general expression are too similar to be coincidental'. The figure on the Tate Gallery drawing is shown as being cut off at the bottom by what may be the decorated edge of a boat, assuming that Charon is portrayed, or the surface of water, in which case he is not. Mary Lynn Johnson, who is also suspicious of the identification with Charon, gives one piece of supporting evidence, however, the pen and ink drawing by George Romney of 'Psyche being rowed across the Styx' in the Fitzwilliam Museum (repr. Essick and Pearce 1978, pl. 171), in which the general pose, the staff and the billowing of the cape of Charon are similar to those in the Tate drawing. The blank eyes support the suggestion that the drawing was made from an antique sculpture; on the other hand, it is just possible that the blind Orion may be the subject.

The verso also shows a detail from what appears to be a carved head with blank eyes, probably also copied from an antique sculpture.

The dating adopted here corresponds with the time that Blake might have copied from the Antique as a student at the Royal Academy. However, he continued to do copies of the Antique later in his life, including the famous occasion when he went to the cast rooms of the Royal Academy Schools to copy the Laocoön in 1815 (see Butlin 1981, no. 679, pl. 898A).

This work was formerly inventoried as no. 3694 xviii.

2(recto)

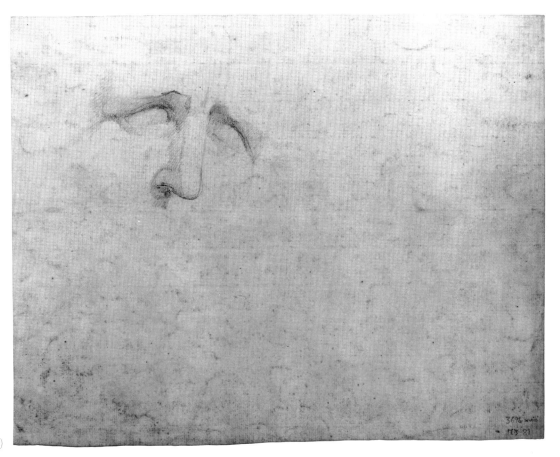

2(verso)

3 **An Allegory of the Bible** *c.*1780–85 (recto)

Part Drawing of a Nude Male Figure (?): Two Shins *c.*1780–85 (verso)

T 01128/B 127
Recto: pen and watercolour over pencil,
irregular, 615 × 349 (24¼ × 13¾); this includes a
strip of paper tapering from 10 (4) to 9 (3⅝)
overlapping the main sheet of paper by 1.5 (½)
added at the top; Verso: pencil.
Bequeathed by Miss Rachel M. Dyer to the
National Portrait Gallery and transferred to
the Tate Gallery 1969

PROVENANCE
…; Alexander Macmillan by 1876; by descent
to his granddaughter Miss Rachel M. Dyer

EXHIBITED
BFAC 1876 (47)

LITERATURE
Rossetti 1880, p.251 no.239 as 'The
Pilgrimage of Christiana'; Essick in Paley and
Phillips 1973, p.58; Bindman 1977, p.31,
pl.23; Butlin 1981, pp.48–9 no.127, pl.147

Although finished in colour this work is close to the large group of pen and wash
drawings that can be dated to the early and mid 1780s, e.g. nos.4 and 6. The
decoration of the parapet at the top of the steps resembles that in the background of
'Joseph Ordering Simeon to be Bound', exhibited at the Royal Academy in 1785
(Butlin 1981, no.156, colour pl.184), and the treatment of hair and the patterned
dress of one of the figures look forward to such works as 'Age Teaching Youth',
no.8, and Blake's illustrations to his poem *Tiriel* of *c.*1789 (Butlin no.198, the series
repr. Bentley *Tiriel* 1967). On the other hand 'An Allegory of the Bible' is
considerably less accomplished than those works of the mid and late 1780s and was
presumably painted earlier.

William Rossetti's title, 'The Pilgrimage of Christiana', presumably refers to the
second part of John Bunyan's *The Pilgrim's Progress*, the first of which was later
illustrated by Blake in a series of watercolours left unfinished at his death (Butlin
no.829, pls.1093–1120). It is, however, impossible to relate this composition to any
part of Bunyan's text, hence the more general title adopted here. The book, from
which rays of light shine forth, is not however necessarily the Bible. A source yet to
be fully explored for the subject of this and other similar early works is Swedenborg.

The drawing on the back of the strip of paper added at the top, upside down as
compared with the main composition, has been cut at both top and bottom, at the
ankles and the knees. This infers that it is a fragment from a complete figure. On the
recto of the added sheet of paper there are pencil lines underneath the watercolour
which continue over the otherwise bare paper which was concealed when the
larger sheet of paper was stuck over the edge. This suggests that these pencil lines
have nothing to do with the final composition, but what they represent is unclear.
In the main composition there is a pentimento round the lower half of the figure
descending the steps. The relative strength of colour in the areas at one time
covered by an old mount suggests that the main part of the design has faded,
particularly the pinks. The drawing was restored at the Tate Gallery in 1988.

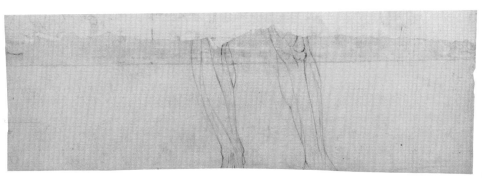

3(verso)

3(recto)

4 **The Good Farmer, Probably the Parable of the Wheat and the
Tares,** *c.*1780–85 (recto)

Rough Sketch of Two or Three Figures in a Landscape *c.*1780–85 (verso)

N 05198/B 123
Recto: pen and wash; Verso: pencil; on paper
267 × 375 (10$\frac{1}{2}$ × 14$\frac{3}{4}$)
Inscribed on verso, not by Blake, 'Sketch/by
Blake R.A.' b.c. and 'N⁰ 9./4.11.0' b.r.
Bequeathed by Miss Alice G.E. Carthew 1940

PROVENANCE
…; Miss Carthew by 1918 (letter in Tate
Gallery files)

LITERATURE
Keynes *Bible* 1957, p.34 no.118, recto repr.;
Butlin 1981, p.47 no.123, recto pl.141, verso
pl.166; David Bindman, review of Butlin 1981
in *Burlington Magazine*, CXXV, 1983, p. 371

Inscribed on the back, not by Blake, are the words 'Sketch by Blake R.A. [?]'; the
last letters are unclear and Blake never was a Royal Academician although he did
exhibit there.

The drawing on the recto is typical of Blake's rather crude pen and wash
drawings of the early 1780s. It is one of a series of drawings in which Blake worked
out the composition of a subject showing a cornfield with a Christ-like figure as
chief protagonist with other figures beseeching his aid or raising their arms
imploringly to heaven; most if not all show a scene of destruction in the distance
(Butlin 1981, nos.120–5, pls.135–142). The Tate Gallery drawing seems to have
been executed after the two drawings on one sheet belonging to Robert N. Essick
(Butlin no.122) and before that belonging to the Humanities Research Center,
University of Texas, Austin (Butlin no.124).

The subject of this series of drawings has been much debated. One of them
(Butlin no.121) has been tentatively identified as an illustration to Ruth, ii, 1–17,
but the figure of a woman gleaning that suggested this identification disappears
between the recto and the verso of the next drawing in the series (Butlin no.122).
William Rossetti gives two alternative interpretations for the more elaborate
drawing that seems to conclude the series (Butlin no.124), firstly as 'The Parable of
the Sower' (Matthew, xii, 18–23) with, behind, 'an angel in the sky … sowing the
seed', and secondly as '"Christ as the Good Farmer", distributing His produce to
the poor; … a group in the background shows a hard-hearted farmer whose goods
are being destroyed by lightning' (1863, p.267 list 2 no.76, and 1880, p.265 list 2
no.100). According to Irene Langridge (*William Blake, a Study of His Life and Art
Work*, 1904, pp.185–6), D.G. Rossetti and Frederic Shields suggested that the
drawings illustrate I Samuel, xii, 16–19, in which Samuel calls upon the Lord to
strike the harvest with thunder and rain as a judgement on the people for wanting a
king. Michael Tolley has suggested (in correspondence) a more general title, 'Pray
ye therefore the Lord of the Harvest' (Matthew, ix, 38), while accepting that there
is a link with I Samuel, xii, 16–19.

Most recently David Bindman has suggested that the drawings illustrate the
Parable of the wheat and the tares (Matthew, xiii, 24–30) in which the good farmer
allows both the wheat and the tares to ripen so that at the harvest they can be
separated and the wheat gathered and the tares burnt. In Christ's explanation of
this Parable 'The field is the world; the good seed are the children of the kingdom;
but the tares are the children of the wicked ones; the enemy that sowed them is the
devil; the harvest is the end of the world and the reapers are the angels. As therefore
the tares are gathered and burned in the fire, so shall it be in the end of this world'
(Matthew, xiii, 37–43). This apocalyptic theme has parallels in some of Blake's
other designs of the mid 1780s, and reflects his links with other Millenarians (for
Blake and Millenarianism see Morton D. Paley, 'William Blake, the Prince of the
Hebrews, and the Woman Clothed with the Sun', in Paley and Phillips 1973,
pp.260–93, Bindman 1977, pp.31–3, and Bindman 1982, pp.16–20, 74–6).

4(recto)

4(verso)

In style this group of drawings seems to date from the earlier 1780s, preceding the fully accomplished neo-classicism of the watercolour illustrations to the story of Joseph exhibited at the Royal Academy in 1785 (Butlin nos.155–7, colour pls.183–5). The drawing of 'St. John the Evangelist before a Vision of Christ' on the back of the first drawing in the series, one of the two in the British Museum (Butlin no.120 recto, the verso repr. pl.144) was engraved early in 1782 but was not necessarily done at the same time as the drawing on the recto.

The drawing on the back seems to show three figures seated in animated conversation in a landscape, but no specific subject can be suggested. In the top right-hand corner, to be seen with the paper turned at a right-angle, is what seems to be a separate sketch of three stooping figures, perhaps connected with the drawing on the recto.

Before restoration this drawing bore green and brown stains matching those to be found on a number of Blake's early drawings including two further ones from the 'Good Farmer' series, suggesting that they were all together in Blake's studio (the drawings are Butlin 1981, nos.94, 104A, 123, 124, 139A and 186).

5 Oberon, Titania and Puck with Fairies Dancing *c.*1785

N 02686 / B 161
Pencil and watercolour, irregular 475 × 675
($18\frac{3}{4}$ × $26\frac{1}{2}$)
Presented by Alfred A. de Pass in memory of his wife Ethel 1910

PROVENANCE
Mrs Blake, sold to Francis Cary, sold Christie's 13 March 1895 (16) £3.10.0 bt. Leggatt; Alfred A. de Pass, given 1910 to the Tate Gallery

EXHIBITED
Carfax 1904 (34); Tate Gallery (45), Manchester (52), Nottingham (34) and Edinburgh (37) 1913–14; *Shakespeare in Art*, Arts Council, April–May 1964 (33); New Haven and Toronto 1982–3 (16, repr.)

LITERATURE
Gilchrist 1863, I, p.366; Rossetti 1863, p.237 no.212, and 1880, p.251 no.240; Blunt 1959, p.10; Gert Schiff, *Johann Heinrich Füssli, ein Sommernachtstraum* 1961, p.20, pl.13; Merchant in *Apollo*, LXXIX, 1964, pp.320–2, pl.6 (reprinted in Essick 1973, pp.241–3, pl.66); Martin Butlin, 'Another Blake Watercolour cleaned at the Tate Gallery' in *Blake Newsletter*, VI, 1972–3, p.43; Bindman 1977, pp.37–8, pl.32; Paley 1978, p.20; Butlin 1981, p.61 no.161, colour pl.182; Warner 1984, p.155, pl.89; Baine 1986, p.4

This watercolour illustrates the closing scene of Shakespeare's *A Midsummer Night's Dream*. It is close in style and handling to the three finished watercolours of events from the life of Joseph exhibited at the Royal Academy in 1785 (Butlin 1981, nos.155–7, colour pls.183–5); there seems no reason to adopt the slightly later dating of *c.*1785–87 proposed by David Bindman (exh. cat.1982–3, *loc.cit.*). Two further watercolours showing 'Oberon and Titania, preceded by Puck' and 'Oberon and Titania on a Lily' are distinct in style and seem to date from the early 1790s (see Butlin 1981, nos.245–6, pls.294–5).

The watercolour was cleaned and restored to something near its original brilliance in 1973.

5

6   **Job, his Wife and his Friends: The Complaint of Job** c.1785 (recto)

Job's Wife and other Sketches c.1785 (verso)

N 05200/B 162
Recto: pen and grey wash; Verso: pencil; on
paper 311 × 451 (12¼ × 17¾)
Inscribed on verso by Frederick Tatham(?),
'Job. his Wife/& 3 friends' b.r.
Bequeathed by Miss Alice G.E. Carthew 1940

PROVENANCE
Mrs Blake; Frederick Tatham, ? sold
Sotheby's 29 April 1862 (in 164 with another
version of this subject and two of 'The Death
of Ezekiel's Wife', Butlin 1981, nos.164–5) bt
F.T. Palgrave; …; ? sold anonymously
Sotheby's 18–23 April 1904, 2nd day (403) bt
W. Daniell; …; Miss A.G.E. Carthew by
1914

EXHIBITED
Manchester (69), Nottingham (52) and
Edinburgh (25) 1914; Paris and Vienna 1937
(2); *British Painting* Hamburg, Oslo,
Stockholm and Copenhagen 1949–50 (1);
Port Sunlight 1950 (17)

LITERATURE
Binyon and Keynes *Job* 1935, I, p.3, recto
pl.4; Keynes *Separate Plates* 1956, p.11; Blunt
1959, p.11; Keynes *Blake Studies* 1971, p.176,
recto repr. p.45; Lindberg *Job* 1973, pp.11–12
nos.iii (recto) and iv (verso), 246–8 nos.10 Fi
(recto) and 10 Fii (verso), pls.32 and 33;
Bindman 1977, p.36; Bindman in Essick and
Pearce 1978, p.94, recto pl.93; Paley 1978,
p.19; Essick *Printmaker* 1980, pp.65–6; Butlin
1981, pp.61–2 no.162, pls.199 and 200; Essick
1982–3, p.30, recto pl.11; Essick *Separate Plates*
1983, p.20, figs.9 and 10; Warner 1984, p.58,
pl.30

This drawing is generally accepted as being a typical example of Blake's style in pen
and ink of the mid 1780s, being more accomplished than works such as no.4. It is an
illustration to Job, vii, 17–18. Job, having lost his children and all his possessions,
and having been smitten with sore boils (see no.70), asks God for justification:
'What is man that thou shouldest … try him every moment?' The theme of Job's
sufferings was later to be illustrated by Blake in two series of watercolours and one
of engravings (see nos.108–130).

This drawing is the first of three connected with the large line engraving entitled,
in the second state, 'Job. What is Man That thou shouldest Try him Every
Moment?' The recto of the Tate Gallery drawing differs from the other versions of
the composition in that Job is seated between his wife and the three friends. On the
back of the drawing the figure of his wife appears, alone, but in the position she was
to occupy in all the subsequent versions of the composition.

The second state of the engraving bears a date 18 August 1793 but there exists an
earlier undated state, which was assigned by Keynes and others to the year 1786
while the second state was accepted, at face value, as dating from 1793 (Keynes
1956, pp.10–12, pls.6 and 7). The Tate drawing and the two subsequent drawings
were also dated c.1785.

However, the datings of the two states of the engravings, and of the two further
drawings, have now been brought into doubt. Lindberg, on the grounds that the
composition of the recto of the Tate drawing and that of its developments in the
other two drawings show a further development of a drawing of c.1793 in Blake's
Notebook (Butlin 1981, no.201 *20*; repr. Lindberg 1973, pl.31), redated the first
state of the engraving to 1793 and the second to c.1798. However, the dependence
on the Notebook drawing is by no means certain. Nevertheless, it is now generally
accepted that Blake's dates on the later states of his engravings refer to the date of
the first state or original conception, not to the revised state. This argument has
been most closely argued by Essick (1980, pp.64–73). The arguments for dating
the first state of the engraving to 1793 are now accepted by most authorities
including myself. The second state is tentatively dated to c.1808–9 in Butlin
1979–80, pp.18–19, while both Essick and Lindberg now date this state even later,
to the 1820s (Essick 1980, pp.65–8, 178–87, 219–20, and definitively, 1983,
pp.17–20 no.v, the two states repr. figs.7 and 9; Lindberg 1981–2, p.142).

6(recto)

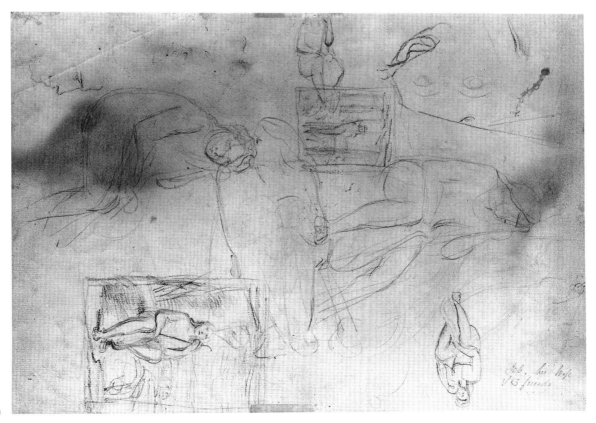

6(verso)

The finished drawing now in the Fine Art Museums of San Francisco (Butlin no.164, pl.201) must now also be accepted as having been executed in the early 1790s (see Essick 1983, p.20, fig.11). An earlier version of the composition reappeared early in 1989; it had been sold from the collection of Miss Brenda G. Warr at Sotheby's, 17–21 December 1928, first day (138) when it was bought by Maggs (Butlin no.163). It corresponds in the placing of the figures to the finished drawing in San Francisco, though in style it parallels the first of two drawings for a companion print to the 'Job' showing 'Ezekiel, I take away from thee the Desire of thine Eyes'. Of this only one state survives, dated 1794 but now presumed to share the later dating of the second state of the Job print, the technique of which it parallels; the putative first state would therefore be the work of 1794. There is a finished drawing in the Philadelphia Museum of Art (Butlin no.166, pl.203) that matches in style the Job drawing at San Francisco, and there is also an earlier drawing, typical in style of works of the mid 1780s, in the collection of George C. Homans (Butlin no.165, pl.202; for the 'Ezekiel' print and related drawings see also Essick 1983, pp.21–3 no.vi, the print and drawings repr. figs.12–14).

To sum up, the various versions of the Job composition and their dates seem to be as follows: the Tate Gallery recto, the Tate Gallery verso, and the Brenda G. Warr drawing, all of *c*.1785; the more richly worked, finished drawing in San Francisco, and the first state of the engraving, of 1793 or thereabouts; the second, drastically reworked state of the print, dating from well into the nineteenth century, either *c*.1801–9 or from the 1820s.

On the verso, besides the drawing of Job's wife, there are a number of rapid pencil sketches, drawn with the paper held in different positions. To the right of Job's wife is what seems to be a sketch for the lower part of the foremost friend. Blake then used the paper to develop other themes. There is a small complete sketch of a figure with lyre and staff seated in a landscape, possibly Orpheus or Apollo, although no finished work of this subject is recorded. Various poses for this seated figure were tried out in four other sketches; two further sketches of this figure appear with other sketches on a drawing now in the collection of Edwin Wolf 2nd (Butlin no.81, pl.81). Possibly related to this theme is the minute composition sketch of a figure apparently standing before a screen of columns or trees. Finally there are two sketches of profiles and two more of eyes seen full-face.

The early history of the three drawings relating to the engraving of Job is confused, particularly as two drawings of this subject were bought by F.T. Palgrave at Sotheby's in 1862, and as all three are of much the same size, but the provenance given above seems to be the most probable one. The drawing sold anonymously in 1904 was described as 'Job, his Wife and Three Friends. "What is a man that thou shouldest try him every moment?" Drawing, $17\frac{1}{2}$ in. × 12 in. This important drawing was formerly in the collection of Mr. Palgrave. It is fully described in Gilchrist's *Life*, 1863, vol.i, p.137 [the reference here is in fact to the engraving], and vol.ii, p.240. On the back are several of Blake's designs in pencil.' This sounds like the Tate Gallery's drawing. William Rossetti's listing in Gilchrist's *Life* of 1863, ii, p.240 list 2 no.6, of a work from Palgrave's collection in fact sounds more like the Brenda G. Warr drawing in that Rossetti describes it as being 'In outline; rather empty in manner'; he does not mention any drawings on the back, though there is in fact a sketch for 'The Bard', presumably related to the lost R.A. exhibit of 1785 (see no.60). It is just possible, though not very likely, that the drawing sold in 1904 could subsequently have belonged to Thomas Woolner, R.A, before being acquired by Miss Carthew. It was sold from Woolner's collection at Sotheby's on 20 December 1912 (97, as 'Job and his comforters', pen and ink, $12 × 17\frac{3}{4}$ in) where it was bought by Tregaskis, appearing in his catalogue of January 1913. However, Woolner was a close personal friend of F.T. Palgrave, even sharing a house with him in 1861–2 (Amy Woolner, *Thomas Woolner R.A.* 1917, pp.205–6, 213), and he could more likely have acquired his drawing direct from Palgrave. Either way, the San Francisco drawing does not seem to have been that sold in 1904 as it seems to have no drawings on the back, nor can it have been owned by Woolner as it was bought by W. Graham Robertson in 1906 and retained by him until his death and its subsequent sale at Christie's in 1949.

7 **Lower Half of a Woman Playing a Harp** *c*.1785 (recto)

Seraphim and Other Drawings *c*.1807(?) (verso)

A 00044 / B 77
Pencil 268 × 450 (10$\frac{9}{16}$ × 17$\frac{3}{4}$): the verso is upright in format
Inscribed on verso by Frederick Tatham
'William Blake vouched by Frederick Tatham' b.r.
Presented by Mrs John Richmond 1922

PROVENANCE
Mrs Blake; Frederick Tatham; his brother-in-law George Richmond, sold Christie's 29 April 1897 (in 147, with 22 other items, see no.2) £2.10.0 bt Dr Richard Sisley; his daughter, Mrs John Richmond

LITERATURE
Butlin 1981, p.29 no.77, pls.68 and 70

The sketch on the recto is the bottom half of a drawing the rest of which is on a sheet in the Rosenbach Museum, Philadelphia (Butlin 1981, no.76 verso, pl.67; in Butlin 1981 the recti and versi of these two drawings are transposed). Although slightly smaller, 11$\frac{1}{4}$ × 16$\frac{9}{16}$ in, the Rosenbach sheet shows the upper half of the seated girl playing the harp which connects, allowing for a small loss in between, with the seated figure with harp, seen from the waist down, on the Tate Gallery sheet. On the left of the Tate Gallery drawing there are two partly erased sketches of hands which seem to be alternative ideas for the girl's right hand plucking the harp strings in the Rosenbach drawing.

The drawings on the backs of the sheets in the Tate Gallery and the Rosenbach Museum are not connected with each other and must have been done after the drawing of the woman playing the harp had been cut in two. In earlier editions of this catalogue and in Butlin 1981 the drawing on the back of the Rosenbach sheet was dated *c*.1780 but this seems to be an error. It is related to the small relief-etching of 'Joseph of Arimathea Preaching to the Inhabitants of Britain' at present known only in two colour-printed versions of *c*.1795 (Butlin 1981, nos.262 *6* and 286, pl.366 and colour pl.340). Although the underlying relief-etching may have been executed a few years earlier there is nothing stylistically about the drawing to prevent it from having been executed in the first half of the 1790s.

Similarly the sketches on the back of the Tate Gallery sheet seem to have been executed considerably later than 1780. The seraphim, if such they are, appear in a tight group in the lower right-hand corner. The drawing at the top of the sheet is perhaps related to that in Blake's Notebook called by Keynes 'The Trinity' (Butlin no.201 *104*, repr. Keynes 1970, no.15, and Erdman and Moore *Notebook* 1973); through this it is related to the figures of God the Father embracing the Son in 'Christ offers to Redeem Man' from the illustrations of 1807 and 1808 to *Paradise Lost* (Butlin nos.529 *3* and 536 *3*, colour pls.634 and 647). In the Tate Gallery drawing the ascending figure seems to be accompanied by two smaller figures, perhaps angels. The drawing in the lower right-hand corner could also be related to the two *Paradise Lost* series, showing some resemblance to the seated manacled figure seen full-face in 'Satan Calling up his Legions' (Butlin nos.529 *1* and 536 *1*, colour pls.632 and 645). The rough sketch in the centre of the sheet is unidentifiable. Some of the Miltonic drawing in Blake's *Notebook* were subsequently

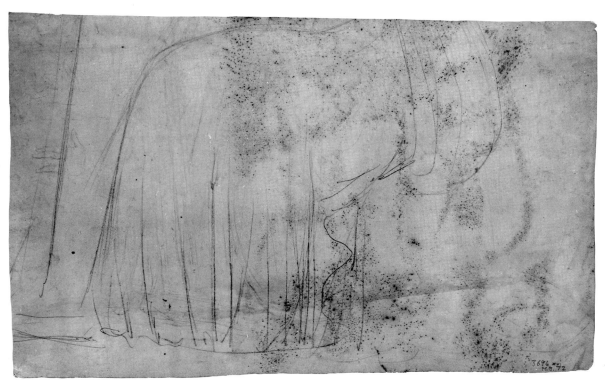

7(recto)

7(verso)

covered by drafts for *Songs of Experience*, first issued by Blake in 1794, and presumably precede this date. However, it seems more likely that the Miltonic drawings on the Tate Gallery sheet are more directly related to the *Paradise Lost* series of 1807 and 1808, hence the tentative dating given above.

The degree of accomplishment shown in the upper part of the drawing of the woman playing the harp on the recti of the two sheets has always made a dating of as early as *c.*1780 difficult to accept. The drawing, not being typical of Blake in its subject, is difficult to date. It is tempting to see it as a life study made in preparation for the several drawings of people playing harps in the illustrations to Gray's *Poems* of *c.*1797–8 (Butlin no.335) and in particular for what one can see of the decorative head-piece of the harp in the watercolour of 'The Welch Bard' accompanying the title page to *The Bard* (Butlin no.335 *53*, repr. Geoffrey Keynes, *William Blake's Water-colour Designs for the Poems of Thomas Gray*, 1971, Irene Taylor, *Blake's Illustrations to the Poems of Gray*, 1971, and Geoffrey Keynes, *William Blake's Water-Colour Designs for the Poems of Thomas Gray*, Blake Trust facsimile in colour, 1972). Even more likely, the drawing could have been done in preparation for the lost watercolour of 'The Bard' exhibited at the Royal Academy in 1785 (Butlin no.160; see also no.60). The upper part of the drawing shows a strong Neo-Classical crispness and sense of line which suggests that date. However, it bears no relationship to the recently rediscovered drawing for 'The Bard' noted under no.6.

This work was formerly inventoried as no.3694 xvi.

8 **Age Teaching Youth** *c.*1785–90

N 05183 / B 91
Pen and watercolour 108 × 80 ($4\frac{1}{2} \times 3\frac{1}{8}$)
Bequeathed by Miss Alice G.E. Carthew 1940

PROVENANCE
?Mrs Blake; ?Frederick Tatham, ?sold Sotheby's 29 April 1862 (? in 185, 2 items 'in colours') 15/- bt Harvey; Harvey by 1863; George A. Smith, sold Christie's 16 July 1880 (102) 14/- bt J. Pearson; ?U.S. collection by 1905; Miss Carthew

EXHIBITED
BFAC 1876 (183); ?*Exhibition of the Works of William Blake*, Grolier Club, New York, January–February 1905 (95 as 'An old man seated teaching a young girl; a youth in gaily coloured raiment seated, in foreground, reading'); Tate Gallery 1978 (39, repr.)

LITERATURE
Rossetti 1863, p.237 no.219, and 1880, p.252 no.249; Binyon 1922, p.22, pl.3; Essick in Paley and Phillips 1973, p.58; Bindman 1977, p.48; Butlin 1981, pp.35–6 no.91, colour pl.179

This small watercolour is close in style and handling to a number of delicate pen and wash drawings of the 1780s, some in colour, others in monochrome. The works in colour include 'A Man and a Woman Kneeling and Warming Themselves at a Fire' in the British Museum, 'An Enthroned Old Man Offering Two Children to Heaven' in the Fogg Art Museum and 'An Old Man and a Woman in Contemplative Adoration' in a private collection (Butlin 1981, nos.87, 88 and 90, pls.95, 97 and 99). The monochrome works include 'A Girl and a Bearded Man Embracing' and 'An Old Man Appearing on a Cloud to a Young Nude Couple', both in the British Museum (Butlin nos.85 and 86, pls.91 and 92). Some of these compositions are based on a group of eight rapid pen sketches on the back of the two last-mentioned British Museum drawings, which were originally on a single piece of paper (Butlin 1981, pls.93 and 94). Michael Tolley has suggested that the series of compositions, which seem to concern two protagonists, one male, one female, set out a story of murder, exile and redemption (Michael J. Tolley, 'Some

8

Blake Puzzles – Old and New' in *Blake Studies*, III, 1971, pp.107–28). 'Age Teaching
Youth' is not however based on one of these composition sketches and Michael
Tolley did not include it in his discussion; but the theme may be connected.

   In style this whole group of drawings seems to date from the later 1780s,
preceding the series of pen and wash illustrations to *Tiriel* of *c.*1789 (Butlin no.198,
the series repr. Bentley *Tiriel* 1967); the boy's decorated garment in 'Age Teaching
Youth' is particularly close to the similar costume in 'Har Blessing Tiriel' (Butlin
no.198 *4*). In its somewhat Stothard-like mood and delicacy it also anticipates the
illustrations to *Songs of Innocence*, issued by Blake in 1789. In particular the
apparently innocent scene of children reading accompanied by an adult is close to
that on the title page. Essick however, linking this work more closely to *Tiriel*, sees
the old man as representing the repression and false wisdom later embodied by
Blake in his character Urizen; the boy absorbed in the book wears a dress
representing Nature uninspired, but the girl points to Heaven as if to contradict the
codified knowledge of the books.

9(recto)

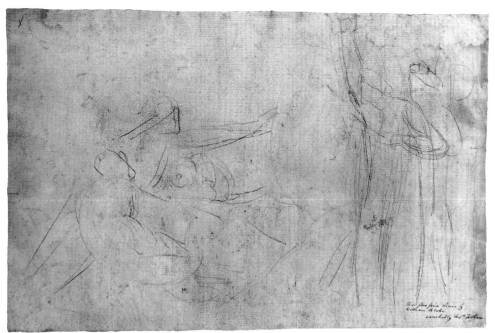

9(verso)

9   **Sketches for 'Tiriel Supporting the Dying Myratana'** *c.*1789
(recto and verso)

A 00040 / B 200
Pencil 291 × 450 (11½ × 17¾)
Inscribed on recto by Frederick Tatham
'These few fine Lines by William Blake
vouched by Fredk Tatham' b.r.
Presented by Mrs John Richmond 1922

PROVENANCE
Mrs Blake; Frederick Tatham; his brother-in-

law George Richmond, sold Christie's 29 April
1897 (in 147, with 22 other works; see no.2)
£2.10.0 bt Dr Richard Sisley; his daughter
Mrs John Richmond

LITERATURE
Michael Tolley, review of 1971 edition of this
catalogue, *Blake Newsletter*, VI, 1972–3, p.29;
Butlin 1981, no.200, pls.227 and 228

The drawings on both the recto and the verso are almost certainly connected with
'Tiriel Supporting the Dying Myratana and Cursing his Sons', one of the twelve

pen and wash drawings illustrating Blake's poem *Tiriel* (Yale Center for British Art, Paul Mellon Collection; Butlin 1981, no.198 *1*, pl.223). The aged Tiriel, with his dying wife Myratana, upbraids and curses their three sons who have driven him into exile (Keynes *Writings* 1957, p.89; Bentley *Tiriel* 1967, pp.60–61). The architectural background of the finished drawing is absent, and the gestures of the figures are somewhat different, but the confrontation of the two groups is very close in feeling. The drawing on the recto also has elements of 'Tiriel Upheld on the Shoulders of Ijim' (Victoria and Albert Museum; Butlin no.198 *7*; repr. Bentley 1967, pl.5).

The twelve finished pen and wash drawings illustrate, more or less closely, the manuscript known as *Tiriel* from the name of its chief protagonist (British Museum, Dept of MS. EG2876; repr. in full Bentley 1967, pp.61–89). They measure approximately $7\frac{1}{4} \times 10\frac{3}{4}$ in, slightly larger than and in the opposite direction to the pages of the manuscript which are $8\frac{1}{4} \times 6\frac{3}{16}$ in. They were probably designed, had the work been published, to have been engraved in the conventional way. This supports a date before Blake's fusion of text and illustration in one technical process in the illuminated books which began in *There is no Natural Religion* and *All Religions are One* of *c.*1788, and, in its fully developed form, in *Songs of Innocence* of 1789. Most authorities, including Anthony Blunt (1959, p.11) and Bentley, have dated both manuscript and drawings to *c.*1789; David Bindman (1977, pp.44–7, and exh. cat. 1982–3, pp.46, 78) suggests that they may have been begun at a rather earlier date, *c.*1786.

This work was formerly inventoried as no.3694 xi.

EARLY WORKS *c*.1779–*c*.1793

10

10 **Two Figures in a Decorative Border** *c*.1790

A 00042 / B 220
Pencil approx. 95 × 160 ($3\frac{3}{4}$ × $6\frac{1}{4}$) on paper
122 × 203 ($4\frac{13}{16}$ × 8)
Inscribed by Frederick Tatham 'William
Blake Frederick Tatham' b.r.
Presented by Mrs John Richmond 1922

PROVENANCE
Mrs Blake; Frederick Tatham; his brother-in-law George Richmond, sold Christie's 29 April 1897 (in 147, with 22 other works; see no.2) £2.10.0 bt Dr Richard Sisely; his daughter, Mrs John Richmond

LITERATURE
Butlin 1981, p.115 no.220, pl.251

The subject is difficult to make out but appears to be a girl, or perhaps a female centaur, looking down at another more sketchily drawn figure reclining in the lower left-hand corner of the scroll-like border. Although the drawing has been attributed to Robert Blake (see p.oo) it seems to be a work by William, of, very roughly, about 1790. It is perhaps connected with one of the early illuminated books or a decorative illustration. The girl's head has some points of similarity to that in the drawing perhaps related to *The Book of Thel*, 1789, in the British Museum (Butlin 1981, no.219, pl.250).

This work was formerly inventoried as no.3694 xiii.

11   After William Hogarth: The Beggar's Opera, Act III   1790

T 01801/ –
Etching and engraving 402 × 539
($15\frac{13}{16} \times 21\frac{3}{16}$) on wove paper, cut irregularly,
470 × 620 ($18\frac{1}{2} \times 24\frac{3}{8}$); platemark 457 × 582
($17\frac{15}{16} \times 22\frac{7}{8}$)
Engraved inscriptions; 'BEGGAR'S OPERA, ACT III.',
'"*When my hero in Court appears, &c.*"', '*From the
Original Picture, in the Collection of his Grace the
Duke of Leeds.*', '*Painted by W<u>m</u> Hogarth.*',
'*Engraved by W<u>m</u> Blake.*', '*Size of the picture* $\frac{1}{24}$ . .
by $\frac{1}{30}$ . . *long.*', '*Publish'd July 1<u>st</u> 1790, by J. and
J. Boydell, Cheapside, & at the Shakspeare Gallery
Pall Mall London*'.
Presented by Sir Geoffrey Keynes 1933;
transferred from the reference collection 1973

PROVENANCE
. . .; Sir Geoffrey Keynes

LITERATURE
Keynes *Separate Plates* 1956, pp.73–4;
Wilmarth Sheldon Lewis and Philip Hofer,
'*The Beggar's Opera*' *by Hogarth and Blake*, 1965;
Bentley *Blake Books* 1977, pp.581–4; Mitchell
1978, pp.45–6; Essick *Printmaker* 1980,
pp.18–19, 50, 58–9; Essick *Separate Plates*
1983, p.252 no.LXI

This is an example of the last of the four known states of Blake's engraving after the famous painting by Hogarth. There are in fact six oil paintings of the subject by Hogarth which fall into two main groups. Blake's engraving is after the first example in the second group which was acquired by the 4th Duke of Leeds at the John Rich sale in 1792 and remained with the Duke of Leeds until 1961; it is now in the Yale Center for British Art, Paul Mellon Collection. The Tate Gallery owns Hogarth's own replica of this version painted two years later in 1731 (N 02437; see Elizabeth Einberg and Judy Egerton, *Tate Gallery Collections: Volume 2: The Age of Hogarth; British Painters born 1675–1709*, 1988, pp.74–81 no.87, all versions repr.).

Blake's engraving was issued both separately and as no.103 of *The Original Works of William Hogarth*, published and sold by John and Josiah Boydell at the Shakespeare Gallery, Pall Mall, and no.90, Cheapside, London in 1790; it reappeared in subsequent editions of the same publication, with varied titles, in ?1795, 1822 and later. The 1790 issue contains impressions of either the third or fourth state; the two earlier states are known only as separate prints.

The first state, which is in etching alone, bears the imprint 'Painted Will<u>m</u> Hogarth 1729', 'Etch'd by Will<u>m</u> Blake 1788', and 'publish'd October 29: 1788: by Ald<u>m</u> Boydell & Co. Cheapside' (repr. Lewis and Hofer 1965, pl.VIII). The rare second state retains the 1788 imprint but the image has been completed (repr. Essick 1980, pl.48). The third state has the same imprint as the fourth except that the size is omitted and the letters of the title are left open rather than filled with hatching. The original copper-plate was in the collection of the late Philip Hofer and a modern restrike was included in each copy of Lewis and Hofer 1965 (pl.XI).

VELUTI IN SPECULUM UTILE DULCI

BEGGAR'S OPERA, Act III.

When my hero in Court appears, &c.

From the Original Picture in the Collection of his Grace the Duke of Leeds.

11

12 **The House of Death** *c*.1790

N 05192 / B 259
Pencil, pen and wash 318 × 451 ($12\frac{1}{2}$ × $17\frac{13}{16}$)
Bequeathed by Miss Alice G. E. Carthew 1940

PROVENANCE
...; ?William Bell Scott, sold Sotheby's 20–25
April 1885, 2nd day (185, as 'Subject from
Milton, pen and ink sketch') £1 bought
Pincott; ...; Miss Carthew

LITERATURE
Collins Baker in *Huntington Library Bulletin*, x,
1936, p.142; Gert Schiff, *Johann Heinrich Füsslis
Milton-Galerie*, 1963, pp.78–9, pl.38;
Hagstrum 1964, pp.67–8, pl.42a; Warner in
Erdman and Grant 1970, pp.186–7, pl.93;
Butlin 1981, p.131 no.259, pl.307

This is a more or less finished drawing illustrating Milton's *Paradise Lost*, xi, lines
477–93 and related to the large colour print, no.32. The drawing has been
damaged and was repaired by Miss Carthew, particularly in the upper left-hand
corner. In the print the recumbent pair on the left are omitted, Death and Despair
completely changed, and the other figures less radically altered.

Collins Baker suggested that the drawing was by Fuseli, who did a number of
versions of the subject including a large picture for his Milton Gallery, completed in
1793. However, although there is some general similarity in mood and in the figure
of Despair on the left, the composition is completely different, with recumbent
figures based on Blake's early studies of Gothic tombs in Westminster Abbey, and
heads on the right that are entirely characteristic of Blake's style. Moreover, the
relationship to the print, which is in reverse, seems to be too close for another artist
to be involved.

The drawing seems to show a later development of the style and technique of the
pen and wash drawings of the 1780s, for example nos.4 and 6. It is close to the *Tiriel*
illustrations of *c*.1789 (Butlin 1981, no.198, the series repr. Bentley *Tiriel* 1967) but
rather more personal, particularly the air-borne figure of Death which is already
Blake's typical Urizen-like type of bearded old man. On the other hand it probably
precedes the somewhat freer style of 'Los and Orc' (no.13). It can therefore be
dated to the beginning of the 1790s.

12

13 **Los and Orc** *c.*1792–3

T 00547/B 255
Pen and watercolour 217 × 295 ($8\frac{9}{16}$ × $11\frac{5}{8}$)
Signed 'W. Blake' b.l.
Presented by Mrs Howard Samuel in memory
of her husband 1962

PROVENANCE
John Linnell, sold Christie's 15 March 1918
(159, as 'A Figure chained to a Rock. A
mountainous landscape, with a figure on the
left [sic] chained to the ground; before him
stands another man with arms raised in
wonderment') £94.10.0 bt Apsley Cherry-
Garrard; his widow, sold April 1960 to
Quaritch, from whom bought by Howard
Samuel in May 1960; his widow, Jane Samuel

EXHIBITED
Hamburg and Frankfurt 1975 (34, repr.)

LITERATURE
Rossetti 1863, p.202 no.11, and 1880, p.208
no.13, as '1793. – A Young Man gazing
remorsefully upon another bound upon a
rock. [Mr Linnell]. Similar to the head-piece
of the "America" but without the female
figure, and a good deal larger. Darkish tone of
colouring'; Martin Butlin, 'Blake's "Vala, or
the Four Zoas" and a new Water-colour in the
Tate Gallery', *Burlington Magazine*, CVI, 1964,
pp.381–2, repr. p.379 fig.30; Raine 1968, I,
pp.346–7; Butlin 1981, p.129 no.255, pl.305;
Jean H. Hagstrum, review of Butlin 1981,
Modern Philology, LXXIX, 1981–2, p.449; Essick
1982–3, p.32

This watercolour is a version of the engraved design for the 'Preludium' to Blake's illuminated book *America*, which is dated 1793 on the title-page, but may have been begun a year or two earlier (repr. Erdman *Illuminated Blake* 1974, p.139). In the watercolour the composition is in reverse and lacks the female figure of the engraving, facts which suggest that it was executed first. It is similar in style, though more subdued in colour, to the watercolour of 'The Good and Evil Angels' in the Cecil Higgins Museum, Bedford (Butlin 1981, no.257, colour pl.197). The Bedford watercolour can be dated *c.*1793–4. It is a slightly later development, in the same direction, of the design of plate 4 of *The Marriage of Heaven and Hell* (repr. Erdman 1974, p.101); this book is dated 1790 on one copy but was almost certainly not completed until 1793, plate 4 being one of the later pages (see David V. Erdman, ed., *The Poetry and Prose of William Blake*, 1965 and subsequent editions, p.723). The watercolour formed the basis for the large colour print of 'The Good and Evil Angels' of 1795 (see no.33). 'Los and Orc' probably dates from slightly earlier, though in style it follows the *Tiriel* wash drawings of *c.*1789 (Butlin no.198, the series repr. Bentley *Tiriel* 1967).

The design in *America* accompanies the fourteen-year-old Orc's account of how he has been bound in chains by his father Urthona, but it prefigures rather a passage in one of Blake's slightly later poems, *Vala*, first drafted 1795–7; here Orc's parents Los (as Urthona is now called) and Enitharmon have come to repent of this deed and lament over their chained son ('Night the Fifth', lines 143–72; Keynes *Writings* 1957, p.309). *Vala*, later retitled *The Four Zoas*, was never published by Blake, but in the much emended manuscript in the British Museum (Butlin no.337, the whole repr. G.E. Bentley Jr, *Vala or the Four Zoas*, 1963, and Cettina Tramontano Magno and David V. Erdman, *The Four Zoas by William Blake*, 1987) this passage, rewritten *c.*1802–3, is accompanied on page 62 by another version of the *America* design in reverse but with all three figures. In Blake's mythology Los represents the 'Poetic Genius' and Enitharmon his inspiration; Orc embodies energy and revolt, and his chaining symbolises a restraint of natural passions.

Enitharmon is absent from the Tate Gallery watercolour but the scene shown is presumably the same. It is an indication of the close relationship between Blake's art and his writings that in this case the theme appears first in the visual form, not in his poetry. Some years later Blake returned to the subject again in the relief etching 'The Chaining of Orc' of 1802 (Essick *Separate Plates* 1983, pp.90–92 no.xvii, fig.45). In addition there is a complex stylistic and iconographic link with the watercolour and colour print of 'The Good and Evil Angels'; see no.33.

13

14 The Penance of Jane Shore in St Paul's Church *c*.1793

N 05898 / B 69
Pen and watercolour, sized, 245 × 295
($9\frac{5}{8} \times 11\frac{5}{8}$)
Presented by the Executors of W. Graham
Robertson through the National Art-
Collections Fund 1949

PROVENANCE
Mrs Blake; Frederick Tatham, sold Sotheby's
29 April 1862 (in 171 with another work)
£1.7.0 bt H. Toovey; C.J. Toovey; Henry
Cunliffe, sold Sotheby's 11 May 1895 (101)
£1.1.0 bt Joseph Grego; E. Parsons, sold July
1908 to W. Graham Robertson, offered at
Christie's 22 July 1949 (59) £273 bt his
executors

EXHIBITED
?Blake's exhibition 1809 (16); Tate Gallery
1913 (62); on loan to Tate Gallery from 1923;

Tate Gallery 1947 (79); Bournemouth,
Southampton and Brighton 1949 (13);
Whitworth 1969 (39, repr.); Tate Gallery
1978 (17, repr.)

LITERATURE
Blake *Descriptive Catalogue* 1809, pp.65–6
(reprinted in Keynes *Writings* 1957,
pp.585–6); Gilchrist 1863, I, p.31; Rossetti
1863, p.201 no.1, and 1880, p.207 no.1;
Russell *Engravings* 1912, p.66; Blunt in
Warburg Journal, VI, 1943, p.194, pl.54b;
Preston 1952, pp.74–6 no.20, pl.20; Blunt
1959, pp.4–9, pl.4a; Erdman 1969, p.47;
Bindman in Paley and Phillips 1973, pp.33–4;
Mellor 1974, pp.106–7, pl.28; Bindman 1977,
pp.24–5, 156–7, 247 n.26; Paley 1978, pp.19,
177, pl.1; Butlin in *Blake*, XIII, 1979–80, p.17,
repr.: Butlin 1981, p.24 no.69, pl.61

On the reverse Henry Cunliffe, one of the earlier owners of this watercolour, has
written, 'Jane Shore doing Penance by William Blake. Obit 28 Aug. 1828 [sic] For
a Biography of this most remarkable man see Cunningham's Lives of British
Painters Purchased Sotheby in Lot. No.171, 28 Ap. 1862, H.C.' Blake in fact died
on 12 August 1827; the year 1828, but not the mistaken date of the month, derives
from Allan Cunningham's *Lives of the Most Eminent British Painters, Sculptors and
Architects*, both the first and second editions of which were published in 1830 (for a
reprint see Bentley 1969, pp.476–507).

This is a later, more accomplished version of the small watercolour that forms
part of the series of illustrations to English history executed *c*.1779 and which is now
on loan to the Tate Gallery (Butlin 1981, no.69, pl.59). This has only two
bystanders on the right and five fully defined figures in the main group; only some
five further heads are suggested behind. There is also a pencil drawing of the main
figures, without any architectural setting, that seems to have been drawn between
the two watercolours; though much closer to the Tate Gallery version, it retains the
somewhat looser grouping of the figures of the earlier watercolour (Keynes
Collection, Fitzwilliam Museum, Cambridge; Butlin 1981, no.68, pl.60).

'The Penance of Jane Shore' appears in a list of titles of subjects from English
history written *c*.1793 in Blake's Notebook. Interestingly enough the drawing from
the Keynes Collection is almost the same size as the large historical engraving of the
same year, 'Edward & Elenor', published on 18 August 1793 ($12\frac{1}{8} \times 18\frac{1}{16}$ in; see
Essick 1983, pp.14–16 no.iv). This suggests a date, supported by style and
technique, for the Tate Gallery watercolour.

However, both Gilchrist and Rossetti assume that it was the watercolour now in
the Tate Gallery that was shown by Blake in his exhibition of 1809 with the note
'This Drawing was done above Thirty Years ago, and proves to the Author, and he
thinks will prove to any discerning eye, that the productions of our youth and of our
maturer age are equal in all essential points'. It is however the smaller, earlier
version of this composition that would seem to date from *c*.1779, but it is of so
tentative a character that it seems unlikely that Blake could have presumed to show
it with such pride in 1809. Blake's attitude to dates was somewhat cavalier; it was
the idea rather than the material execution that really mattered to him, and in his
catalogue he could well have been referring to his original conception as of 'above
Thirty Years ago'. A parallel example is the engraving of 'Joseph of Arimathea
among the Rocks of Albion' of which the second state, probably executed well into

14

the nineteenth century, is inscribed 'Engraved by W. Blake 1773', the presumed
date of the first much less accomplished state which is not dated (see Essick *Separate
Plates* 1983, pp.3–9 no.i). For other examples of Blake's cavalier approach to
dating see under no.6 and also the large colour prints, nos.25–34 in this catalogue.

Jane Shore (d.1527?) was a mistress of Edward IV and was noted for her beauty
and goodness of nature. On Edward's death in 1483 she was attacked by the
Protector, the future Richard III, who imprisoned her in the Tower, seized her
goods, and, to complete her ruin, accused her of harlotry. She was condemned in
the Ecclesiastical Court to do public penance in St Paul's Church and was brought
there in a white sheet, with a wax taper in her hand; there '... she behaved with so
much modesty and decency, that such as respected her beauty more than her fault,
never were in greater admiration of her, than now' – so wrote Rapin de Thoyras in
his *History of England*, probably Blake's chief source for his early historical paintings
(translated N. Tindal, third ed., 1743, I, p.635). Blake probably chose the subject
as a protest against orthodox sexual morality. Another instance is 'The Ordeal of
Queen Emma' (Butlin 1981, no.51, colour pl.177), who in the legend illustrated by
Blake was accused of adultery by her son Edward the Confessor. Erdman has

suggested that there is also an anti-monarchist element in many of the early historical paintings, but this has been denied by Anthony Blunt (review of Erdman (1954 ed.) in *Burlington Magazine*, XCIX, 1957, p.101).

Treatment at the Tate Gallery in 1972 showed that the varnish covering the watercolour was considerably later and it was removed, leaving a much more translucent layer of size below. Finishing in size to give greater depth to the colours was quite common among watercolourists at the end of the eighteenth century and the beginning of the nineteenth, and Blake may have added it for his exhibition in 1809. Gilchrist writes that 'One extrinsic circumstance materially detracts from the appearance of this and other watercolour drawings from his hand of the period 1778–9 : viz. that they were all eventually, in prosecution of a hobby of Blake's, *varnished* – of which process, applied to a watercolour drawing, nothing can exceed the disenchanting, not to say destructive effect'; it is not clear whether what he saw was mainly the size or whether the watercolour had already been varnished by this time.

MISCELLANEOUS PAGES, FRAGMENTS AND SEPARATE DESIGNS FROM THE ILLUMINATED BOOKS 1789–1795

The Tate Gallery possesses no complete illuminated book by Blake but five odd pages from *Songs of Innocence and of Experience* and the fragment of a page from *Europe* give some idea of the innovatory technique of these works. As Blake himself claimed in his prospectus *To the Public* of 10 October 1793, he 'invented a method of Printing both Letter-press and Engraving in a style more ornamental, uniform, and grand than any before discovered' (Keynes *Writings* 1957, p.207). He was able to print both text and illustration from the same copper plate and in most of his books, including those represented by the fragments in the Tate, this was done by relief etching or stereotype rather than intaglio, that is printing from the raised, unetched surface of the plate rather than from lines or areas engraved or etched into the plate; the words or designs to be printed were almost certainly drawn or painted with a resist directly onto the plate.

At the end of *The Ghost of Abel* of 1822 Blake stated that 'Blake's Original stereotype was 1788', and he seems to have claimed that his brother Robert, who died in February 1787, had dictated the technique to him in vision. J.G. Smith wrote in *Nollekens and his Times*, 1828, that 'Blake, after deeply perplexing himself as to the mode of accomplishing the publication of his illustrated songs, without their being subject to the expense of letter-press, his brother Robert stood before him in one of his visionary imaginations, and so decidedly directed him in the way in which he ought to proceed, that he immediately followed his advice, by writing his poetry, and drawing his marginal subjects of embellishments in outline upon the copper-plate with an impervious liquid, and then eating the plain parts or lights away with aquafortis considerably below them, so that the outlines were left as a stereotype. The plates in this state were then printed in any tint that he wished, to enable him or Mrs. Blake to colour the marginal figures up by hand in imitation of drawings' (II, p.461; Bentley *Blake Records* 1969, p.460). John Linnell added a note in the margin of a copy of this book, subsequently deleted, that 'The most extraordinary facility seems to have been attained by Blake in writing backwards ...' (Bentley *loc.cit.*).

Blake's first books in this technique are the tentative and very small *All Religions are One* and *There is no Natural Religion*, which seem to have been etched in 1788. However, the technique seems to have been in the air at the time; indeed the experiments of Blake's friend George Cumberland are referred to in Blake's manuscript *An Island in the Moon* of *c*.1784 (Keynes *Writings* 1957, p.62) The fullest account of Blake's processes is given by Robert Essick though Ruthven Todd made important experiments in the technique.

The intimate connection of text and illustration was not merely a question of technique. Blake, as both poet and artist, used each medium to comment and enlarge upon the other. In view of the peripheral place of these pages in the Tate Gallery's collection no attempt has been made to discuss this interrelationship nor to give references to the vast literature on the subject.

The Tate Gallery's collection also includes three of the colour-printed designs from the illuminated books that Blake issued separately, together with a copy of another. These designs are heavily printed in opaque colours in the technique that reached its height in the large colour prints dated by Blake to 1795 (see nos.25–34). Here however the basis is still the relief etching on copper of the original book.

That Blake issued at least one set of a number of such designs is shown by a passage in his letter to Dawson Turner of 9 June 1818: 'those [works] I Printed for Mr. Humphry are a selection from the different Books of such as could be Printed without the writing, tho' to the loss of some of the best things. For they, when Printed perfect, accompany Poetical Personifications & Acts, without which Poems they never could have been executed.' Ozias Humphry, the miniaturist (1742–1810), went blind in 1797; his set of the designs was presumably executed before then. Keynes and Wolf have reconstructed three such sets, two *Small Books of Designs* of 1794 and 1796 (Butlin 1981, no.260 and 261) and one *Large Book of Designs* of *c.*1794 (Butlin no.262). Similar designs were also issued separately (Butlin nos.263–87). Two of the designs in the Tate Gallery (nos.21 and 22) seem to have been issued separately, while that from *Urizen* (no.23) seems to have once been part of the second copy of *A Small Book of Designs*.

LITERATURE
Smith 1828, II, p.461 (reprinted Bentley *Blake Records* 1969, p.460); Ruthven Todd, 'The Techniques of William Blake's Illuminated Printing', *Print Collector's Quarterly*, XX, 1948, pp.25–36 (reprinted Essick 1973, pp.19–44); Keynes *Engravings* 1950, pp.18–20; Keynes and Wolf *Illuminated Books* 1953, pp.84–90; Keynes *Writings* 1957, pp.269, 356–8; Raymond Lister *Infernal Methods; A Study of William Blake's Art Techniques* 1975, pp.67–70; Bindman 1977, pp.96–8; Bindman *Graphic Works* 1978, pp.13–15; Paley 1978, pp.36–7; Essick *Printmaker* 1980, pp.85–120, 125–30, 151

15–19   ***Songs of Innocence and of Experience*: Miscellaneous Pages** 1789 and 1794/1831 or later

A 00035–9/ –
5 relief etchings, printed in grey
Presented by Mrs John Richmond 1922

PROVENANCE
?Mrs Blake; Frederick Tatham; his brother-in-law George Richmond, sold Christie's 29 April 1897 (in 147 with 22 other works; see no.2) £2.10.0 bt Dr Richard Sisley; his daughter Mrs John Richmond

LITERATURE
Keynes *Bibliography* 1921, pp.114–28; Erdman *Illuminated Blake* 1974, pp.41–97, book repr.; Bentley *Blake Books* 1977, pp.364–432 no.139 (Tate works pp.371, 430); Bindman *Graphic Works* 1978, pp.468–9 nos.40–70, 474 nos.214–69, two books repr.

Blake published his *Songs of Innocence* on their own in 1789. In his prospectus *To the Public* of 10 October 1793 he advertised both *Songs of Innocence* and, as a separate item, *Songs of Experience*; however the separate title-page for *Songs of Experience* is dated 1794 (Keynes *Writings* 1957, p.208). Most though not all of the existing copies of *Songs of Experience* are bound up with *Songs of Innocence* with a joint title-page reading *Songs of Innocence and of Experience Shewing the Two Contrary States of the Human Soul*; this is undated. In some of these joint copies certain poems originally included in *Songs of Innocence* are moved to *Songs of Experience*. Even within the two sets, the order of the poems was frequently altered.

No.17 is watermarked '1831' and, as all these pages show the same palish grey inking and type of paper, all were presumably printed after Blake's death in 1827, probably by Frederick Tatham from the plates that Mrs Blake would have brought with her when she went to stay with him in September 1828, though not necessarily before her death on 18 October 1831.

These works were formerly inventoried as nos.3694 vii, viii, vi, v, va and iv respectively.

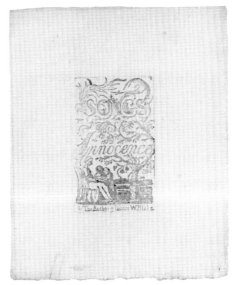 

15   16

15   **_Songs of Innocence_: Title-Page** 1789/1831 or later

A 00038/–
Relief etching, printed in grey 120 × 64
$(4\frac{3}{4} \times 2\frac{7}{8})$ on paper, irregular 245 × 201
$(9\frac{5}{8} \times 7\frac{7}{8})$

This title-page normally comes second in copies of _Songs of Innocence_, following the frontispiece, and third in the combined _Songs of Innocence and of Experience._

16   **_Songs of Innocence:_ Title-Page (second copy)** 1789/1831 or later

A 00039/–
Relief etching, printed in grey 120 × 64
$(4\frac{3}{4} \times 2\frac{7}{8})$ on paper 245 × 202 $(9\frac{11}{16} \times 8\frac{13}{16})$

17   **_Songs of Innocence:_ 'Spring'** 1789/1831 or later

A 00037/–
Relief etching, printed in grey 115 × 79
$(4\frac{1}{2} \times 3\frac{1}{8})$ on paper 248 × 200 $(9\frac{3}{4} \times 7\frac{7}{8})$
Watermarked '[JWHATMAN]/1831'

This is the first of two pages devoted to this poem and normally occur as page 25 in

17

18

19

copies of *Songs of Innocence* and as page 22 in the combined *Songs of Innocence and of Experience*. For the rest of the poem see Erdman 1974, Bindman 1978 or Keynes *Writings* 1957, p.123.

18 **Songs of Innocence and of Experience: 'Infant Sorrow'** 1794/1831 or later

A 00035 / –
Relief etching, printed in grey 112 × 97
($4\frac{7}{16} \times 3\frac{13}{16}$) on paper 245 × 201 ($9\frac{5}{8} \times 7\frac{15}{16}$)
Watermarked 'JW[HATMAN]'.

This poem, one of those added in 1794, normally occurs as page 40 in the combined *Songs of Innocence and of Experience*.

19 **Songs of Innocence and of Experience: 'Infant Sorrow' (second copy)** 1794/1831 or later

A 00036/–
Relief etching, printed in grey 112 × 97
$(4\frac{7}{16} \times 3\frac{13}{16})$ on paper 241 × 202 $(9\frac{1}{2} \times 8)$

20(recto)

20(verso)

20 **Europe: Fragment of Pages 3 and 4** 1794/*c*.1830–5 (recto and verso)

A 00034/–
Relief etching, printed in grey and finished in
watercolour (probably not by Blake), cut
irregularly 92 × 166 $(3\frac{5}{8} \times 6\frac{1}{2})$
Presented by Mrs John Richmond 1922

PROVENANCE
?Mrs Blake; Frederick Tatham; his brother-
in-law George Richmond, sold Christie's 29
April 1897 (in 147 with 22 other items; see

no.2) £2.10.0 bt Dr Richard Sisley; his
daughter Mrs John Richmond

LITERATURE
Keynes *Bibliography* 1921, pp.139–44; Erdman
Illuminated Blake 1974, pp.155–73, book repr.;
Bentley *Blake Books* 1977, pp.141–64 no.33
(this work pp.143, 162 (as pages 6–7));
Bindman *Graphic Works* 1978, pp.472–3
nos.167–184, book repr.

Europe is dated 1794 on the title-page and is not included in Blake's prospectus *To the Public* of 10 October 1793 (Keynes *Writings* 1957, pp.207–8). This fragment may well have been printed posthumously (see nos.15–19) and the colouring appears too harsh to be by Blake himself. For the full text of pp.3 and 4 see Keynes *Writings* 1957, pp.239–40.

This work was formerly inventoried as no.3694 iv.

21 **Frontispiece to *Visions of the Daughters of Albion*** 1793/*c*.1795

N 03373 / B 264
Colour-printed relief etching finished in ink and watercolour 170 × 120 (6¾ × 4¾) on paper 355 × 267 (14 × 10½)
Purchased with the assistance of a special grant from the National Gallery and donations from the National Art-Collections Fund, Lord Duveen and others, and presented through the National Art-Collections Fund 1919

PROVENANCE
John Linnell, sold Christie's 15 March 1918 (174) £52.10.0 bt Martin for presentation to the Tate Gallery

EXHIBITED
Tate Gallery (93), Manchester (80), Nottingham (60) and Edinburgh (47) 1913–14; Paris and Vienna (4); *English Romantic Art* Arts Council tour 1947 (8)

LITERATURE
Rossetti 1863, p.202 no.12, and 1880, p.208 no.14, as 'Design for the Frontispiece to the "Daughters of Albion"'; Damon 1924, pp.330, 332; Wright 1929, II, p.51, repr. I, pl.14; Erdman in *Warburg Journal*, XV, 1952, p.246; Keynes and Wolf 1953, pp.26–8, 89; Digby 1957, p.75, pl.67; Blunt 1959, p.53; Hagstrum 1964, p.96; Beer 1968, pp.40–2; Erdman 1969, pp.233–4; Duerksen in *Blake Newsletter*, VI, 1972–3, p.72; Mellor 1974, pp.62–3, 142; Jackson, Murray and Duerkson in *Blake Newsletter*, VIII, 1974–5, pp.91–6; Bentley *Blake Books* 1977, pp.469, 478; Bindman 1977, pp.73–4, pl.56; Beer in Phillips 1978, pp.211–15; Paley 1978, p.177; Morton D. Paley, '"Wonderful Originals" – Blake and Ancient Sculpture', Essick and Pearce 1978, p.178; Butlin 1981, p.146 no.264, colour pl.337

The title-page of *Visions of the Daughters of Albion* is dated 1793. The earliest copies, of 1793–4, were printed in monochrome and finished in watercolour. The only known colour-printed copy probably dates from 1795; this is also the approximate date of the two separate designs in the Tate Gallery. No.14 corresponds to page 5 of the *Large Book of Designs* in the British Museum which probably dates from a year earlier (Butlin 1981, no.262 5, pl.362).

Visions of the Daughters of Albion is an allegory of the sinfulness of subjecting love to the bonds of orthodox morality. This full-page design is usually taken as showing Oothoon, 'the soft soul of America', bound back to back to Bromion, who has raped her; Theotormon, her lover, persuaded by Bromion's moralistic arguments that Oothoon is now impure, crouches in despair on the right. The setting is Bromion's cave. Duerksen, while accepting the identification of Theotormon on the right, suggests less convincingly that the other figures are not so specific, being two prisoners in Bromion's cave representing terror and meekness, the two principles by which Bromion maintains his tyrannical power. As well as an attack on orthodox morality Erdman also sees *Visions of the Daughters of Albion* as a condemnation of slavery and the temporising of Abolitionists such as Wilberforce.

21

22 **Plate 4 of *Visions of the Daughters of Albion*** 1793/*c*.1795

N 03374 / B 265
Colour-printed relief etching finished in ink
and watercolour 75 × 115 ($2\frac{7}{8}$ × $4\frac{5}{8}$) on paper
282 × 245 ($11\frac{1}{4}$ × $9\frac{5}{8}$)
Purchased with the assistance of a special
grant from the National Gallery and
donations from the National Art-Collections
Fund, Lord Duveen and others, and presented
through the National Art-Collections Fund
1919

PROVENANCE
John Linnell, sold Christie's 15 March 1918
(175) £17.17.0 bt Martin for presentation to
the Tate Gallery

EXHIBITED
Paris and Vienna 1937 (5)

LITERATURE
Damon 1924, p.333; Wright 1929, II, p.18;
Erdman in *Warburg Journal*, XV, 1952, p.246;
Keynes and Wolf 1953, pp.26, 89; Digby
1957, p.76, pl.68; Beer 1968, pp.43–4;
Erdman 1969, p.233; Duerksen in *Blake
Newsletter*, VI, 1972–3, p.72; Jackson, Murray
and Duerksen in *Blake Newsletter*, VIII, 1974–5,
pp.91–6; Bentley *Blake Books*, 1977, pp.471,
478; Beer in Phillips 1978, pp.211–15;
Mitchell 1978, pp.66–7, 158; Butlin 1981,
p.146 no.265, colour pl.338

This design fills a bit over the upper third of the page in the original book and seems
to have illustrated Oothoon's lament from plate 2 (Keynes *Writings* 1957, p.190),

Why does my Theotormon sit weeping upon the threshold;
And Oothoon hovers by his side, perswading him in vain.

This corresponds to page 4 of the large *Book of Designs* in the British Museum
(Butlin 1981, no.262 *4*, pl.365). There are two rough sketches for the composition
in Blake's *Notebook* (Butlin 1981, no.201 *50* and *92*, repr. Erdman and Moore 1973).

23

"Teach these Souls to Fly."

23 **Plate 2 of *Urizen*: 'Teach these Souls to Fly'** 1794/?1796

N 03696/B 261 5
Colour-printed relief etching finished in ink
and watercolour 109 × 102 ($4\frac{5}{16}$ × 4) on paper
208 × 187 ($8\frac{3}{16}$ × $7\frac{3}{8}$)
Inscribed '"Teach these Souls to Fly"' below
design
Purchased from Mrs John Richmond (Grant-
in-Aid) 1922

PROVENANCE
John Giles, sold Christie's 2–5 February 1881,
3rd day (440) £2.6.0 bt Dr Richard Sisley; his
daughter Mrs John Richmond

EXHIBITED
Paris and Vienna 1937 (6, repr.); *English
Romantic Art*, Arts Council tour 1947 (7)

LITERATURE
Damon 1924, p.355; Keynes and Wolf 1953,
pp.70–3, 84–6; Beer 1969, p.79; Paul Miner,
'Visions in the Darksome Air: Aspects of
Blake's Biblical Symbolism', Rosenfeld 1969,
p.264; Bentley *Blake Books* 1977, pp.176, 183;
Mitchell 1978, p.144; Butlin 1981, p.139
no.261 5, pl.354

This design illustrates the 'Preludium' of *The First Book of Urizen* of which the first
copies were made in 1794 (repr. Erdman *Illuminated Blake* 1974, p.184). It was
reissued in *A Small Book of Designs*, the copy of which in the British Museum is also

dated 1794 on the first design (Butlin 1981, no.260 *1*; this design is no.260 *12*, pl.316). The version in the Tate Gallery almost certainly comes from the second copy of this collection, in which the date on the first design has been altered to 1796 (Butlin no.261 *1*, pl.350). The designs in this second set were given titles by Blake in matching inscriptions below each composition; many also show signs of having been stitched for binding, as in the case of the Tate Gallery design.

In Urizen, only one book of which was issued, Blake recounts the creation of the world by Urizen, the embodiment of reason unenlightened by the imagination; in this way the Creation is equated with the Fall (Damon 1924, pp.116–21; see also no.25). This design, which occupies the upper part of the page with the writing omitted, shows Enitharmon and her son by Los, Orc; they typify Pity, Poetry and Revolt respectively.

COPY AFTER BLAKE

24 **Plate 3 of *Urizen*: 'Oh! Flames of Furious Desires'**

N 05190/–
Watercolour 60 × 99 ($2\frac{3}{8} \times 3\frac{5}{8}$) on paper
213 × 206 ($8\frac{3}{8} \times 8\frac{1}{8}$)
Inscribed, not by Blake, 'Oh! Flames of
furious desires' below design
Bequeathed by Miss Alice G.E. Carthew 1940

PROVENANCE
?Carfax and Co. 1904; Miss Carthew

EXHIBITED
?Carfax 1904 (15); ?Carfax 1906 (79b);
Wartime Acquisitions, 2nd Exhibition, CEMA tour
1944–5 (4); Port Sunlight 1950 (14);
Edinburgh 1969 (52)

LITERATURE
Piloo Nanavutty, 'A Title-Page in Blake's
illustrated Genesis Manuscript', *Journal of the
Warburg and Courtauld Institutes*, x, 1947, p.114;
Beer 1969, p.79: Mitchell 1978, p.145

Although this was included in the first edition of this catalogue (1957, p.38 no.10) it was doubted in the second (1971, p.33 no.13). It is in fact a copy of the design in the second set of *A Small Book of Designs* of 1796 (Butlin 1981, no.261 *4*, pl.353). It is on different, thicker paper than nos.21, 22 and 23 and seems to be entirely executed in watercolour, including what should be the printed outlines of the design. Nor can its history be traced earlier than 1904, if that far.

The original design occurs at the top of plate 3 of *Urizen* (repr. Erdman *Illuminated Blake* 1974, p.185) and it is included in both copies of *A Small Book of Designs*, that already mentioned and the first issue of 1794 (Butlin no.260 *9*, pl.314). The version from the second, dismembered *Small Book of Designs* (Keynes Collection, Fitzwilliam Museum, Cambridge) has been trimmed and lacks the usual title in Blake's hand. It is however inscribed on the back, not by Blake, 'Oh! Flames of Furious Desires'; the supposed lost title is presumably the origin of that inscribed on the Tate's copy.

24

The Keynes copy of this design was acquired by W. Graham Robertson in 1904 (Preston 1952, pp.253-4 no.136) and would have been acknowledged as belonging to him had he lent it to the Carfax exhibitions of that year and 1906. The work exhibited by Carfax is therefore presumably the Tate's copy, unless it was yet another copy such as that sold at Sotheby's on 17 December 1970 (14 as by 'Blake' and therefore presumably thought not to be by him) bt C. Fry.

The design does not represent any particular passage in *Urizen* though the motif of fire recurs frequently in association with Los and Urizen, particularly the former. Damon suggests that it shows Los in the flames of inspiration (1924, p.355), the 'flames of fierce desire' evoked by Blake in his address 'To the Public' at the beginning of *Jerusalem* (Keynes *Writings* 1957, p.621). Keynes and Wolf hesitantly suggest Urizen as an alternative to Los (1953, p.70). Piloo Nanavutty's identification of the figure as Orc is less convincing; Orc, the red light of revolution in *Europe*, also of 1794, has only a minor, passive rôle in *Urizen*.

There is what seems to be a preliminary sketch in reverse, known as 'Pestilence', in the Rosenwald collection, National Gallery of Art, Washington (Butlin no.230, pl.272).

THE LARGE COLOUR PRINTS *c*.1795–1805

These large colour prints represent the culmination, both artistic and technical, of Blake's development of colour-printing in the first half of the 1790s. Their execution involved both printing and the direct application of ink and water-colour. (For the way in which Blake's work in his illuminated books helped bring about the creation of these prints see Butlin 1969, pp.110–16; since this article was written several important discoveries have been made about the prints, these being discussed below).

The first description of Blake's technique in these prints was given by Frederick Tatham, quoted by D.G. Rossetti in the 'Supplementary' chapter to Gilchrist's *Life of William Blake* 1863: 'Blake, when he wanted to make his prints in oil, took a common thick millboard, and drew in some strong ink or colour his design upon it strong and thick. He then painted upon that in such oil colours and in such a state of fusion that they would blur well. He painted roughly and quickly, so that no colour would have time to dry. He then took a print of that on paper, and this impression he coloured up in water-colours, re-painting his outline on the millboard when he wanted to take another print. This plan he had recourse to, because he could vary slightly each impression; and each having a sort of accidental look, he could branch out so as to make each one different.'

A letter from Tatham of 6 November 1862 to William Rossetti, who reprinted it in 1903, complements this account: 'They were printed in a loose press from an outline sketched on paste-board; the oil colour was blotted on, which gave the sort of impression you will get by taking the impression of anything *wet*. There was a look of accident about this mode which he afterwards availed of, and tinted so as to bring out and favour what was there rather blurred.'

In fact Tatham, who was not born until 1805, seems to have erred in several respects. Blake did not use oil paint but rather a medium much like that of his temperas (see pp.00); on some of the colour prints, though not any of those in the Tate Gallery, he added the inscription 'fresco', a somewhat misleading reference to the technique of early Italian tempera paintings. The thick, tacky medium Blake used for his colours, which often produced a reticulated surface, was the same as that used in his illuminated books. In at least one case, the copy of 'Lamech and his Two Wives' in the collection of Robert N. Essick, chemical analysis has shown that this vehicle is a vegetable based gum (see Essick 1980, pp.259–60, and Lindberg 1980–1, p.146).

Nor is it certain that his 'plate' was of millboard, the flexibility of which for works of this size would have presented difficulties. In fact it has recently been demonstrated that the three versions of 'God Judging Adam' were printed from a metal plate with areas of relief-etching defining the main forms of the figures as in such illuminated books as *Urizen* (Patrick Noon's discovery was reported by David Bindman in *Blake, an Illustrated Quarterly*, 1982–3, p.224; that Blake had used a printed outline for this composition had already been suggested in Butlin 1981, p.156). A printed outline has also been suggested for the New York version of 'Pity' (Sue Welsh Reed, 1980, p.86), but this is not visible to the eye of the present compiler. No other copies of the prints show signs of an initial printing in relief etching, and this has led to the suggestion that 'God Judging Adam' was the first design to be executed and that Blake subsequently abandoned using metal plates, perhaps for reasons of economy. On the other hand, the presence of a small version of 'Pity' in the British Museum (Butlin no.314, pl.413) in which Blake seems to be experimenting with the technique of colour printing in a brand new design, suggests that it was 'Pity' that was the first composition that Blake tackled (see no.30).

Nor does Tatham seem to have been correct in suggesting that Blake repainted his plate before taking each impression. In at least some cases Blake seems to have printed two or even three copies of a print without renewing his application of paint to the plate, each impression being therefore weakened in intensity. Any deficiencies could be made up when Blake completed the work in pen and watercolour. (See Butlin 1969, pp.110, 115, and, for a detailed examination of the three successive pulls of 'God Judging Adam', then known as 'Elijah in the Fiery Chariot', Butlin in *Burlington Magazine*, c, 1958, p.24 (this article mistakenly refers to the print in New York as being in the Rosenwald Collection); further researches and experiments on Blake's colour-printed technique have been done by W. Graham Robertson and Ruthven Todd, *loci cit.*, the former's experiments being included in the exhibition of his work, Carfax 1906 (56–61), an example of which, after Blake's 'Paolo and Francesca (?)' (Butlin no.816), is in the Tate Gallery Archive; see p.249.) As a result of this technique, repetition of each design was limited, none being securely traced in more than three examples (but see no.28), and each version is unique. In fact, Blake seems to have used this technique more for its textural qualities than as a means of reproduction.

Many of the prints, including more than one version of the same composition, are dated 1795; no print with any other date has been traced. However, the recent discovery that nos.28 and 29 are on paper watermarked 1804 (reported by Butlin in *Blake, An Illustrated Quarterly*, xv, 1981–2, pp.101–3, and xvii, 1983–4, p.159) shows that in a number of cases the actual printing, not just the finishing off in pen and watercolour, was done some ten years later than the date inscribed on the work. This does not conflict with the fact that the first record of any of the prints is the debtor-and-creditor account between Blake and Thomas Butts of 3 March 1806, which includes the payment of a guinea each for eight prints, including these two examples, under 5 July and 7 September 1805; the prints were presumably finished shortly before their sale.

There are several examples of Blake using an 'ideal' date that refers to the conception rather than the execution of a design. However, this discovery extends Blake's use of colour printing by about ten years, it having previously been thought that he discontinued its use after about 1796. This in its turn has an important bearing on the evolution of Blake's style in the early years of the nineteenth century, the full implications of which have not yet been worked out. Far from radically switching from a technique that relied considerably upon texture to one relying on clear outline and flat areas of colour, a development related to Blake's 'conversion' during his three years at Felpham from 1800–1803, Blake is now seen to have been still using a technique embodying a lot of 'blurring demons', albeit tamed by a bounding pen outline. Taking the examples of 'Newton' and 'Nebuchadnezzar' in the Tate Gallery as touch-stones for prints pulled in 1804–5 it is possible to date one or two other examples to this period, including 'Elohim Creating Adam' (no.25). At the other extreme are the Tate Gallery's versions of 'Pity' and 'Hecate' (nos.30 and 31) which, with their flatter, more overall application of pigment producing a less variegated texture, are much closer to the separate colour-printed designs from the illuminated books such as nos.21–3. The use of a separately printed, relief-etched monochrome outline in 'God Judging Adam' also suggests an early date. Other pulls of the designs can be tentatively dated according to which of these two poles they most resemble; a tentative attempt to date many of the known pulls both in the Tate Gallery and elsewhere can be found in the appendix to the printed version of my lecture on 'The Physicality of William Blake', to be published in a forthcoming issue of the *Huntington Library Quarterly*.

The Tate Gallery possesses examples of ten of the twelve designs that make up what seems to be a unified series despite the subjects being at first sight an apparently haphazard collection including events from the Old Testament and the life of Christ, illustrations to Shakespeare and Milton, designs previously used in Blake's prophetic books, and the completely unprecedented appearance of Newton as a figure of universal significance, all raised by Blake's genius to an equal level of importance. As yet there has been no fully convincing analysis of the meaning of the series as a whole, but it seems likely that Blake is drawing indiscriminately on a number of sources to find images to express various aspects of his own universal philosophy. Most if not all of the prints seem to have been designed as complementary pairs. The two titles not represented in the Tate Gallery are 'Naomi Entreating Ruth and Orpah to Return to the Land of Moab', of which there are examples in the Victoria and Albert Museum and in the Keynes collection (Butlin nos. 229 and 300, pls. 392 and 404, the first in colour), and 'Satan Exulting over Eve', of which there are examples in the Craxton collection and in the Getty Museum (Butlin nos. 291 and 292, pls. 348 and, in colour, 389).

LITERATURE
Gilchrist 1863, I, pp. 375–6; John Ruskin, 'Arthur Burgess', *Century Guild Hobby Horse*, II, 1887, pp. 51–2; Rossetti 1903, pp. 16–17; Cook and Wedderburn *Works of Ruskin*, XIV, 1904, pp. 354–5, XXXVI, 1909, pp. 32–3; Robertson in Gilchrist 1907, pp. 405–6; Figgis 1925, pp. 24–7; Ruthven Todd, 'The Techniques of William Blake's Illuminated Printing', *Print Collector's Quarterly*, XXIX, November 1948, pp. 25–36 (revised reprint in Essick 1973, pp. 19–44); Keynes *Writings* 1957, p. 867; Blunt 1959, pp. 57–63; Bentley *Blake Records* 1969, pp. 572–3; Butlin in Rosenfeld 1969, pp. 109–16; Kostelanetz in Rosenfeld 1969, pp. 117–30; Todd 1971, pp. 37–40; Warren Jones, 'Blake's Large Color-Printed Designs of 1795', doctoral dissertation, Northwestern University, 1972; Mellor 1974, pp. 87, 89, 102–3, 150–64; Bindman 1977, pp. 98–100, 106, 117; Bindman *Graphic Works* 1978, nos. 324–36; Paley 1978, pp. 36–8; Butlin in *Blake*, XIII, 1979–80, p. 22; Essick *Printmaker* 1980, pp. 130–5, 259–60; Sue Welsh Reed, 'Monotypes in the Seventeenth and Eighteenth Centuries', exh. cat., *The Painterly Print*, Metropolitan Museum of Art, New York, 1980, pp. 6–7, 84–9; La Belle in *Blake*, XIV, 1980–1, pp. 66–84; Lindberg in *Blake*, XIV, 1980–1, p. 167; Butlin 1981, pp. 156–8; Heppner in *Bulletin of Research in the Humanities*, LXXXIV, 1981, pp. 337–9: Butlin in *Blake*, XV, 1981–2, pp. 101–3; Lindberg in *Blake*, XV, 1981–2, pp. 141–2, 145–6; Bindman 1982, pp. 110–11, 115–18; Morris Eaves, *William Blake's Theory of Art*, 1982, pp. 41–2; Bindman in *Blake*, XVI, 1982–3, pp. 224–5; Essick in *Blake*, XVI, 1982–3, pp. 34–7; Martin Butlin, 'The Physicality of William Blake: the Large Colour Prints of "1795"', *Huntington Library Quarterly*, forthcoming.

25 **Elohim Creating Adam** 1795/*c*.1805

N 05055 / B 289
Colour print finished in ink and watercolour
431 × 536 (17 × 21⅛) on paper approx.
515 × 595 (20¼ × 23½)
Signed '1795 WB inv [in monogram]' b.c. and inscribed 'Elohim creating Adam' below design
Presented by W. Graham Robertson 1939

PROVENANCE
Thomas Butts; Thomas Butts jun.; Capt. F.J. Butts; his widow, sold through Carfax April 1906 to W. Graham Robertson

EXHIBITED
BFAC 1876 (205); Carfax 1904 (18); Carfax 1906 (30); *Century of Art* Grafton Galleries 1911 (55); Tate Gallery (1), Manchester (1), Nottingham (1) and Edinburgh (5) 1913–14; on loan to Tate Gallery 1923–7; BFAC 1927 (1, pl.2); *British Art* RA 1934 (771, pl.87; 701, pl.164); Whitechapel 1934 (51); *Wartime Acquisitions* National Gallery 1942 (8); Paris (1, repr. in colour facing p.6), Antwerp (1, pl.2), Zurich (1, repr. in colour) and Tate Gallery (2) 1947; Tate Gallery 1978 (85, repr. in colour)

LITERATURE
Rossetti 1863, p. 203 no. 18, and 1880, p. 209 no. 20; Robertson in Gilchrist 1907, pp. 406–7, repr. facing p. 406; Binyon and Keynes *Job* 1935, I, p. 10; Percival 1938, p. 214, repr.; Collins Baker in *Huntington Library Quarterly*, IV, 1940–1, p. 366, repr. p. 363 (reprinted in Essick 1973, pp. 124–5, pl. 48); Blunt in *Warburg Journal*, VI, 1943, pp. 198–9, 226; Keynes *Faber Gallery* 1946, pp. 4, 24, colour pl. 1; Frye 1947, p. 130; Preston 1952, pp. 29–31 no. 1, pl. 1; Digby 1957, pp. 32–3, pl. 34; Keynes *Bible* 1957, p. 2 no. 3 repr.; H. M. Margoliouth 'Blake's Drawings for Young's Night Thoughts', Pinto 1957, pp. 202–3; Blunt 1959, p. 58, pl. 26b; Damon 1965, pp. 5, 119; Beer 1968, pp. 192, 256, pl. 34; Keynes *Letters* 1968, p. 118; Raine 1968, II, p. 13, pl. 127; Bentley *Blake Records* 1969, p. 573; Kostelanetz in Rosenfeld 1969, p. 124, pl. 2; Warner in Erdman and Grant 1970, pp. 184, 189, pl. 94; Tolley in *Blake Newsletter*,

25

VI, 1972–3, pp.28–9; Mellor 1974, pp.151–2, pl.39; Rosenblum 1975, pp.43–4, pl.47; Bindman 1977, pp.98–9, colour pl.1; Klonsky 1977, p.57, repr. in colour; Bindman *Graphic Works* 1978, no.324, repr.; Paley 1978, p.37, colour pl.28; Butlin in *Blake* XIII, 1979–80, p.16; Essick *Printmaker* 1980, p.132; La Belle in *Blake* XIV, 1980–1, pp.67–72, pl.3; Butlin 1981, pp.158–9 no.289, colour pl.388; Raine 1982, pp.30, 226, 308 and at pl.104, repr.; Warner 1984, pp.20, 30–1, 42–3, 87, 95–6, 105, 121, pl.17; Hoagwood 1985, p.69, pl.6. *Also repr*: *Mizue*, no.816, 1973, 2/3, p.13, colour pl.1

Listed in Blake's account with Thomas Butts of 3 March 1806 as 'God Creating Adam', apparently as having been delivered on 7 September 1805. There are no other known versions but, this version having already been sold to Butts, there could have been a second copy when, on 9 June 1818, Blake offered a complete set of the 12 large prints to Dawson Turner (Butlin 1981, no.290). The Tate print, on account of the similarity in handling and colouring to nos.28 and 29, seems to have been executed in 1804–5, shortly before being sold to Butts; the untraced version could have been executed when the design was first conceived, in the 1795 of the inscribed date. There is a pencil sketch for this composition on p.54 of Blake's Notebook (Butlin no.201 *54*, repr. Erdman and Moor 1973).

Elohim is one of the Hebrew names for God, the creator in Genesis and representing God in his aspect as Justice; the name can also be translated as 'judges'. In Night the Eighth of *Vala or the Four Zoas* Elohim appears as the third of the seven Eyes of God sent by the Eternals to lead Man out of the error of selfhood: 'They sent Elohim who created Adam To die for Satan' (Keynes *Writings* 1957, p.351). In this design the non-conformist Blake stresses the negative aspect of the Creation: Man's enslavement to the material world is symbolised by the worm, emblem of mortality, that entwines Adam. The mystery of creation is paralleled by the account in *Urizen*, published the year before the design was conceived, 1794.

Collins Baker suggests that the figure of Elohim is derived from an engraving after the Skiron of the Temple of the Winds (R. Dalton's engraving repr. Collins Baker 1940–1, p.363; 1973, pl.49).

26 **God Judging Adam** 1795

N 05063 / B 294
Colour-printed relief etching finished in ink and watercolour 432 × 535 ($17 \times 21\frac{1}{8}$) on paper approx. 545 × 770 ($21\frac{1}{2} \times 30\frac{1}{4}$)
Signed 'WB inv [in monogram] 1795' b.l. and inscribed 'God speaking to Adam' below design
Presented by W. Graham Robertson 1939

PROVENANCE
Thomas Butts; Thomas Butts jun.; Capt. F.J. Butts; his widow, sold through Carfax April 1906 to W. Graham Robertson

EXHIBITED
Carfax 1906 (27); *Century of Art* Grafton Galleries 1911 (60); Tate Gallery 1913 (14); on loan to the Tate Gallery 1920–7; BFAC 1927 (8, repr. p.8); *British Art* RA 1934 (781, repr. in 2nd ed. pl.87; 702); Whitechapel 1934 (48); *British Painting* Paris 1938 (158); *Wartime Acquisitions* National Gallery 1942 (15); Tate Gallery 1947 (54) (all above as 'Elijah'); Tate Gallery 1978 (87, repr.)

LITERATURE
Rossetti 1863, p.203 under no.21, p.208 no.66, and 1880, p.210 under no.23, p.216

no.72; Robertson in Gilchrist 1907, p.411, repr. facing p.140; Preston 1952, pp.34–6 no.3, pl.3; Digby 1957, p.66, pl.62; Keynes *Bible* 1957, p.2 no.13, p.18 no.65a repr.; Butlin in *Burlington Magazine*, C, 1958, p.42; Blunt 1959, p.61, pl.28b; Martin Butlin 'Blake's "God Judging Adam" Rediscovered', in *Burlington Magazine*, CVII, 1965, pp.86–9, fig.43 (reprinted in Essick 1973, pp.303–10, pl.103); Keynes *Letters* 1968, p.118; Beer 1969, p.xv; Bentley *Blake Records* 1969, p.572; Kostelanetz in Rosenfeld 1969, p.125, pl.3; Tolley in *Blake Newsletter*, VI, 1972–3, pp.28–9; Mellor 1974, pp.153–5, pl.40; Bindman 1977, pp.98–9; Klonsky 1977, p.58, repr. in colour; Paley 1978, p.37; Butlin in *Blake*, XIII, 1978–80, p.16; Essick *Printmaker* 1980, p.132; La Belle in *Blake*, XIV, 1980–1, p.72, pl.7; Butlin 1981, pp.160–1, colour pl.390; Bindman in *Blake*, XVI, 1982–3, p.224; Essick in *Blake*, XVI, 1982–3, pp.32–3; Robert N. Essick, 'A Supplement to *The Separate Plates of William Blake: A Catalogue*, in *Blake*, XVII, 1983–4, p.139; Boime 1987, pp.357–60, pl.4.52. *Also repr*: *Mizue*, no.816, 1973, 2/3, p.34 in colour: *Mizue*, no.882, 1978, 9, p.18 in colour

Listed in Blake's account with Butts of 3 March 1806 as 'God Judging Adam' with 'Judging' replacing the deleted word 'Creating' ('God Creating Adam' was listed separately below; see no.25); 'God Judging' was apparently delivered to Butts on 5 July 1805. There are two other pulls of the subject, in the Metropolitan Museum of Art, New York (Butlin 1981, no.295, pl.385) and the Philadelphia Museum of Art (Butlin no.296, pl.386). The first pull seems to be that in the Metropolitan Museum, the second that in the Tate, and the third at Philadelphia which may have been finished off in watercolour by another hand (see Essick in *Blake* XVI, 1982–3, p.36, repr.; my own view, because of the correspondence of the colouring to the related lines in *Urizen* (see below), is that the somewhat odd appearance of the Philadelphia version may be the result of time). The first two pulls, if not the third, appear for stylistic reasons to date from about 1795; in this design, the only example in which the outline seems to have been etched in relief, the initial printing of the first two pulls is in dark grey, and in the third an orange-brown. In addition

26

to the three copies of the colour print there is an earlier version of the composition in watercolour in the collection of George Goyder (Butlin no.258, colour pl.198).

Until 1965 this design was known as 'Elijah in the Fiery Chariot', with Elisha standing before him. This identification seems to have originated in the middle of the nineteenth century: the catalogue of the sale of works from Frederick Tatham's collection held at Sotheby's on 29 April 1862 included the version now at Philadelphia as lot 189, 'Elijah about to ascend in his Chariot', and Rossetti's lists, published the following year, included the New York version as 'Elijah mounted in the Fiery Chariot' (1863, p.203 no.21, and 1880, pp.209–10 no.23). Rossetti also lists 'God Judging Adam' but merely gives the ownership as 'From Mr Butts' with a reference to the Butts account, showing that he had not seen the actual work (1863, p.208 no.66, and 1880, p.216 no.72). In addition he lists (1863, p.232 no.203, starred as of considerable size, no owner listed, and 1880, p.245 no.228) a 'Judgment. *Colour-printed*. Presumed to be a "*Last* Judgment"'; or, possibly, the "Judgment of Paris"?', which may also be a faint echo of the same print though there is a watercolour of 'The Judgment of Paris' of 1811(?) in the British Museum (Butlin no.675, colour pl.964). The discovery of the faintly pencilled title previously hidden under the mount of no.26 has established the connection with the hitherto unaccounted-for 'God Judging Adam' of the Butts account; no 'Elijah' was known from early records, though not all the large prints from the Butts collection are listed in the accounts (see nos.30 and 31).

Like 'Elohim Creating Adam', this design reflects Blake's negative attitude to the God of the Old Testament in the mid 1790s, when his thought was at its most pessimistic. The stern embodiment of unyielding justice imposes his law on the stooping figure of Adam, who is shown transformed into God's own Urizen-like image. Much of the imagery of the design, and in particular the book on God's lap and the flames, which in the Philadelphia design burn darkly against a black sky, is paralleled in the verses of *Urizen* of the year before, 1794, in which Urizen is heard declaiming the laws of 'the Book Of eternal brass ... One command, one joy, one desire, ... One King, one God, one Law', upon which appear 'All the seven deadly sins of the soul ... In the flames of eternal fury ... But no light from the fires: all was darkness In the flames of Eternal fury' (Keynes *Writings* 1957, pp.224–5). The last line is on a page (plate 5) headed by an illustration showing Urizen surrounded by flames and holding the book of eternal brass, different in composition but similar in imagery to 'God Judging Adam'. Urizen is described with 'his chariot of fire' in *Vala* or *The Four Zoas*, written *c.*1796 onwards (Keynes *Writings* 1957, p.273). The design seems, in its depiction of the perverted energy of fire, to be the companion to 'The Good and Evil Angels' (see no.33): the two compositions condemn on the one hand the sameness imposed by Jehovah-Urizen's imposition of a single law and on the other the frustration of vital energy resulting from the opposition of the two angels, both being the result of the division of Man in the fallen world.

Boime makes an interesting comparison between the composition of this print and the combination of round wheels and straight driving arms in such machines as James Watt's double-acting rotative engine (an example of which was used in, perhaps significantly, the Albion Mills Company's flour mill) and Robert Fulton's adaptation of such a machine for use in a steam boat (both repr. Boime 1987, pls.4.53 and 4.54).

There is another interesting parallel, with the composition of George Stubbs's 'Fall of Phaeton' (version repr. Constance Anne Parker *Mr Stubbs the Horse Painter* 1971, p.31, and Basil Taylor *Stubbs* 1971, pls.94–5). A version of this may well have been known to Blake and the design could have been interpreted by him as representing the consequences of the Orc-like Phaeton letting his energies run away with him. 'God Judging Adam' shows the reverse; everything is static and dead.

27 **Lamech and his Two Wives** 1795

N 05061 / B 297
Colour print finished in ink and watercolour 431 × 608 (17 × 23$\frac{15}{16}$), the corners cut across approx. 55 (2$\frac{1}{4}$) from each corner, on paper approx. 545 × 755 (21$\frac{1}{2}$ × 29$\frac{3}{4}$)
Signed 'WB inv [in monogram] 1795' b.l. and inscribed 'Lamech and his two Wives' below design
Presented by W. Graham Robertson 1939

PROVENANCE
Thomas Butts; Thomas Butts jun.; Capt. F.J. Butts, offered Sotheby's 24 June 1903 (1) £156 bought in Stephens; his widow, sold through Carfax April 1906 to W. Graham Robertson

EXHIBITED
BFAC 1876 (171); Carfax 1904 (1); Carfax 1906 (35); *Wartime Acquisitions* National Gallery 1942 (12); Tate Gallery 1947 (53); Tate Gallery 1978 (93, repr.)

LITERATURE
Rossetti 1863, p.203 no.19, and 1880, p.209 no.21; Robertson in Gilchrist 1907, p.410, repr. facing p.366; Preston 1952, pp.32–3 no.2, pl.2; Keynes *Bible* 1957, p.6 no.17a repr.; Blunt 1959, p.59; Damon 1965, pp.4–5, 223, 458; Hagstrum in Hilles and Bloom 1965, p.329 n.30; Keynes *Letters* 1968, p.117; Bentley *Blake Records* 1969, p.572; Kostelanetz

27

in Rosenfeld 1969, p.128; Mellor 1974,
pp.160–1; Bindman 1977, p.99; Bindman
Graphic Works 1978, no.330, repr.; Paley 1978,
p.37; Essick *Printmaker* 1980, pp.134–5,

pl.130; La Belle in *Blake*, XIV, 1980–1, p.77,
pl.12; Butlin 1981, pp.162–3 no.297, colour
pl.391; Warner 1984, p.68

Listed in Blake's account with Thomas Butts of 3 March 1806 as 'Lamech'; it had
apparently been delivered on 5 July 1805. There is a second copy of this print,
almost certainly the second pull, in the collection of Robert N. Essick (Butlin 1981,
no.298, pl.387). The format of the Tate Gallery's print, with the corners cut across
diagonally, is also found in the version of 'Naomi entreating Ruth and Orpah to
Return to the Land of Moab' in the Victoria and Albert Museum (Butlin no.299,
colour pl.392). The colouring and manner of printing of these two works is also
similar and suggests that they were both pulled in 1795.

The format and manner of treatment also suggests that the two works were
designed by Blake as pendants, but it is difficult to see any connection in subject
beyond the fact that each deals with a family relationship: Lamech with his two
wives, and Naomi with her two Moabite daughters-in-law. David Bindman groups
these two designs with two other Old Testament subjects (nos.26 and 28) as
representing consequences of Jehovah's moral law.

The obscure subject of this print is from Genesis, iv, 23–4. Lamech, Cain's great-
great-great-grandson, tells his wives that he has slain a man: 'If Cain shall be
avenged sevenfold, truly Lamech seventy and seven fold'. There was a tradition,

partly derived from the text in Genesis, iv, 15 and 13, and spelt out in full in the Apocrypha, that Lamech did in fact accidently kill Cain (see Denis Grivot and George Zarnecki, *Gislebertus, sculptor of Autun*, 1961, p.70, quoting Byzantine and Romanesque prototypes). Bindman suggests that the reason Blake chose Lamech rather than Cain himself to epitomise murder and vengeance was that Lamech was father by his two wives of Jubal, representing music, and Tubalcain, 'an instructor of every artifice in brass and iron'; the two wives would thus represent the state of the arts in the Fallen World.

Janet Warner, demonstrating that one of Blake's sources for his visual language of gesture was the English pantomime, likens the gesture of Lamech's hands passionately applied to his forehead to the standard motif of indignation described by the dancing master John Weaver in his *History of the Mimes and Pantomimes* of 1728. This gesture is also found in Blake's 'Body of Abel found by Adam and Eve', no.69.

This similarity is presumably the reason for David Erdman's mistaken relating of the Emblem drawing no.28 on p.49 of Blake's sketchbook to the figure of Cain in Blake's depictions of this subject rather than directly to the figure of Lamech in the colour print, to which it is much closer though, as one would expect, in reverse (Butlin no.201 *49*, repr. Erdman and Moore 1973).

28 **Nebuchadnezzar** 1795/*c.*1805

N 05059 / B 301
Colour print finished in ink and watercolour, irregular 446 × 620 ($17\frac{5}{8}$ × $24\frac{3}{8}$) on paper approx. 545 × 725 ($21\frac{1}{2}$ × $28\frac{1}{2}$)
Signed '1795 WB inv [in monogram]' b.r. and inscribed 'Nebuchadnezzar' below design
Watermarked 'JWHATMAN/1804'
Presented by W. Graham Robertson 1939

PROVENANCE
Thomas Butts; Thomas Butts jun.; Capt. F.J. Butts; his widow, sold through Carfax April 1906 to W. Graham Robertson

EXHIBITED
Carfax 1906 (33); Tate Gallery 1913 (17); on loan to Tate Gallery 1923–7; BFAC 1927 (11, pl.11); *Wartime Acquisitions* National Gallery 1942 (10); Paris, Antwerp (pl.7), Zurich and Tate Gallery (repr.) 1947 (12); *Romantic Movement* Arts Council 1959 (611); Tate Gallery 1978 (91, repr.)

LITERATURE
Gilchrist 1863, I, p.88; Rossetti 1863, p.202 no.13, and 1880, p.202 no.15; Robertson in Gilchrist 1907, pp.408–9, repr. facing p.90; Russell *Engravings* 1912, p.20; Figgis 1925, at pl.77, repr. in colour; Blunt in *Warburg Journal*, VI, 1943, pp.203–4, pl.60a; Keynes *Faber Gallery* 1946, pp.4–5, 8, colour pl.3; Grigson in *Architectural Review*, CVIII, 1950, p.218; Preston 1952, pp.37–8 no.4, pl.4; Digby 1957, p.102; Keynes *Bible* 1957, p.26 no.84a repr.; Blunt 1959, pp.51, 60, pl.31c; Preston in *Apollo*, LXXXIV, 1966, pp.384–6, pl.6; Keynes *Letters* 1968, p.118; Bentley *Blake Records* 1969, p.573; Erdman 1969, pp.193–4; Kostelanetz in Rosenfeld 1969, pp.125–6; Mellor 1974, pp.97, 155; Bindman 1977, pp.98–100; Klonsky 1977, p.63, repr. in colour; Bindman *Graphic Works* 1978, no.332, repr.; Paley 1978, pp.11, 37, 178; La Belle in *Blake*, XIV, 1980–1, p.76, pl.9; Butlin 1981, pp.164–5 no.301, colour pl.393; Butlin in *Blake*, XVII, 1983–4, p.159; Warner 1984, p.44, pl.19; Boime 1987, pp.326–30, pl.4.28 in colour; *Also repr: Mizue*, no.882, 1978, 9, p.9.

Listed in Blake's account with Thomas Butts of 3 March 1806, apparently as having been delivered on 7 September 1805. There are two other versions, in the Minneapolis Institute of Arts and the Museum of Fine Arts, Boston (Butlin 1981, nos.302 and 303, pls.406 and 407). In 1981, before the discovery of the 1804 watermark, I suggested that the Tate copy of the print was probably the first of the known pulls of this design. The variations between the three copies, and the general nature of the two other prints, suggests that this view is still the most likely one, and that none of the known copies of the design can therefore have been executed before

28

1804. There is however a possibility, though an unlikely one, that there was, uniquely, a fourth copy of this design belonging *c.*1880 to Arthur Burgess (see Butlin no.304).

This is an illustration to Daniel, iv, 31–3. Blake had already used this composition on a smaller scale on p.24 of *The Marriage of Heaven and Hell*, *c.*1790–3 (repr. Erdman *Illuminated Blake* 1974, p.121). There are two pencil sketches on pages 44 and 48 of Blake's Notebook (Butlin nos.201 *44* and *48*, repr. Erdman and Moore 1973). An untraced sepia drawing was in the William Bell Scott sale at Sotheby's on 21 April 1885 (181); see Butlin no.305.

The figure of Nebuchadnezzar also appears, in a modified form, in one of the watercolour illustrations to Young's *Night Thoughts*, 1796–7 (Night VII, page 27; Butlin no.330 *299*, repr. David V. Erdman, ed., *William Blake's Designs for Edward Young's Night Thoughts*, 1980). The pose of the figure is probably based on Dürer's engraving of 'The Penance of St John Chrysostomus'. Blake greatly admired Dürer's prints and there is also an iconographic connection: St John Chrysostomus deliberately based his penance on Nebuchadnezzar's bestial madness (see Edgar Wind, 'The Saint as Monster' in *Journal of the Warburg Institute*, I, 1937–8, p.183, the Dürer repr.; also repr. Preston 1966, p.8).

Geoffrey Grigson has demonstrated the influence of John Hamilton Mortimer's engraving of 'Nebuchadnezzar Recovering his Reason' of *c.*1778 (repr. Grigson *loc. cit.*, Erdman 1969, pl.7a, and Blunt *op. cit.*, pl.31b). Erdman associates Nebuchadnezzar with Blake's own character Urizen; thus Blake is seen to be representing

'Reason losing his reason'. This work and 'Newton' (no.29) seem to have been designed as a pair and may therefore represent two aspects of the rational will. On the other hand, as Blunt has suggested, Nebuchadnezzar may be seen as slave to the senses, with Newton as slave to Reason. This is supported by the text accompanying the earlier version of the design in *The Marriage of Heaven and Hell*, which illustrates the last 'Memorable Fancy' in which Blake, speaking through a Devil, asserts that the greatest men should be especially loved and honoured and demonstrates how Christ transcended and broke the Ten Commandments; the design is captioned 'One Law for the Lion and Ox is Oppression', the sense being that in this instance Man, in the person of Nebuchadnezzar, is being subjected to the Law of the Beast, in other words to the senses alone. What appear to be massive twisted roots behind the figure, with some foliage, were perhaps suggested by the great tree of Nebuchadnezzar's dream in Daniel, iv, 10–16, and in particular by 'the stump of his roots' which were to remain when the rest had been hewn down; in addition these forms give a feeling of oppressive materialism to the design.

Boime points out that, whereas in the illustration to *The Marriage of Heaven and Hell* Nebuchadnezzar is shown wearing a crown, an allusion to the recent downfall of the French Monarchy which is also alluded to in 'The Song of Liberty' that begins on the next page of the book, the colour prints omit this detail. Presumably this was to make the meaning of the composition more general, less topical.

29 Newton 1795/*c*.1805

N 05058 / B 306
Colour print finished in ink and watercolour
460 × 600 (18⅛ × 23⅝) on paper approx.
545 × 760 (21½ × 30)
Signed '1795 wb inv [in monogram]' b.r. and inscribed 'Newton' below design
Watermarked 'JWHATMAN/1804'
Presented by W. Graham Robertson 1939

PROVENANCE
Thomas Butts; Thomas Butts jun.; Capt. F.J. Butts; his widow, sold 2 June 1905 to W. Graham Robertson

EXHIBITED
BFAC 1876 (172); Carfax 1906 (29); Tate Gallery 1913 (63); on loan to Tate Gallery 1923–7; BFAC 1927 (54, pl.40); *Wartime Acquisitions* National Gallery 1942 (11, repr.); Paris, Antwerp (pl.25), Zurich (repr.) and Tate Gallery (repr.) 1947 (36); *Romantic Movement* Arts Council 1959 (612); Paris 1972 (14, repr.): Hamburg and Frankfurt 1975 (61, repr.); Tate Gallery 1978 (92, repr.); New Haven and Toronto 1982–3 (56b, colour pl.VI)

LITERATURE
Gilchrist 1863, I, pp.375–6; Rossetti 1863, p.203 no.22, and 1880, p.210 no.24; Robertson in Gilchrist 1907, pp.407–8, repr. facing p.396; Blunt in *Warburg Journal*, II, 1938, p.61, pl.11a (reprinted in Essick 1973, pp.84–5, pl.29); Saxl and Wittkower 1948, at pl.67, repr. no.6; Preston 1952, pp.53–6

no.10, pl.10; Digby 1957, pp.44–5, pl.45; Martin K. Nurmi, 'Blake's "Ancient of Days" and Motte's Frontispiece to Newton's *Principia*', Pinto 1957, pp.207–16; Blunt 1959, pp.35, 60, pl.30c; Paul Miner, 'The Polyp as a Symbol in the Poetry of William Blake', *Studies in Literature and Language*, University of Texas, II, 1960, pp.198–205; Damon 1965, pp.91, 298–9; Beer 1968, pp.191, 257, pl.48; Keynes *Letters* 1968, p.118; Raine 1968, II, pp.64–5, 136, pl.159; Bentley *Blake Records* 1969, p.573; Kostelanetz in Rosenfeld 1969, p.126; Robert N. Essick, 'Blake's Newton', *Blake Studies*, III, 1971, pp.149–62, pl.1; Gage in *Warburg Journal*, XXXIV, 1971, pp.372–7, pl.66b; Helmstadter in *Blake Studies*, V, 1972–3, p.108; Donald Ault, *Visionary Physics: Blake's Response to Newton*, 1974, pp.2–4, repr. as frontispiece; Mellor 1974, pp.97, 155–7, pl.41; Bindman 1977, pp.98, 100, pl.82; Klonsky 1977, p.62, repr. in colour; Bindman *Graphic Works* 1978, no.336, repr.; Mitchell 1978, pp.49, 51–2, 63, 73; Paley 1978, p.37, pl.30; Essick *Printmaker* 1980, pp.132, 148, pl.148; La Belle in *Blake*, XIV, 1980–1, pp.77–81, pl.17; Butlin 1981, pp.166–7 no.306, colour pl.394; Butlin in *Blake*, XV, 1981–2, pp.101–3, repr.; Bindman 1982, p.55, colour pl.VI; Morton Paley, review of 1982–3 exhibition, *Burlington Magazine*, CXXIV, 1982, pp.789–90; Bindman in *Blake*, XVI, 1982–3, pp.224–5; Essick in *Blake*, XVI, 1982–3, pp.35–6; Ruth E. Fine, review of 1982–3 exhibition, *Blake*, XVI, 1982–3, p.228; Behrendt 1983, pp.169–70; W.J.T. Mitchell, 'Metamorphoses of the Vortex: Hogarth,

29

Turner, and Blake', Richard Wendorf, ed.,
*Articulate Images: The Sister Arts from Hogarth to
Tennyson* 1983; Warner 1984, p.102;
Hoagwood 1985, p.69; Baine 1986, p.127,

pl.57; Boime 1987, pp.352–5, pl.4.49; *Also
repr*: Figgis 1925, p.75; *Mizue*, no.812, 1973,
2/3, p.13, colour pl.2

Listed in Blake's account with Thomas Butts of 3 March 1806, apparently as having been delivered on 7 September 1805, as is the probable companion 'Nebuchadnezzar'. The only other known copy of this print, formerly in the collection of Mrs William T. Tonner, now belongs to the Lutheran Church in America, Glen Foerd at Torresdale, Philadelphia (Butlin 1981, no.307, pl.408). Before the discovery of the 1804 watermark I had assumed that the Tate Gallery copy of the design was the first to be pulled. However, unlike 'Nebuchadnezzar', where the character of all three known copies is very similar, the Glen Foerd copy of 'Newton' is very different, being closer to the Tate Gallery copies of 'Pity' and 'Hecate', nos.30 and 31. It therefore seems more likely that the Glen Foerd copy was executed in or about 1795, as indeed was suggested by David Bindman in the catalogue of the exhibition held at New Haven and Toronto 1982–3, when both versions were exhibited (the Glen Foerd version as no.56a, repr.). As Bindman points out, the form of signature on the Glen Foerd copy, 'Fresco WBlake inv', corresponds to the version of 'God Judging Adam' in the Metropolitan Museum (see no.26) which seems to be the first pull of that composition and again is likely to have been executed in or around 1795; this is so despite the fact that this form of signature is not known to have been used by Blake before 1810, in Butlin nos.667 and 669, and would therefore have been added at a later date, when the print was finished in pen and watercolour for a prospective client. (Morton Paley, in his review of the New Haven, Toronto exhibition of 1982–3, reports a suggestion that the Tate Gallery's 'Newton' was not colour printed at all but executed entirely in ink and watercolour, but further examination during the exhibition showed this to be unfounded.)

A pencil sketch in reverse is in the Keynes Collection, Fitzwilliam Museum, Cambridge (Butlin no.308, pl.409).

The figure of Newton is related to Michelangelo's Abias, one of the Ancestors of Christ in the lunettes of the Sistine Chapel; Blake had made a copy of this *c*.1785 from an engraving by Adamo Ghisi (Butlin no.168 verso, pl.207; the engraving is repr. Blunt 1959, pl.30a). The design was also developed from plate 10 of the second issue of *There is no Natural Religion* of *c*.1788, which shows an old man kneeling on the ground and drawing with a pair of compasses to illustrate the text 'Application. He who sees the Infinite in all things sees God. He who sees the Ratio only sees himself only'. This illustration also led to the famous 'Ancient of Days', frontispiece to *Europe* of 1794 (repr. Erdman *Illuminated Blake* 1974, p.156), in which the Creator in the guise of Urizen imposes a rational order on the universe. 'The Ancient of Days', although completely different in composition to 'Newton', is also related through having apparently been derived, as a deliberate visual counter-blast, from A. Motte's frontispiece to the 1729 edition of Newton's *Principia*, in which Newton is elevated to the heavens. Another source, as Bindman suggests, may have been Blake's own commercial engraving after Stothard for the frontispiece to John Bonnycastle's *An Introduction to Mensuration, and Practical Geometry*, published in 1782 (Bindman 1978, no.2, repr.). The compasses, which are shown both in 'Newton' and 'The Ancient of Days', appear in *Urizen*, 1794, as one of the instruments created by Urizen to define the material world (Keynes *Writings* 1957, p.234); in *The Song of Los*, 1795, Urizen entrusts the 'Philosophy of the Five Senses' to Newton and Locke (Keynes 1957, p.246). If, as it appears at least in the Tate Gallery copy of the print, Newton is shown under water this is another symbol of materialism (Boime has drawn attention to Newton's comparison of himself to a boy playing on a sea shore, 'diverting myself in now and then finding a smoother pebble or a prettier shell than ordinary, while the great ocean of truth lay all undiscovered before me'). But Newton was also seen by Blake as contributing towards Man's redemption, if only by giving a tangible form to error; in *Europe* he blows 'The Trump of the Last Doom', one of the events leading up to the French Revolution (Keynes 1957, p.243).

29 (detail of signature, date and watermark)

30 **Pity** *c.*1795

N 05062 / B 310
Colour print finished in ink and watercolour,
irregular 425 × 539 (16¾ × 21¼) on paper
approx. 545 × 775 (21½ × 30½)
Signed 'Blake' incised b.r.
Presented by W. Graham Robertson 1939

PROVENANCE
Thomas Butts; Thomas Butts jun.; Capt F.J.
Butts; his widow, sold through Carfax April
1906 to W. Graham Robertson

EXHIBITED
Carfax 1906 (28); Cambridge 1910; Tate
Gallery 1913 (48); on loan to Tate Gallery
1920–7; BFAC 1927 (46, pl.34); *British Art*
RA 1934 (786; 704, pl.165); Whitechapel
1934 (46); *Two Centuries of English Art*
Amsterdam 1936 (188, repr.); *British Painting*
Paris 1938 (159); *Wartime Acquisitions* National
Gallery 1942 (14); Paris, Antwerp (pl.21),
Zurich (repr.) and Tate Gallery 1947 (31);
Tate Gallery 1978 (95, repr.); *The Painterly
Print*, Metropolitan Museum, New York, and
Museum of Fine Arts, Boston, October
1980–March 1981 (17, repr.); New Haven
and Toronto 1982–3 (52, repr.)

LITERATURE
Rossetti 1863, p.237 under no.218; Robertson
in Gilchrist 1907, p.407, repr. facing p.188;
Blunt in *Warburg Journal*, VI, 1943, pp.201,
207–8, 212, pl.57b; Keynes *Faber Gallery* 1946,
p.5, 10, colour pl.4; Grigson in *Architectural
Review*, CVIII, 1950, p.218; Preston 1952,
pp.44–6 no.7, pl.7; Blunt 1959, pp.39, 60–1,
pl.28a; Merchant in *Apollo*, LXXIX, 1964,
p.322, pl.9 (reprinted in Essick 1973,
pp.244–6, pl.69); Damon 1965, p.370;
Hagstrum in Hilles and Bloom 1965, p.311,
316, 318–20, 329 n.40; Kostelanetz in
Rosenfeld 1969, p.129, pl.4; Mellor 1974,
pp.161–3, pl.45; Bindman 1977, pp.98–9,
106; Klonsky 1977, p.61, repr. in colour;
Bindman *Graphic Works* 1978, no.326, repr.;
Paley 1978, p.38; Essick *Printmaker* 1980,
p.134, pl.126; Sue Welsh Reed, catalogue
entries on three versions of 'Pity' in exh. cat.
The Painterly Print, 1980, pp.84–9; La Belle in
Blake, XIV, 1980–1; Butlin 1981, pp.168–9
no.310, colour pl.395; Heppner in *Bulletin of
Research in the Humanities*, LXXXIV, 1981,
pp.337–54, repr. p.349; Butlin in *Blake*, XV,
1981–2, p.102; Bindman in *Blake*, XVI,
1982–3, p.162

There are two other full-size versions of this design, one in the Metropolitan
Museum, New York, and one at the Yale Center for British Art, Paul Mellon
Collection, New Haven (Butlin 1981, nos.311 and 312, pls.410 and 411). None of
the prints are dated, nor do they bear dated watermarks, but all seem to date from
the initial phase of Blake's work on his large colour prints, *c.*1795. The sequence of
the three pulls seems to have been Tate Gallery, Metropolitan Museum and Yale
Center.

There is also a smaller colour print of the same composition, measuring
7¼ × 10¹³⁄₁₆ in, in the British Museum (Butlin no.313, pl.412) which seems to have
been a try-out not just for this composition but for the technique of the series of
large colour prints as a whole.

In composition the smaller colour print lies mid-way between the large printed
versions of the composition and two preliminary pencil drawings with the
composition reversed which are also in the British Museum (Butlin nos.314 and
315, pls.413 and 414). The earlier of these two drawings (no.314) is upright in
composition, suggesting that Blake had not yet fixed a format of the proportions of
the composition. The second drawing in the British Museum is however in the
oblong format of the later colour prints, as is what may be another sketch for the
same composition, much rougher and partly obscured by writing, in Blake's
Notebook (Butlin no.201 *106*, and Erdman and Moore 1973, Caption 2 N106
repr.). On the back of the second, oblong British Museum drawing there is another
sketch related at least in part, recently uncovered when the drawing was
remounted. At the bottom of the composition the same small child appears leaping
upwards, towards however a completely different figure of a nude woman
apparently clambering up rocks.

The first, upright British Museum drawing is inscribed by Frederick Tatham
with the words 'Shakespeares Pity/. And Pity like a naked new-born Babe/ &c
&c[?]/ F. Tatham –'. Although no title seems to have been inscribed by Blake on

the margin of the Tate Gallery print, and no account between Butts and Blake giving the title can be traced, it seems to be universally accepted that Tatham was correct in his identification with the verses from Shakespear's *Macbeth*, i, vii:

> Besides, this Duncan
> Hath borne his faculties so meek, hath been
> So clear in his great office, that his virtues
> Will plead, like angels, trumpet-tongu'd against
> The deep damnation of his taking off;
> And Pity, like a naked new-born babe,
> Striding the blast, or heav'n's cherubin hors'd
> Upon the sightless couriers of the air,
> Shall blow the horrid deed in ev'ry eye;
> That tears shall drown the wind – I have no spur
> To prick the sides of my intent, but only
> Vaulting ambition, which o'er leaps itself,
> And falls on th'other –.

Blake, rather than illustrating the incident in Shakespeare's play, illustrates his figures of speech, recreating his imagery, as Christopher Heppner says, 'in the form of a dramatized episode implying a supportive narrative'. This illustration of the figure of speech rather than the dramatic situation had been anticipated by John Hamilton Mortimer (see Grigson, *loc. cit.*) and Fuseli (see Bindman 1977, p.106). Both of Shakespeare's alternative similes for pity are illustrated, the babe and the female cherubin leaning from the horse's back to snatch it up from the mother lying below. In one sense the design is an amazingly literal illustration of Shakespeare's images, including the 'sightless couriers of the air', with the 'tears' being shown as rain. However, the mother does not appear in Shakespeare's text but forms part of Blake's new narrative context.

Until recently the design has more usually been seen as negative in content, illustrating pity as a divisive force as in the line 'For pity divides the soul' from *Urizen* of 1794. In this book Pity appears as the first woman, Blake's character Enitharmon, who divides off from Los, a division paralleling the creation of Eve from Adam, and this leads, through her mating with Los, to 'Man begetting his likeness, On his own divided image' (Keynes *Writings* 1957, pp.230–2). However, in part anticipated by A.S. Roe (exh. cat., *William Blake: An Annotated Catalogue*, Andrew Dixon White Museum of Art, Cornell University, Ithaca, February–March 1965, p.28 no.32, the Metropolitan Museum version repr.), Christopher Heppner, who has given the fullest and probably the closest analysis of the design up to the present, sees the design as positive in intent, demonstrating the possibilities of salvation through pity in the fallen world typified by the abandoned mother. Certainly the general impression is positive, as opposed to the negative impact of the companion print usually identified as 'Hecate' (no.31). Pity, as embodied in the figure of the babe, is one of Blake's typical figures of positive energy, that personified most usually by Orc in his earliest, innocent state.

The farther horseman or cherubin, with arms outstretched, who seems to be male in contrast to the female figure on the nearer horse, is probably based on one of Raphael's representations of God the Father in the Vatican Loggie (e.g. that repr. Blunt 1959, pl.32d). At this period in his life Blake saw God the Father, the God of the Old Testament, as a negative force in contrast to Christ, and Heppner has suggested that the two cherubim are similarly contrasted, the nearer one being Pity, the farther one Wrath. On the other hand the attitude of the farthest figure may merely have been adopted by Blake to stress a sense of continuing movement against which is set the momentarily more static action of the nearer figure snatching up the babe.

30

31 **Hecate** (?) *c.*1795

N 05056/B 316
Colour print finished in ink and watercolour
439 × 581 ($17\frac{1}{4}$ × $22\frac{7}{8}$) on paper approx.
545 × 770 ($21\frac{1}{2}$ × $30\frac{1}{4}$)
Signed 'Blake' incised b.l.
Watermarked '1794/JWHATMAN'
Presented by W. Graham Robertson 1939

PROVENANCE

Thomas Butts; Thomas Butts jun.; Capt. F.J. Butts; his widow, sold through Carfax April 1906 to W. Graham Robertson

EXHIBITED

BFAC 1876 (204); Carfax 1904 (22); Carfax 1906 (31); Cambridge 1910; Tate Gallery (67) and Manchester (51) 1913–14; on loan to Tate Gallery 1920–7; BFAC 1927 (56, pl.42); *British Art* RA 1934 (776, repr. in 1st ed. pl.87; 703); Whitechapel 1938 (49); *Wartime Acquisitions* National Gallery 1942 (9); Paris, Antwerp (pl.26), Zurich (repr.) and Tate Gallery 1947 (37); Tate Gallery 1978 (99, repr.); New Haven and Toronto 1982–3 (55, repr.)

LITERATURE

Rossetti 1863, p.238 no.228, and 1880, p.253 no.257; Robertson in Gilchrist 1907, p.410, repr.; Cook and Wedderburn *Works of Ruskin*, XXXVI, 1909, pp.32–3; Percival 1938, p.70, repr.; Collins Baker in *Huntington Library Quarterly*, IV, 1940–1, p.360 (reprinted in Essick 1973, pp.118–19, pl.68); Preston 1952, pp.47–9 no.8, pl.8; Roe 1953, p.67; Blunt 1959, pp.59–60, pl.26a; Merchant in *Apollo*, LXXIX, 1964, p.322, pl.8 (reprinted in Essick 1973, pp.243–4, pl.68); Damon 1965, p. 370; Hagstrum in Hilles and Bloom 1965, pp.320, 329 nn.30 and 34, pl.6; Raine 1968, II, pp.7–8, pl.125; Kostelanetz in Rosenfeld 1969, pp.126–7; Mellor 1974, pp.157–8, pl.42; Bindman 1977, pp.98, 100; Klonsky 1977, p.60, repr. in colour; Bindman *Graphic Works* 1978, no.334, repr.; Paley 1978, pp.38, 178, pl.26; La Belle in *Blake*, XIV, 1980–1, pp.77–80, pl.15; Butlin 1981, p.171 no.316, colour pl.396; Heppner in *Bulletin of Research in the Humanities*, LXXXIV, 1981, pp.337–8, 355–65, repr. p.362; Butlin in *Blake*, xv, 1981–2, p.102; Bindman in *Blake*, XVI, 1982–3, p.225; Hilton 1983, p.162, detail repr. pl.40; Warner 1984, p.120. *Also repr*: *Mizue*, no.882, 1978, 9, p.11 in colour

Two other copies of this print are known, in the National Gallery of Scotland, Edinburgh, and in the Huntington Library and Art Gallery, San Marino (Butlin 1981, nos.317 and 318, pls.415 and 416). None of these is dated, though the Tate Gallery copy is watermarked 1794, and in this case, as in that of 'Pity', it seems possible to accept, partly for stylistic reasons, that all three copies were executed *c.*1795, the Tate copy being the first pull, that in Edinburgh the second, and that at San Marino the last. A pencil sketch in reverse was formerly in the collection of Ian L. Phillips (Butlin no.319, pl.419).

This work seems to have been designed as a companion to 'Pity'. In the case of the copies in the Tate Gallery the form of signature and the general colouring are similar. The two designs probably represent aspects of the feminine role in the Fallen World.

Until recently the traditional title, 'Hecate', has been generally accepted; the only difference of opinion seems to have been over whether the title referred to Puck's closing speech in *A Midsummer Night's Dream* or to the figure in *Macbeth*. However, as Christopher Heppner had pointed out, the title 'Hecate' was not used until William Rossetti's lists in Gilchrists's *Life of William Blake*, 1863. No title is inscribed on the mount unlike others of the colour prints that belonged to Thomas Butts, nor does it figure in any surviving account between Blake and Butts. In fact the first title to be applied to his design, in a reference by John Ruskin in a letter of *c.*1843 to the copy in the Huntington Library, was 'The Owls'. In all traditional representations of Hecate the three heads of what is a single figure face outwards; here the seated female figure partly obscures totally distinct younger figures, a girl on the left and a boy on the right. One's instinctive reaction, as Heppner points out, is that this is a depiction of shame, and in this the design would be on a par to that representing pity. To some extent this identification is supported visually by comparison with the frontispiece to *Visions of the Daughters of Albion* (no.21) which definitely represents shame, with figures seated in somewhat similar poses at the

31

mouth of a cave. However, it is difficult to be precise about this identification. Jean Hagstrum saw the scene as representing jealousy while his pupil Warren Jones, in an unpublished dissertation reported by Heppner, sees it as representing institutional religion. Heppner himself is reluctant to go beyond identifying the main figure as that of a witch though not specifically Hecate; the strange creature hovering in the air above would be her familiar, while the owl and toad shown on the left are also to be associated with witchcraft.

Heppner suggests further that, just as Blake illustrated pity in the companion print as a sort of narrative, so this composition should also be seen as a point in time, with the ass on the left standing for a means of travel. The fact that it is derived from an engraving of 'The Rest on the Flight into Egypt' in Alexander Browne's *Ars Pictoria*, 1675 (repr. Collins Baker 1940–1, p.361; 1973, pl.43), and reappears in Blake's watercolour of the same subject of 1806 in the Metropolitan Museum (Butlin no.472, colour pl.543), seems to have no iconographic significance; it also appears in the illustration showing the Good Samaritan in Young's *Night Thoughts* (Night II, p.35; Butlin no.330 *68*, repr. Erdman *Night Thoughts* 1980).

Shame is quite often associated with pride in Blake's writings as in 'Shame is Prides cloke' (*The Marriage of Heaven and Hell*, 1790–93, plate 7; Keynes *Writings* 1957, p.151) and 'The Sexes sprung from Shame & Pride' ('To Tirzah' added *c.*1805 or later to *Songs of Experience*; Keynes 1957, p.220). It is also yet another devisive element: 'Shame divides Families. Shame hath divided Albion in sunder!' (*Jerusalem, c.*1804–15; Keynes 1957, p.643).

Blake's composition may have influenced Fuseli's 'The Witch and the Mandrake', both the oil exhibited at the Royal Academy in 1812 and the engraving of probably about the same date (repr. Gert Schiff, *Johann Heinrich Füssli*, 1973, II, p.489 no.1497 and p.499 no.1510), though, as Fuseli had already exhibited a lost work called 'The Mandrake; a Charm' in 1785, the influence may have been the other way round.

32 **The House of Death** 1795/*c*.1805

N 05060/B 320
Colour print finished in ink and watercolour
485 × 610 (19⅛ × 24) on paper approx.
545 × 770 (21½ × 30¼)
Signed 'WB 1795' b.l. and inscribed 'The House of Death Milton' below design
Watermarked '1794/I TAYLOR'
Presented by W. Graham Robertson 1939

PROVENANCE
Thomas Butts; Thomas Butts jun.; Capt. F.J. Butts; his widow, sold through Carfax April 1906 to W. Graham Robertson

EXHIBITED
Carfax 1906 (26); Tate Gallery (51a), Manchester (56), Nottingham (39) and Edinburgh (42) 1913–14; on loan to Tate Gallery 1923–7; BFAC 1927 (49, pl.37); *Wartime Acquisitions* National Gallery 1942 (13); Tate Gallery 1947 (55); Cambridge 1971 (73); Tate Gallery 1978 (101, repr.)

LITERATURE
Rossetti 1863, p.202 no.17, and 1880, p.209 no.19; Robertson in Gilchrist 1907, p.409, repr. facing p.338; Blunt in *Warburg Journal*, VI, 1943, p.212, pl.63b; Keynes *Faber Gallery* 1946, pp.5, 12, colour pl.5; Preston 1952, pp.50–2 no.9, pl.9; Digby 1957, pp.46–7, pl.46; Blunt 1959, pp.20, 41, 59, pl.27a; Gert Schiff, *Johann Heinrich Füsslis Milton-Galerie*, 1963, pp.78–9, pl.38; Hagstrum 1964, pp.67–8, pl.42b; Beer 1968, p.192; Keynes *Letters* 1968, p.17; Raine 1968, II, p.96, pl.151; Taylor and Grant in *Blake Studies*, I, 1968–9, pp.42–6, 195–6, repr. p.43; Bentley *Blake Records* 1969, p.572; Kostelanetz in Rosenfeld 1969, p.128, pl.5; Pointon 1970, p.135, pl.124; Tomory *Fuseli* 1972, pp.211–2; Mellor 1974, pp.160–1, pl.44; Bindman 1977, pp.98, 100, 104, pl.81; Klonsky 1977, p.59, repr. in colour; Bindman *Graphic Works* 1978, no.335, repr.; Paley 1978, pp.37–8, pl.33; La Belle in *Blake*, XIV, 1980–1, pp.73–6, pl.8; Butlin 1981, pp.172–3 no.320, colour pl.397; Raine 1982, at pl.64, repr.; Behrendt 1983, pp.143, 179–81; Butlin in *Blake*, XVII, 1983–4, p.159; Warner 1984, pp.87, 94, 102, 121; Hoagwood 1985, pp.69, 76, pl.1. *Also repr*: Figgis 1925, pl.73; *Mizue*, no.882, 1978, 9, p.19 in colour

This copy of the design was listed in Blake's account with Thomas Butts of 3 March 1806 as 'House of Death', apparently having been delivered on 5 July 1805. There are two other known copies of the design, at the British Museum and in the Fitzwilliam Museum, Cambridge (Butlin 1981, nos.321 and 322, colour pls.398 and 399). The Tate Gallery copy of the print may be the first pull, the British Museum one the second, and the Fitzwilliam Museum one, in which the left-hand of the foremost reclining figure is made much more expressive by being open, with extended figures, instead of resting on a shoulder, the third. This ordering is the case if one holds that all the pulls were made at the same time, in 1795; the modelling of the right-hand figure in the British Museum pull in particular has affinities with other works attributed to *c*.1795. Alternatively however, it could be that the British Museum pull and that in the Fitzwilliam Museum were made in about 1795, in that order, while the Tate Gallery copy was done afresh *c*.1804–5. For a related pen and wash drawing of *c*.1790 see no.12.

The composition, also known as 'The Lazar House', illustrates Milton's *Paradise Lost*, XI, 477–93. Death hovers above; Despair stands on the right. The latter figure recurs on page 51 of *Jerusalem*, probably etched *c*.1804–7 (repr. Erdman *Illuminated Blake* 1974, p.330), a design that also exists as a separate coloured print, 'Vala, Hyle and Skofeld' of *c*.1820 (see Butlin 1981, nos.578 and 579, pl.812 and colour pl.961). The figure of Death is based on a figure in the copy of Fuseli's 'Fertilisation

32

of Egypt' made by Blake for his engraving published in Erasmus Darwin's *The Botanic Garden* in 1791; this was probably based in its turn on the Jupiter Pluvius on the Column of Marcus Aurelius and is modified from Fuseli's original figure (both drawings are in the British Museum; the Blake, Butlin no.173, pl.213, and the Fuseli are repr. Blunt 1959, pls.21b and 21a respectively). The position of the figure, right across the top of the design instead of in one corner as in no.12, is common to Fuseli's pen and wash drawing of the same subject in the Kunsthaus, Zurich, presumably made for the oil completed for his Milton Gallery in 1793 (repr. Schiff 1963, pl.37, Tomory, *op. cit.*, p.101, and Schiff 1973, II, p.305 no.1023; see also *ibid.* p.569 no.1764), but Blake's composition is otherwise different.

Death is shown in the guise of Blake's character Urizen, close to the depiction of God the Father in 'Elohim Creating Adam' (no.25) and 'God Judging Adam' (no.26). Blake's meaning is perhaps to show the Creator presiding over the inevitable decay of his material creation; He blasts them with the scroll of Law, its ends transformed into thunder-bolts, as has been suggested by Kathleen Raine. Visually the design seems to be the counterpart of 'Christ Appearing to the Apostles' (no.34): the wrath of the Old Dispensation is contrasted with the mercy of the New.

33 **The Good and Evil Angels** 1795/?*c.*1805

N 05057 / B 323
Colour print finished in ink and watercolour
445 × 594 (17½ × 23⅜) on paper approx.
545 × 760 (21½ × 30)
Signed 'WB inv [in monogram] 1795' b.l. and
inscribed 'The Good and Evil Angels' below
design
Presented by W. Graham Robertson 1939

PROVENANCE

Thomas Butts; Thomas Butts jun.; Capt. F.J.
Butts; his widow, sold 2 June 1905 to W.
Graham Robertson

EXHIBITED

BFAC 1876 (202); Carfax 1906 (32); Tate
Gallery 1913 (68); on loan to Tate Gallery
1923 onwards; *Wartime Acquisitions* National
Gallery 1942 (7); *English Romantic Art* Arts
Council tour 1947 (9); Tate Gallery 1947
(56); Tate Gallery 1978 (102, repr.)

LITERATURE

Rossetti 1863, p.203 no.20, and 1880, p.209
no.22; Robertson in Gilchrist 1907, p.408,
repr. facing p.142; Damon 1924, p.327; Figgis
1925, at pl.71, repr.; Preston 1952, pp.41–3
no.6, pl.6; Digby 1957, pp.38–9, pl.38; Blunt
1959, pp.42, 61–2, pl.31b; Butlin in *Burlington
Magazine*, CVI, 1964, p.382; Beer 1968,
pp.191, 256, pl.30a; Keynes *Letters* 1968,
pp.117; Raine 1968, I, pp.365–6, colour
pl.120; Bentley *Blake Records* 1969, p.572;
Kostelanetz in Rosenfeld 1969, pp.127–8;
Warner in Erdman and Grant 1970, pp.184,
187; Mellor 1974, pp.120, 158–60, pl.43;
Bindman 1977, pp.69, 98–9; Klonsky 1977,
p.64, repr. in colour; Bindman *Graphic Works*
1978, no.328, repr.; Paley 1978, pp.38, 178,
colour pl.32; La Belle in *Blake*, XIV, 1980–1,
p.76, pl.9; Butlin 1981, pp.174–5 no.323,
colour pl.400; Heppner in *Bulletin of Research in
the Humanities*, LXXXIV, 1981, pp.388, 349–50;
Raine 1982, at pl.53, repr.; Essick in *Blake*,
XVI, 1982–3, pp.32–3; Warner 1984,
pp.95–6, 102. *Also repr*: *Mizue*, no.882, 1978,
9, p.14 in colour

Listed in Blake's account with Thomas Butts of 3 March 1806 as 'Good and Evil
Angel', having apparently been delivered on 5 July 1805. This is probably the
second pull of the print, following that in the John Hay Whitney collection (Butlin
1981, no.324, pl.405). It could be one of the later pulls of *c.*1805, but if, as seems
likely, it can be paired with 'God Judging Adam', it may date from 1795, as is
supported by its general appearance. There is an earlier watercolour version of the
composition, in reverse, probably painted *c.*1793–4, in the Cecil Higgins Museum,
Bedford (Butlin no.257, colour pl.197).

The earliest version of the composition, however, also in reverse but on a smaller
scale, occurs on page 4 of *The Marriage of Heaven and Hell, c.*1790–3, where it
appears to illustrate 'the following Errors. 1. That Man has two real existing
principles Viz: a Body & a Soul. 2. That Energy calld Evil is alone from the Body.
& that Reason. calld Good. is alone from the Soul. 3. That God will torment Man
in Eternity for following his Energies'. Blake goes on to assert that the 'following
Contraries ... are True 1. Man has no Body distinct from his Soul ... 2 Energy is
the only life and is from the Body and Reason is the bound or outward
circumference of Energy. 3 Energy is Eternal Delight'. The design is thus an
assertion of the error of dividing Man, originally unified, into his different elements,
a concept that Blake developed and refined in his Lambeth Books, in which he
symbolised these elements of the divided Man by different personifications. In the
large colour print it is possible to identify the two main figures with two such
personifications. The fettered figure is Orc, Blake's symbol for Energy, now older
but demonstrably developed from the figure in 'Los and Orc', no.13, by way of the
headpiece to the 'Preludium' of *America* (repr. Bindman 1978, no.148). As Mellor
has demonstrated, Energy is now in 1795 seen as a negative force, a Urizenic will to
power. The other figure is also a development of that in the earlier watercolour 'Los
and Orc': Los, normally the personification of the Imagination, is also like Orc
shown in his fallen state as a repressive force. The child is not paralleled in Blake's
contemporary writings but may represent the lost innocence of the unified Man,
now torn between the two fallen 'angels'. As compared with the first version of the

33

composition in *The Marriage of Heaven and Hell* the sun is lower in the sky, sinking below the horizon, another indication of Blake's increased pessimism at this time.

If one accepts the theory that Blake designed the series of large colour prints in pairs, this composition would seem to be the complement to 'God Judging Adam'. In the latter 'the flames of eternal fury' emit no light, whereas in 'Good and Evil Angels' the fire represents energy as 'the only Life . . . Eternal delight'. Here light is positive, even if the scene shows one stage in the breaking up of Man into his different elements, while in 'God Judging Adam' the fire without light is part of a completely negative scene.

34 **Christ Appearing to the Apostles after the Resurrection** *c.*1795

N 05875/B 327
Colour print finished in ink and watercolour,
varnished and trimmed 406 × 499 (16 × 19⅝)
Bequeathed by W. Graham Robertson 1948

PROVENANCE
?Mrs Blake; ?Frederick Tatham;? Joseph
Hogarth, sold Southgate's 7–30 June 1854,
17th evening (7112 as 'Our Saviour appearing
to His Disciples, in colours') 8/- bt M. Sharp;
...; J.W. Pease, bequeathed 1901 to Miss S.H.
Pease, sold Christie's 2 December 1938 (57)
£75 bt. Martin for W. Graham Robertson

LITERATURE
Rossetti 1903, pp.16–17; Preston 1952,
pp.39–40 no.5, pl.5; Preston *Letters from
W.G.R.* 1953, pp.400, 405–6, 424; Keynes
Bible 1957, p.46 no.151a repr.; Kostelanetz in
Rosenfeld 1969, pp.129–30; Keynes *Blake
Studies* 1971, p.156; Helmstadter in *Blake
Studies*, v, 1972–3, p.132; Mellor 1974, p.163;
Bindman 1977, p.100; Paley 1978., p.37;
Essick *Printmaker* 1980, p.134, pl.128; La Belle
in *Blake*, XIV, 1980–1, p.81; Lindberg in *Blake*,
XIV, 1980–1, pp.167, 173 n.48; Butlin 1981,
pp.176–7 no.327, pl.418

Unlike other prints from this series in the Tate Gallery this example is not that from the Butts collection, which was mentioned in the Butts accounts of 3 March 1806 apparently as having been delivered on 7 September 1805. This had passed to J.C. Strange by 1863 and is now in the Yale University Art Gallery (Butlin 1981 no.325, colour pl.401). There is a third version of the design in the National Gallery of Art, Washington, D.C. (Butlin no.326, pl.417). The Tate Gallery copy is one of five designs from this series that were in the collection of J.W. Pease when he died in 1901, some or all of which were part of a larger, if not complete, set from the Tatham collection. All the Pease prints, together with one or two further examples traceable back to Tatham, have been varnished, either by Blake himself or subsequently, causing the prints to become much darker and more obscure. In addition the Tate's 'Christ Appearing to the Apostles after the Resurrection' has been trimmed and the lower corners made up. The Tate Gallery's pull, which bears relatively little colour printing and is hardly finished at all in pen and watercolour, seems to be the last, with the Washington one first and the Yale Center one second. All seem to date from about 1795 although the Yale Center version was probably finished in pen and watercolour shortly before being delivered to Butts in 1805; it bears the 'WB inv' monogram common to other works of this date though only traces, if that, of a date, and it is also mounted on fine linen as were formerly the Butts prints at the Tate, though lacking the paper margins of the other Butts colour prints.

The print illustrates Luke, xxiv, 36–40, the Apostles 'terrified and affrighted' at Christ's appearance. Most if not all of the other prints in this series seem to be condemnatory in character, showing the divided Man in his fallen state. It is tempting therefore to see this apparently more positive scene also in a negative sense, as showing Doubting Thomas. Rossetti indeed lists this as a separate subject seen by him in the Butts collection, 'Christ overcoming the incredulity of Thomas', a tempera, 'Great in the expression of speechless, unspeakable adoration in the other ten Apostles, earth bowed' (Rossetti 1863, p.229 no.165, and 1880, p.241 no.189; Butlin no.328). This is untraced and may well be a mistake for the Yale version of the colour print. In support of this interpretation is the similarity pointed out by Helmstadter between the figure of Christ in the colour print and that in the illustration to Young's *Night Thoughts*, 1796–7 (Butlin no.330 *265*; repr. Helmstadter 1972–3, pl.5, and Erdman and Moore 1973) which is identified by him as showing Christ with St Thomas; the only important difference (possibly significant?) is that in the print Christ's left foot is forward rather than his right. David Bindman on the other hand stresses the opposition between the one young apostle who regards the risen Christ with adoration and the others who bow themselves before Him as if He were an idol. The fact that the layout of the composition resembles that of 'The Good Farmer' (see no.4) is probably without significance.

34

On the other hand the fact that the design seems to be a counterpart to 'The House of Death' (no.32) suggests that the meaning may be a positive one, contrasting the merciful god of the New Testament with the vengeful god of the old. Michael Tolley, in conversation in 1988, suggests that the figures looking upwards in the two compositions represent Hope and Fear respectively.

Early titles given to this design are no help. In the Butts account the design was called simply 'Christ appearing'. What seems to be this version, though it may perhaps have been the version now in Washington, was sold with the stock of Joseph Hogarth at Southgate's in 1854 as 'Our Saviour appearing to His Disciples', and seems also to have been referred to by Frederick Tatham in a letter of 6 November 1862 to William Rossetti, mentioning seven prints that he had offered to 'Mr Ferguson of Tynemouth' some years earlier, as 'the Saviour'. That this version is that subsequently sold from the Hogarth collection is probable in view of the likely history of the other large colour prints later in the Pease collection (see Butlin 1981, p.158).

TEMPERA PAINTINGS OF BIBLICAL SUBJECTS *c.*1799–1800

Blake painted over 135 illustrations to the Bible for Thomas Butts (1757–1845), Blake's most important patron, at least until the last years of his life. Butts was a clerk in the office of the Commissary General of Musters. Alexander Gilchrist suggests that they met as early as *c.*1793 (1863, I, p.115) but there is no record of any actual dealing between them until 1799. A number of receipts for payment made by Butts to Blake in 1803 and between 1805 and 1810 survive and there is a debtor and creditor account, drawn up on 3 March 1806, for part of 1805 (see nos.25–9, 32 and 33). During this period Butts seems to have made regular payments in advance for work in hand. In 1806 Blake began to give lessons in engraving to Butts's son, though the father probably profited as much or more. Butt's patronage seems to have slackened after about 1816 but continued until Blake's death; he bought a set of the Job engravings in 1825 and subscribed to the Dante engravings in 1827.

Of the biblical subjects painted for Butts about fifty were in tempera, either on canvas or, more rarely, on metal. These seem to have been done largely before the watercolours, there being dated examples from 1799 (including no.37; the full list is Butlin 1981, nos.380, 384, 396, 398, 402, 404, 406, 413, 419 and 428) and 1800 (Butlin nos. 409 and 422); one was exhibited at the Royal Academy in 1799 (Butlin no.424) and another in 1800 (Butlin no.416). However it is possible that Blake painted further examples at Felpham, where he lived from 1800 to 1803. He sent 'Two Pictures' to Butts on 22 November 1802 and asked, in a second letter of the same date, 'what subject you choose to be painted on the remaining Canvas which I brought down with me (for there were three)'. This third picture was probably 'The Riposo' sent to Butts on 6 July 1803 (this is presumably 'the Repose in Egypt' listed by Rossetti as being in the Butts collection but now untraced; Butlin no.405). It is possible however that at least the first two of these canvases were used for totally different subjects, for instance other works from the Butts collection that were included in Blake's exhibition of 1809 (e.g. no.58).

Blake refers to what seem to be these tempera paintings in a letter to George Cumberland of 26 August 1799: 'As to Myself about whom you are so kindly Interested, I live by a Miracle. I am Painting small Pictures from the Bible . . . My Work pleases my employer & I have an order for Fifty small Pictures at One Guinea each.' Thirty temperas are known today and over twenty further biblical subjects can be more or less definitely identified as having been painted in tempera, either from William Rossetti's descriptions or from other early accounts.

The medium of these works seems to have been similar to that used in the colour prints such as nos.25–34. Indeed Blake used the same word 'fresco' both for some of his colour prints and for some of the temperas (see nos.58–60, 64 and 69, and also, for the colour prints, Butlin nos.299, 307, 317 and 326, and, temperas, Butlin nos.667, 669, 673, and 674). According to J.T. Smith, 'Blake's modes for preparing his ground, and laying them over his panels for painting, mixing his colours, and manner of working, were those which he considered to have been practised by the earliest fresco-painters, whose productions still remain, in numerous instances, vivid and permanently fresh. His ground was a mixture of whiting and carpenters's glue, which he passed over several times in thin coatings: his colours he ground himself, and also united them with the same sort of glue, but in a much weaker state. He would, in the course of painting a picture, pass a very thin transparent wash of glue-water over the whole of the parts he had worked upon, and then proceed with his finishing. This process I have tried, and find, by using my mixtures warm, that I can produce the same texture as possessed in Blake's pictures of the

Last Judgment [see Butlin no.648], and others of his productions, particularly in Varley's curious picture of the personified Flea [no.64]. Blake preferred mixing his colours with carpenter's glue, to gum, on account of the latter cracking in the sun, and becoming humid in moist weather. The glue-mixture stands the sun, the change of atmosphere has no effect upon it' (reprinted Bentley *op. cit.*, p.472). Frederick Tatham, writing in about 1832, gives what appears to be an independent acount of the same technique, though unlike Smith he could not have known Blake as early as the first tempera paintings of *c.*1799–1800: 'Blake painted on Panel or canvas covered with 3 or 4 layers of whitening & carpenters Glue; [sic] as he said the nature of Gum was to crack, for as he used several layers of colour to produce his depths, the Coats necessarily in the deepest parts became so thick, that they were likely to peel off. Washing his Picture over with glue in the manner of a Varnish, he fixed the Colours, and at last varnished with a white hard varnish of his own making.' Blake also touched his 'lights with white compound of whiting & glue, of which material he laid the ground of his Panel' (reprinted in Bentley *op. cit.*, pp.515, 517). Blake's use of carpenter's glue instead of the egg yolk of true tempera probably brought about the darkening of so many of his paintings in this technique, which he seems fundamentally to have altered in his later works (see nos.68–70).

Whereas most of the known examples of the temperas painted for Butts measure approximately $10\frac{1}{2} \times 15$ inches, or the vertical equivalent, a few are larger, approximately $12\frac{3}{4} \times 19\frac{1}{2}$ inches (Butlin nos.415, 416, 422 and 424). Both groups include temperas on metal (no.38 and Butlin nos.379, 392, 401, 414, 416 and 422), so perhaps the two sizes were chosen because they were standard copper-plate dimensions. Ruthven Todd has suggested that Blake may even have used engravers' copper plates for his temperas on copper (letter to the compiler of 7 January 1970).

LITERATURE
Smith *Nollekens and his Times* 1828, II, 480–1; Gilchrist 1863, I, p.115; Keynes *Writings* 1957, pp.795, 813, 816; Blunt 1959, pp.64–8, 104–5; Keynes *Letters* 1968, pp.32, 57, 59–60; Bentley *Blake Records* 1969, pp.67, 472, 515, 517, 570–8, 591, 606; Todd 1971, pp.19, 49–50, 100–2, 128; Bindman 1977, pp.117–30, 171; Paley 1978, pp.42, 55; Butlin 1981, pp.316–35

35 **Moses Indignant at the Golden Calf** *c.*1799–1800

T 04134 / B 387
Tempera on canvas 380 × 266 (15 × 10½) on
stretcher 387 × 273 (15¼ × 10¾)
Signed 'wʙ [inv?]' in monogram, damaged,
? with traces of a date, b.l.
Bequeathed by Ian L. Phillips 1986

PROVENANCE
Thomas Butts: Thomas Butts jun.; Capt. F.J.
Butts; his widow, sold April 1906 through
Carfax to W. Graham Robertson, sold
Christie's 22 July 1949 (10) £462 bt Ian L.
Phillips (d. 1984), by whom bequeathed to the
Tate Gallery with a life interest to his wife,
relinquished 1986

EXHIBITED
Century of Art Grafton Galleries 1911 (56); on
loan to Tate Gallery from before 1939 to 1949;
Tate Gallery 1947 (52); Bournemouth,
Southampton and Brighton 1949 (22); Arts
Council 1951 (13); Tate Gallery 1978 (134,
repr.)

LITERATURE
Rossetti 1863, p.224 no.117, and 1880, p.236
no.140; Preston 1952, p.126 no.43, pl.43;
Keynes *Bible* 1957, p.14 no.42 repr.; Blunt
1959, p.66; Bindman 1977, p.125; Butlin
1981, pp.316–8, 320 no.387, pl.487; Warner
1984, pp.68, 161

This is an illustration to Exodus, xxxii, 19. Moses, having come down after his forty days on Mount Sinai, protests at the Israelites' idolatrous worship of the Golden Calf, set up by Aaron during his absence; the Tables of the Law, thrown down by Moses in his fury, lie broken at his feet. The striking angular figure of Moses is contrasted with the graceful naked dancers on the left, behind whom stands Aaron. Janet Warner has pointed out that the pose of Moses follows the second part of the description of Indignation given in John Weaver's *History of the Mimes and Pantomimes* of 1728. As she says, it is not necessary for Blake to have read Weaver; rather, this is an example of the common language of gesture (or 'pathos formulae') used by history painters in the eighteenth century.

It is possible, but unlikely, that William Rossetti lists this work a second time as his no.127 (1880, no.152), 'The Plague Stayed at the Threshing-floor of Araunah the Jebusite', an otherwise untraced painting (see Butlin 1981, no.391). The 'gigantic ancient man' and the sky with 'as much red as blue in it' of Rossetti's description would well fit 'Moses Indignant at the Golden Calf'.

What appear to be the tops of the four digits of a date can be seen in front of the signature: from these it is unclear whether the date would be '1799' or '1800', though the former is perhaps slightly more likely. The painting was restored at the Tate Gallery on acquisition.

35

36 **Bathsheba at the Bath** *c.*1799–1800

N 03007/B 390
Tempera on canvas, previously relined and
now mounted on board 263 × 376 ($10\frac{3}{8}$ × $14\frac{13}{16}$),
cut down from approx. 265 × 380 ($10\frac{1}{2}$ × 15)
Signed 'WB inv' in monogram b.r.
Presented by the National Art-Collections
Fund 1914

PROVENANCE
Thomas Butts; Thomas Butts, jun.; Capt. F.J.
Butts, sold Sotheby's 24 June 1903 (8) £80 bt
Knowles; Carfax 1904; F.P. Osmaston by
1906, sold 1914 to the National Art-
Collections Fund

EXHIBITED
Carfax 1904 (8); Carfax 1906 (8); Tate
Gallery 1913 (13); Paris, Antwerp, Zurich
and Tate Gallery 1947 (4); Arts Council 1951
(14, pl.4); Hamburg and Frankfurt 1975 (99,
colour pl.6); Tate Gallery 1978 (135, repr.)

LITERATURE
Rossetti 1863, p.225 no.125, and 1880, p.237
no.150; Fry in *Burlington Magazine*, IV, 1904,
p.206, repr. p.210; *N.A.-C.F. Report for 1914*,
1915, p.37, repr.; Keynes *Bible* 1957, p.18
no.60 repr.; Blunt 1959, pp.65–6, pl.34a;
Damon 1965, pp.38–9; John E. Grant, 'Two
Flowers in the Garden of Experience',
Rosenfeld 1969, p.489 n.36; Bindman 1977,
pp.120, 126–7; Klonsky 1977, p.70, repr.;
Paley 1978, p.55; Butlin 1981, p.321 no.390,
colour pl.498; Baine 1986, p.161

This is an illustration to II Samuel xi, 2. King David observes the naked
Bathsheba, wife of Uriah, from the roof of his palace. The two children, one male,
one female, were added by Blake, not being mentioned in the text, though
Bathsheba did eventually bear a son to David after he had arranged the death of
her husband. The imagery is particularly sensuous and suggests the influence of
Parmigianino or Correggio, whose work would have been known to Blake through
engravings if not through actual paintings.

This picture was restored by W.G. Littlejohn in 1914 and again at the Tate
Gallery in 1957 (a detail is repr. before and after restoration in *Tate Gallery Annual
Report 1957–8*, 1958, between pp.18 and 19).

36

37 **Christ Blessing the Little Children** 1799

N 05893/B 419
Tempera on canvas, relined 260 × 375
($10\frac{1}{4}$ × $14\frac{3}{4}$) cut down from approx. 270 × 390
($10\frac{5}{8}$ × $15\frac{3}{8}$)
Signed 'WB [?'inv', as monogram] 1799' b.l.
Presented by the Executors of W. Graham
Robertson through the National Art-
Collections Fund 1949

PROVENANCE
Thomas Butts; Thomas Butts jun., sold
Foster's 29 June 1853 (?71, as 'Christ and
Little Children') 10/– bt Sir William Stirling-
Maxwell, Bt. *or* (?96, as 'The Church and
Christ') 10/– with lot 97 ('The Flight into
Egypt', Butlin no.404) bt Golding; the Rev.
Samuel Prince, sold Sotheby's 11–14
December 1865, 1st day (in 281 with Butlin
no. 404) £12.15.0. bt Hayes; Alfred Aspland
by 1876, sold Sotheby's 27 January 1885 (93)

£16 bt Gray; J. Annan Bryce, sold 1904 to W.
Graham Robertson, offered Christie's 22 July
1949 (27) £399 bt his executors

EXHIBITED
BFAC 1876 (139); Carfax 1904 (30); Carfax
1906 (15); Tate Gallery 1913 (24); BFAC
1927 (21, pl.16); Tate Gallery 1947 (49);
Bournemouth, Southampton and Brighton
1949 (33); Arts Council 1951 (25)

LITERATURE
Rossetti 1863, p.226 no.142 and ?p.255 list 3
no.14, and 1880, p.208 no.11 and ?p.275 list 3
no.14; anon., 'Art Sales', *The Times*, 3
February 1885, p.13; Preston 1952, pp.57–8
no.11, pl.11; Keynes *Bible* 1957, p.34 no.120
repr.; Bindman 1977, pp.123, 127–8; Paley
1978, p.55; Butlin 1981, pp.330–1 no.419,
colour pl.507

This is almost certainly an illustration to Mark, x, 13–16: Christ takes the little
children into his arms and blesses them, after refuting his disciples, who had tried to
rebuff them, with the words, 'Suffer the little children to come unto me, and forbid
them not: for of such is the kingdom of God'.

There is a problem with the provenance of this painting. Although there was a
picture entitled 'Christ and Little Children' in the Butts sale at Foster's on 29 June
1853, lot 71, this was bought by Sir William Stirling-Maxwell, Bt., whose collection
is not known to have been dispersed until well into the twentieth century. It is
possible therefore that the work in the Tate Gallery was lot 96 in the same sale, 'The
Church and Christ'. This was sold to Golding together with the following lot,
'Flight into Egypt', which shares the subsequent provenance from Samuel Prince
down to W. Graham Robertson (see Butlin 1981, no.404). The names of the owners
given by William Rossetti in his 1863 lists are no help in this case. He lists 'Christ
Blessing the Little Children' merely as 'From Mr. Butts' while giving the 'Flight
into Egypt' to 'Mr. Strange', who is otherwise not known to have owned that work;
Rossetti subsequently amended this to 'Aspland' when he annotated his own copy
of Gilchrist's *Life*, now in the Houghton Library, Harvard University. From this it
is clear that Rossetti did not know the Golding or Prince collections though he did,
on the basis of Foster's sale of 1853, make a separate entry for 'Christ and the
Church [Mr. Golding, from Mr. Butts.]' in his list 3 of 'Works of Unascertained
Method', this list being presumably of works that he had not seen. The subject of
'Christ Blessing the Little Children' can indeed by seen as an allegory of the Church
and Christ, though there is no concrete evidence to support the identification of this
tempera with the title listed by Rossetti. However, there is no evidence to suggest
that pictures describable as either 'Christ Blessing the Little Children' or 'The
Church and Christ' were subsequently in the Stirling-Maxwell collection, so the

37

answer may simply be that Sir William resold 'Christ Blessing the Little Children' immediately after the 1853 sale and that this is indeed the Tate Gallery picture.

William Rossetti, in his 1863 list, remarked of this picture, 'The surface cracked'. In his revised list of 1880 he added 'but repaired' and dated the work 1790. He had already annotated his own copy of the 1863 edition of Gilchrist's *Life* to this effect some time before 1876. Since the removal at the Tate Gallery in 1952 of the oil paint that seems to have been added during the restoration reported by Rossetti it has become clear that the last figure of the date, though damaged by the trimming of the edge of the canvas, is definitely a '9'. It may also be the early damage to this picture that accounts for the fact that what otherwise looks like Blake's usual monogram lacks the letters 'inv', his normal abbreviation for 'invenit'.

38   **The Agony in the Garden**   *c.*1799–1800

N 05894 / B 425
Tempera on iron 270 × 380 (10⅝ × 15), 3 (⅛)
cut off diagonally at each corner
Signed 'WB inv' in monogram, damaged, b.r.
Presented by the Executors of W. Graham
Robertson through the National Art-
Collections Fund 1949

PROVENANCE
Thomas Butts; Thomas Butts jun.; Capt. F.J.
Butts, offered Sotheby's 24 June 1903 (14) £28
bt in Dimsdale; his widow, sold April 1906
through Carfax to W. Graham Robertson,
offered Christie's 22 July 1949 (30, repr.)
£420 bt his executors

EXHIBITED
Carfax 1904 (11); Carfax 1906 (3); Arts
Council 1951 (30, pl.9); Tate Gallery 1978
(139, repr.)

LITERATURE
Rossetti 1863, p.227 no.153, and 1880, p.240
no.177; Preston 1952, p.59, no.12 pl.12;
Keynes *Bible* 1957, pp.xiii, 38 no.134 repr. and
colour pl.vii; Blunt 1959, p.67; Kremen 1972,
pp.154, 253 n.128, pl.10; Bindman 1977,
p.124; Paley 1978, p.55; Butlin 1981,
pp.332–3 no.425, colour pl.509

This is an illustration to Luke, xxii, 41–4. Blake seems to suggest the detail of
Christ's sweat 'as it were red drops of blood falling down to the ground'.

The picture was restored in 1917 (repr. before and after, *Burlington Magazine*,
XXXII, 1918, p.17) and again in 1949. The original paint is missing in many places.
William Rossetti lists this work, under the title 'Christ in the Garden, sustained by
an Angel', as an 'Oil picture (?) on copper'. Blake was, of course, averse to the use of
oil paint and seems never to have used it.

Although most of Blake's tempera paintings on metal seem to be on copper
recent analysis by Brian Gilmore of the New Armouries at the Tower of London has
shown that the support in this case is iron, almost certainly coated with a form of
tin. On the painted side, underlying Blake's usual white ground, there is a layer of
red paint, probably red lead. This suggests that Blake used a piece of metal already
used in some completely unrelated artefact.

38

39 **The Body of Christ Borne to the Tomb** *c.*1799–1800

N 01164/B 426
Tempera on canvas, mounted on cardboard
267 × 378 (10½ × 14⅞)
Signed 'WB inv' in monogram b.l.
Presented to the National Gallery by F.T.
Palgrave 1884; transferred to the Tate Gallery
1934

PROVENANCE
Thomas Butts; Thomas Butts jun., sold *c.*1852
to F.T. Palgrave

EXHIBITED
Tate Gallery (28), Manchester (21),
Nottingham (14) and Edinburgh (17)

1913–14; Paris and Vienna 1937 (11); Paris,
Antwerp (pl.9), Zurich and Tate Gallery 1947
(17); Arts Council 1951 (31, pl.7); Tate
Gallery 1978 (140, repr.)

LITERATURE
Rossetti 1863, p.228 no.158, and 1880,
pp.240–1 no.182; Blunt in *Warburg Journal*, VI,
1943, p.204 n.3; Keynes *Bible* 1957, p.42
no.142 repr.; Blunt 1959, pp.66–7, pl.33;
Robert Rosenblum, *Transformations in Late
Eighteenth-Century Art*, 1967, pp.161–2, pl.191;
Bindman 1977, pp.124, 129, pl.103; Butlin
1981, p.333 no.426, colour pl.510; Essick in
Blake, XVI, 1982–3, p.42, pl.20

The title given to this picture is William Rossetti's. The actual procession from Calvary is not described in the Gospels. As David Bindman points out, Joseph of Arimathea, who is seen on his own beside the bier holding a long staff, was both an archetype of the artist and, in legend, the first of Christ's followers to come to England. Robert Rosenblum suggests the influence of John Flaxman's engraving of 'Elektra leading Procession to Agamemnon's Tomb' published in *Chöephoroe* of 1795 (repr. *op. cit.*, pl.190).

An inscription on the mount reads '*W. Blake* Bought of Mr. Butts of Fitzroy Square – about 1852. F.T. Palgrave'.

39

ILLUSTRATIONS TO THE BIBLE AND OTHER WATERCOLOURS AND DRAWINGS 1800–1805

This section includes eight watercolours of biblical subjects painted for Thomas Butts together with three copies from works in the series, one of the originals being in the Tate Gallery. There are also four drawings related to this series, one to a work in the Tate (though one may in fact illustrate a subject from Milton). The section concludes with three miscellaneous drawings of this period.

Blake painted over eighty watercolours of biblical subjects for Thomas Butts. These seem to have followed the tempera paintings of similar subjects of which examples are included in the previous section. Blake seems to have turned from tempera to watercolour during 1800: he dated examples in both media in that year. Others of the watercolours are dated 1803 (including no.49) and 1805. Further examples dated 1806 and 1809 are signed in a different form and may fall outside the main series (the significance of the form of Blake's signature for the dating of his works was elaborated by the compiler in a paper on 'Cataloguing William Blake' given at a symposium organised by the University of California, Santa Barbara, on 3 March 1976, published in expanded form in Essick and Pearce 1978, pp.82–4). Certain of the watercolours are mentioned in Blake's letters to Thomas Butts of 25 April 1803 and 6 July 1803 and others, to judge from a financial reckoning of 3 March 1806, were apparently delivered to him on 12 May 1805. Two were exhibited at the Royal Academy in 1808 and four were included in Blake's own exhibition of 1809 (see next section). There is a considerable variation of style within the series and it is possible to trace a development from the rather bold watercolours of 1800, often with considerable chiaroscuro, to the pale colours and soft stipple technique, usually with an unusually prominent use of pencil, of 1803, and from these to the more linear, flatly coloured watercolours of 1805. However, datings within this group are of necessity somewhat tentative.

It seems that Blake wrote an abbreviated reference to the appropriate biblical text below the bottom right-hand corner of each watercolour, but in many cases the paper has been trimmed and the inscription lost. However, the matts of at least some of the watercolours were also inscribed, in a copperplate hand, with similar references where the original references had been cut away, together with titles above the designs and texts below. For examples of such inscriptions see nos.44 and 48; another example, 'The Burial of Moses', Butlin no.449, is reproduced in Christie's sale catalogue of 26 July 1929 (15). Graham Robertson attributed these inscriptions to Mrs Blake; alternatively they may have been done while the watercolours belonged to the Butts family; they definitely existed in 1852 when the Butts family began to disperse the series.

Although the watercolours differ in size they seem to have been intended as a unified series, perhaps embodying Blake's own commentary on their texts, though no detailed analysis has yet been made. Certain sub-groups within the main series can be distinguished, for example groups dealing with the Passion (see nos.47 and 48). The series seems to have petered out with the works of 1806 and 1809 mentioned above, when Butts turned to commissioning other subjects.

The other works in this section are the visionary 'Landscape near Felpham', a portrait drawing of his wife Catherine, and a drawing done in connection with the project to illustrate Robert Blair's *The Grave*.

LITERATURE
Preston 1952, pp.122, 160; Keynes *Writings* 1957, pp.584–5, 822–4, 826; Blunt 1959, pp.69–73, 106–8; Keynes *Letters* 1968, pp.66, 68, 72, 75, 115, 117–18; Bentley *Blake Records* 1969, pp.570–4; Mellor 1974, pp.193–7; Bindman 1977, pp.130–1, 137–8, 141–4, 164–5; Paley 1978, pp.55–6; Butlin 1981, pp.335–6, 454–5

40

40 **The Blasphemer** *c*.1800

N 05195 / B 446
Pen and watercolour 381 × 340 (15 × 13⅜)
Signed 'wB inv' in monogram b.l.
Bequeathed by Miss Alice G.E. Carthew 1940

PROVENANCE
Thomas Butts; Thomas Butts jun., sold
Sotheby's 26 March 1852 (149 as 'The
Blasphemer') £1.19.0 bt Sir Charles
Wentworth Dilke, Bt.; his son, sold Christie's
10 April 1911 (125) £48.6.0 bt Miss Carthew

EXHIBITED
On loan to the Victoria and Albert Museum
1860; BFAC 1876 (76); Carfax 1906 (53);
Tate Gallery (8), Manchester (7),
Nottingham (5) and Edinburgh (8) 1913–14;
Paris and Vienna 1937 (7); *British Painting*

Hamburg, Oslo, Stockholm and Copenhagen
1949–50 (5); Port Sunlight 1950 (3); Tate
Gallery 1978 (164, repr.)

LITERATURE
Rossetti 1863, p.224 no.119, and 1880, p.236
no.142; Collins Baker in *Huntington Library
Quarterly*, IV, 1940–1, p.365; Digby 1957, p.51,
pl.51; Keynes *Bible* 1957, p.15 no.48 repr.;
Blunt 1959, pp.72–3, 80, pl.36a; Taylor in
Blake Studies, I, 1968–9, pp.63–7, repr. p.65;
Tomory *Fuseli* 1972, p.211; Wilton in *British
Museum Yearbook*, I, 1976, p.198, pl.234;
Bindman 1977, pp.143–4; Klonsky 1977,
p.73, repr.; Paley 1978, p.67; Paley in Essick
and Pearce 1978, pp.171–2; Butlin 1981,
pp.341–2 no.446, pl.520. *Also repr*: *Mizue*
no.882, 1978, 9, p.25 in colour

This is an illustration to Leviticus, xxiv, 23. The old matt, now replaced, bore an
inscription in the copperplate hand (see headnote to this section) giving the title

'The Blasphemer' and the text from Leviticus which refers to the story that begins in verses 10 to 16 of the condemnation by Moses to death of the Israelite woman's son for blaspheming the name of the Lord. However, William Rossetti retitled the watercolour 'The Stoning of Achan' (Joshua, vii, 1, 18–25) on the grounds that, though 'the subject *might* be the "Stoning of the Blasphemer" ..., or even of Stephen ... the figure seems less adapted for the latter: and a peculiar detail – a lurid wreath of smoke above his head, mingled with fire – would indicate the "burning with fire" of all that belonged to Achan'; no burning takes place in the passage from Leviticus. On the other hand Taylor, *loc. cit.*, and John E. Grant and Michael Tolley in verbal communications have supported the original identification given by the early inscription, which was also retained for the 1852 sale and the 1876 and 1913–14 exhibitions. The flames may have been added by Blake to strengthen the symbolism of what is surely a condemnation of the Mosaic law of an eye for an eye and a tooth for a tooth; that law was in fact dictated by the Lord to Moses as a result of the Blasphemer's offence (Leviticus, xxiv, 13–22).

Collins Baker has suggested that the Michelangelesque central figure may be derived from Flaxman, while Andrew Wilton traces it back, in more general terms, to the Antique 'Fallen Warrior' type as engraved in Stuart's *Antiquities of Athens*, 1762 (repr. *loc. cit.* pl.233). This figure reappears in an otherwise different context in a pencil drawing from the Keynes collection now in the Fitzwilliam Museum (Butlin 1981, no.564, pl.801) and in a red chalk drawing in the Fogg Museum (Butlin no.565, pl.802). Blake used this figure again, making the pose still more agonised, on page 25 of *Jerusalem*, engraved between 1804 and 1818, where the figure appears to be suffering disembowelment; the accompanying text is, significantly, an attack on Vengeance. Tomory compares the head of the Blasphemer to that of Sloth in Fuseli's engraved illustration to Lavater of *c*.1779 (repr. *op. cit.* pl.166).

The loan in 1860 to the Victoria and Albert Museum, at that time known as the South Kensington Museum, was reported in the *Critic* for 14 April 1860: 'There are also three drawings by that wonderful man William Blake. One is (we suppose) "The High Priests Stoning a Prophet"; the uplifted arms of the former have all that imaginative suggestiveness and rich appeal to the imagination characteristic of this painter'.

41 **David Delivered out of Many Waters: 'He Rode upon the Cherubim'** *c*.1805

N 02230 / B 462
Pen and watercolour 415 × 348 (16$\frac{3}{8}$ × 13$\frac{11}{16}$)
Signed 'WB' b.l.
Presented to the National Gallery by George Thomas Saul 1878; transferred to the Tate Gallery 1909

PROVENANCE
Thomas Butts; Thomas Butts jun., sold Foster's 29 June 1853 (121) £1.2.0 bought Money; G.T. Saul by 1876

EXHIBITED
BFAC 1876 (97); Tate Gallery (12), Manchester (12), Nottingham (9) and Edinburgh (11) 1913–14; *British Painting* Hamburg, Oslo, Stockholm and Copenhagen 1949–50 (6); Port Sunlight 1950 (4); *English Water-Colours* Norwich 1955 (28)

LITERATURE
Rossetti 1863, p.255 list 3 no.1, and 1880, p.237 no.153 and p.275 list 3 no.2; Graham Robertson in Gilchrist 1907, p.491 no.3; Digby 1957, p.43, pl.42; Keynes *Bible* 1957, p.22 no.75 repr.; Blunt 1959, p.71; Damon 1965, p.98; Raine 1968, II, pp.21–3, pl.130; Taylor in *Blake Studies*, I, 1968–9, pp.78–83, repr. p.81; Grant in *Blake Studies*, I, 1968–9, pp.200–1; Butlin in *Blake Studies*, I, 1968–9, p.212; Wark *Ten British Pictures* 1971, p.88, pl.68; Tolley in *Blake Newsletter*, VI, 1972–3, pp.29–30; Bindman 1977, pp.141–2, pl.113; Butlin 1981, p.347 no.462, pl.552; Raine 1982, p.26 and at pl.26, repr.; Essick in *Blake*, XVI, 1982–3, p.44; Warner 1984, pp.95–6

41

This is an illustration to Psalms, xviii, 4, 10, 16. However, Blake multiplies the single cherub of the text as given in the Authorised Version; it is interesting that when the watercolour was sold at Foster's in 1853 it was entitled 'He rode upon the Cherubim' in the plural, perhaps reflecting the lost title in the copperplate hand (see headnote to this section). Blake shows cherubim of four distinct ages, that in the middle being sometimes identified as David as a young man. They are, as Michael Tolley has pointed out, the Seven Eyes of God, who, acting in concert with Christ, represent the ideal form of redemption. At the bottom of the composition David appears again as an older man, being delivered from the waters, bound in the attitude of the Crucified and looking up towards the figure of Christ with similarly outstretched arms; by this Blake makes plain the psalmist's foreshadowing of Man's salvation through Christ. The ropes by which David are bound are not in the main text of the King James translation of the Bible but are the alternative (and more correct) translation from the original Hebrew given in the margin, which reads 'The cords of death' instead of the Authorised Version's 'sorrows' (verse 4).

William Rossetti's first mention of this watercolour, in his 1863 'List No.3. Works of Unascertained Method' (presumably works he had not managed to see), was under the title used in the 1853 Foster's sale catalogue. In 1880, by which time he must have seen the work, he inserted it in his main 'List No.1' as 'David delivered out of Many Waters. – Psalm xviii. 16', while retaining his previous listing in List 3.

For a copy of this work in the Tate Gallery see the next item.

COPY AFTER BLAKE

42 David Delivered out of Many Waters

N 05197 / –
Pencil and watercolour 422 × 355 (16⅝ × 14)
Bequeathed by Miss Alice G.E. Carthew 1940

A copy of no.41 above, done in the late 19th or early 20th century, perhaps even by Miss Carthew herself.

42

43 (recto)

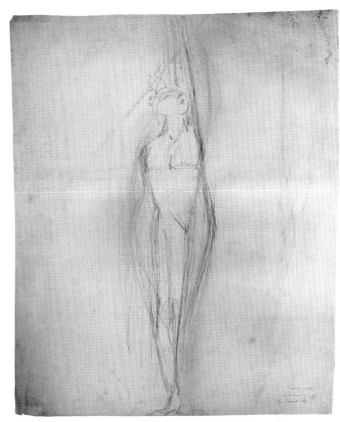

43 (verso)

43 **Preliminary Sketch for 'Christ Girding Himself with Strength'** *c.*1805 (recto)

Standing Figure with One Arm Raised *c.*1805–10(?) (verso)

A 00043 / B 465
Pencil approx. 400 × 335 ($15\frac{3}{4}$ × $13\frac{3}{4}$) on paper
505 × 425 ($19\frac{7}{8}$ × $16\frac{3}{4}$); the drawing on the
verso is upside down
Inscribed on verso by Frederick Tatham,
'William Blake slight beginning Frederick
Tatham' b.r.
Presented by Mrs John Richmond 1922

PROVENANCE
Mrs Blake; Frederick Tatham; his brother-in-
law George Richmond, sold Christie's 29 April
1897 (in 147 with 22 other items; see no.2)
£2.10.0 bt Dr Richard Sisley; his daughter
Mrs John Richmond

LITERATURE
Butlin 1981, p.348 no.465, pls.549 and 550

The recto is a study for the watercolour delivered to Thomas Butts on 12 May 1805 and now in the City Art Gallery, Bristol (Butlin 1981, no.464, pl.551). This is an illustration to Psalms xciii. The figure on the verso is similar in character to those on the backs of nos.50, 53 and 54.

This work was formerly inventoried as no.3694 xv.

44 Satan in his Original Glory: 'Thou wast Perfect till Iniquity was Found in Thee' *c.*1805

N 05892 / B 469
Pen and watercolour 429 × 339 ($16\frac{7}{8}$ × $13\frac{3}{8}$)
Signed 'WB inv' in monogram b.r. and inscr.
on old mount, now replaced, with a damaged
copperplate inscription in pencil with the title
'Thou wast perfect . . .' above, the reference
'Ezekiel ch.28th v.13th & . . . &c' b.r. and with
part of the text from Ezekiel, xxviii, below
Presented by the Executors of W. Graham
Robertson through the National Art-
Collections Fund 1949

PROVENANCE
Thomas Butts; Thomas Butts jun., offered
Foster's 29 June 1853 (103) 11/– bt in
Thomas, and Foster's 8 March 1854 (in 14
with nos.47 and 48) 10/– bt in; Capt. F.J.
Butts; his widow, sold April 1906 through
Carfax to W. Graham Robertson, offered
Christie's 22 July 1949 (23, repr.) £1,260 bt
his executors

EXHIBITED
BFAC 1876 (170); Carfax 1906 (36);
Cambridge 1910; Tate Gallery (16) and
Manchester (14) 1913–14; BFAC 1927 (10,
pl.10); Paris, Antwerp, Zurich and Tate
Gallery 1947 (11); Bournemouth,
Southampton and Brighton 1949 (9); *The
Devil in Figurative Art* Stedelijk Museum,
Amsterdam, June–September 1952; *English
Drawings and Water Colours from British
Collections*, National Gallery of Art,
Washington, and Metropolitan Museum,
New York, February–June 1962 (2);
Whitworth 1969 (32, repr.)

LITERATURE
Rossetti 1863, p.330 no.181 and p.255 list 3
no.13, and 1880, p.243 no.205 and p.275 list 3
no.13; Preston 1952, pp.60–1 no.13, pl.13;
Digby 1957, pp.15–17, pl.23; Keynes *Bible*
1957, p.26 no.82 repr.; Beer 1968, pp.195,
257, pl.44; Raine 1968, II, p.222, pl.179;
Bindman 1977, p.142; Butlin 1981, p.350
no.469, pl.554; Warner 1984, pp.5, 197 n.15,
pl.3

This is an illustration to Ezekiel, xxviii, 14–15. The text refers to 'The Prince of Tyre' but has been read as a general reference to Satan. Blake makes this equation in *Milton*, dated 1804 but written and etched *c.*1803–10, echoing the Prince of Tyre's 'I am God' (plate 9, line 25; Keynes *Writings* 1957, p.490). Blake shows Satan in his original beauty as the covering Cherub of the Biblical text and personifies the precious stones and musical instruments with which he was endowed in the Garden of Eden, but Blake adds the orb and sceptre, symbols of Satan's role as Prince of this World. Janet Warner notes the probable derivation of the figure of Satan from the Apollo in Vincenzo Cartari's emblem book *Imagini delli Dei gl'Antichi* of 1556; the linking of Satan and Apollo is perhaps a meaningful one.

Rossetti seems to have been confused by the two titles under which this watercolour has been known. His first reference, in both 1863 and 1880, is under the title 'Thou wast perfect till iniquity was found in thee – Ezek. xxviii. 15', reflecting the inscription that he would have seen on the matt when he examined Captain Butts's collection. The second reference, in his List 3, 'Works of Unascertained Method', is by the title under which the watercolour was offered at Foster's in 1853, 'Satan in his Former Glory', as belonging to 'Mr. Thomas from Mr. Butts'.

The blue washes that have faded from much of the background can be seen at the bottom where they were covered by the old mount.

44

COPY AFTER BLAKE

45 Christ in the Carpenter's Shop: The Humility of the Saviour

N 05193/–
Pencil and watercolour 330 × 335 (13 × 13¾)
on paper 485 × 355 (19½ × 14)
Bequeathed by Miss Alice G.E. Carthew 1940

PROVENANCE
?Carfax and Co. by 1906; Miss Carthew, ?after
1914

EXHIBITED
?Carfax 1906 (41); ?Manchester (23),
Nottingham (16) and Edinburgh (10) 1914

LITERATURE
Gage in *Warburg Journal*, XXXIV, 1971, p.376;
Butlin 1981, pp.352–3 under no.474

This is a late 19th- or early 20th-century copy after the watercolour painted for Thomas Butts and now in the Walsall Museum and Art Gallery (Garman-Ryan Collection), Staffordshire (Butlin 1981, no.474, pl.558). The matt of the original bears, in the copperplate hand, the title 'The Humility of the Saviour', a reference to 'Luke ch: 2ⁿᵈ v.51ˢᵗ' and the text from Luke, ii, 51. The text in fact merely states 'And He [Christ] went down with them [his parents], and came to Nazareth …' without mentioning the later legend of the Carpenter's Shop.

Blake shows Christ with a set-square and compasses, symbols of rational knowledge, instead of the traditional carpenter's tools. The compasses or dividers link this watercolour with the symbolism of the frontispiece to *Europe*, the famous 'Ancient of Days' (repr. Erdman *Illuminated Blake* 1974, p.156) and the 'Newton' colour print (no.29, *q.v.*). Although such symbolism usually has a negative connotation in Blake's works, Blunt suggests that in this case the interpretation could be a positive one, the dividers now representing the synthesis of reason with the imagination under the new dispensation of Christ. However Gage more convincingly stresses their divisive function, pointing to a passage in *The Marriage of Heaven and Hell*, *c.*1790–93, where Blake writes that 'Jesus Christ did not wish to unite but to seperate [sic] them' – the Prolific and Devouring aspects of Man (Keynes *Writings* 1957, p.155; the imagery recurs earlier in the same book when Blake states that 'in Milton … the Son [is] a Ratio of the five senses', Keynes *op. cit.*, p.150). The design can also be compared with one of the illustrations to Young's *Night Thoughts* 1796–7 (Butlin no.330 *360*, repr. Erdman *Night Thoughts* 1980). This shows Reason instructing Youth and again includes a geometrical design being set out with the aid of compasses.

COPY AFTER BLAKE

46 The Raising of Lazarus

N 05199/–
Pencil and watercolour 430 × 320 (17 × 12⅝)
Bequeathed by Miss Alice G.E. Carthew 1940

PROVENANCE
?Carfax and Co. by 1906; Miss Carthew, ?after
1914

EXHIBITED
?Carfax 1906 (64); ?Manchester (27),
Nottingham (19) and Edinburgh (29) 1914

LITERATURE
Butlin 1981, p.357 under no.487

This is a late 19th- or early 20th-century copy of the watercolour painted for Thomas Butts and now in the Aberdeen Art Gallery and Museums (Butlin 1981, no.487, pl.564). This is an illustration to John, xi, 43–4. The subject is often seen as a prefiguration of the Resurrection and Blake may have painted this watercolour as one of the series of depictions of the Passion. He had already treated this subject in *Night Thoughts* (Butlin no.330 *148*, repr. Erdman *Night Thoughts* 1980).

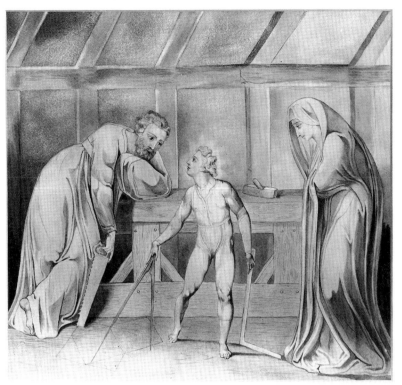

45

46

47 **The Crucifixion: 'Behold Thy Mother'** *c.*1805

N 05895 / B 497
Pen and watercolour 413 × 300 (16¼ × 11¹³⁄₁₆)
Signed 'WB inv' in monogram b.l.
Presented by the Executors of W. Graham
Robertson through the National Art-
Collections Fund 1949

PROVENANCE
Thomas Butts; Thomas Butts jun., offered
Foster's 29 June 1853 (in 124 with no.48, as
'The Crucifixion') £1.10.0 bt in Thomas, and
Foster's 8 March 1854 (in 14 with nos.44 and
48 as 'The Crucifixion') 10/– bt in; Capt. F.J.
Butts; his widow, sold April 1906 through
Carfax to W. Graham Robertson, offered
Christie's 22 July 1949 (34, repr.) £1,155 bt
his executors

EXHIBITED
BFAC 1876 (71); Carfax 1906 (43); Tate
Gallery (27) and Manchester (29) 1913–14;
BFAC 1927 (24, pl.19); Paris, Antwerp,
Zurich and Tate Gallery 1947 (16);
Bournemouth, Southampton and Brighton
1949 (37); Tate Gallery 1978 (178, repr.)

LITERATURE
Rossetti 1863, p.228 no.157, and 1880, p.240
no.181; Preston 1952, pp.62–3 no.14, pl.14;
Keynes *Bible* 1957, p.42 no.141 repr.; Butlin
1981, pp.360–1 no.497, pl.600; Warner 1984,
pp.88–91

This is an illustration to John, xix, 26–7; the old matt bore slight traces of an inscription in a copperplate hand. Christ commends the Virgin to the care of his favourite disciple, St John. The title used by William Rossetti, 'Christ taking leave of His Mother', is misleading in that this usually refers to the incident earlier in Christ's life when He first leaves home.

David Bindman has pointed out that this watercolour seems to belong to a distinct sub-group within the large series of Biblical watercolours painted for Thomas Butts. Similar in their size and upright format, near-symmetrical composition and dark near-monochromatic colouring, they are all of subjects associated with the Crucifixion and Resurrection. Other examples include 'The Entombment' (no.48), 'Christ in the Sepulchre, Guarded by Angels' and 'The Angel Rolling the Stone from the Sepulchre' in the Victoria and Albert Museum (Butlin 1981, nos.500 and 501, pl.603 and colour pl.572), 'The Resurrection' in the Fogg Art Museum, Harvard University, Mass. (Butlin no.502, colour pl.573) and 'The Magdalene at the Sepulchre' in the Yale Center for British Art, Paul Mellon Collection, New Haven, Conn. (Butlin no.504, pl.604). 'The Raising of Lazarus' (see no.46), a prefiguration of the Resurrection, may also be one of this group. For further works rather more doubtfully identified with this group see Butlin, *loc. cit.*

47

48 **The Entombment** *c.*1805

N 05896 / B 498
Pen and watercolour 417 × 310 ($16\frac{7}{16}$ × $12\frac{3}{16}$)
Signed 'WB inv' in monogram b.r. and inscr.
on mount 'Luke ch: 23rd v.53rd' b.r. and, in the
copperplate hand, with the title 'Joseph
burying Jesus' above and the text from Luke,
xxiii, 53 below
Presented by the Executors of W. Graham
Robertson through the National Art-
Collections Fund 1949

PROVENANCE
Thomas Butts; Thomas Butts jun., offered
Foster's 29 June 1853 (in 124 with no.47 as
'Christ in the Sepulchre') £1.10.0 bt in
Thomas, and Foster's 8 March 1854 (in 14
with nos.44 and 47 as 'Christ in the
Sepulchre') 10/- bt in; Capt. F.J. Butts,
offered Sotheby's 24 June 1903 (15) £305 bt in
Fowler; his widow, sold April 1906 through
Carfax to W. Graham Robertson, offered
Christie's 22 July 1949 (35, repr.) £1,102.10.0
bt his executors

EXHIBITED
BFAC 1876 (166); Carfax 1904 (12); Carfax
1906 (65); Cambridge 1910; ?St George's
Gallery 1911 (untraced); Tate Gallery (30),
Manchester (31), Nottingham (20) and
Edinburgh (19) 1913–14; on loan to Tate
Gallery 1923–7; BFAC 1927 (25, pl.20);
British Art, RA 1934 (773; 709); Whitechapel
1934 (55); *British Painting*, Paris 1938 (162);
Paris, Antwerp (pl.11), Zurich and Tate
Gallery 1947 (18); Bournemouth,
Southampton and Brighton 1949 (7); Tate
Gallery 1978 (179, repr.)

LITERATURE
Rossetti 1863, p. 228 no.160, and 1880, p.241
no.184; Preston 1952, pp.64–5 no.15, pl.15;
Keynes *Bible* 1957, p.42 no.144 repr.; Blunt
1959, p.73; Bindman 1977, p.131; Butlin
1981, p.361 no.498, pl.601; Essick in *Blake*,
XVI, 1982–3, p.42, pl.18

This is an illustration to Luke, xxiii, 53. Blake also illustrates verse 55, the arrival of
the three Maries who stand in the archway at the back. The two bearded figures on
the left, one kneeling, one standing, are presumably, as Essick points out, Joseph of
Arimathea and Nicodemus, both described as being present at Christ's tomb in
John, xix, 38–39. This latter text seems to be the basis for Blake's earlier treatment
of 'The Entombment', one of the small tempera paintings done for Thomas Butts
*c.*1799–1800 (Butlin 1981, no.427, pl.516), in which the central figure shown at the
entrance to the tomb has been identified both as Joseph of Arimathea and
Nicodemus.

This work is one of the series of companion watercolours of the theme of the
Passion listed under no.47.

48

49 **The Death of the Virgin** 1803

N 05899/B 512
Watercolour 378 × 371 ($14\frac{7}{8} \times 14\frac{5}{8}$)
Signed 'wb inv [in monogram] 1803' b.r.
Presented by the Executors of W. Graham
Robertson through the National Art-
Collections Fund 1949

PROVENANCE
Thomas Butts; Thomas Butts jun.; Capt. F.J.
Butts; his widow, sold April 1906 through
Carfax to W. Graham Robertson, offered
Christie's 22 July 1949 (42) £1,050 bt his
executors

EXHIBITED
BFAC 1876 (216); Carfax 1906 (46);
Cambridge 1910; *Century of Art*, Grafton
Galleries 1911 (126); Tate Gallery (37),
Manchester (38), Nottingham (27) and
Edinburgh (23) 1913–14; on loan to Tate
Gallery 1923–7; BFAC 1927 (35); *English
Water-Colour Paintings*, Institute of Art
Research, Ueno, Tokyo, October 1929
(pl.21); Whitechapel 1934 (57); Paris,
Antwerp, Zurich and Tate Gallery 1947 (24);
Bournemouth, Southampton and Brighton
1949 (34); Whitworth 1969 (38, repr.)

LITERATURE
Rossetti 1863, p.206 no.42, and 1880, p.213
no.46; Preston 1952, pp.66–7 no.16, pl.16;
Keynes *Bible* 1957, p.50 no.173 repr.; Keynes
Writings 1957, p.824; Keynes *Letters* 1968,
p.68; Raine 1968, I, p.413 n.37; Bentley *Blake
Records* 1969, pp.570–1; Gage in *Warburg
Journal*, XXXIV, 1971, p.375; Mellor 1974,
pp.193–4, pl.55; Bindman 1977, pp.137–8;
Butlin 1981, p.366 no.512, pl.611

Blake, in a letter to Thomas Butts of 6 July 1803, wrote that this watercolour and six
others were 'now on Stocks . . . They are all in great forwardness and I am satisfied
that I improve very much & shall continue to do so while I live'. One of the other
works mentioned in this letter is the companion watercolour of 'The Death of St.
Joseph', also signed and dated 1803 (Butlin 1981, no.511, pl.610). On 16 August
1803 Blake sent Butts these two drawings together with five others, presumably the
same as those listed in the letter of 6 July.

According to William Rossetti 'The Death of the Virgin' was inscribed 'Then
saith He to the Disciple, "Behold thy Mother!" and from that hour that Disciple
took her unto his own home' (John, xix, 27; see no.47), while 'The Death of St.
Joseph' was inscribed 'Into Thine hand I commend my spirit; Thou hast redeemed
me, O Lord God of Truth' (partly taken from Luke, xxiii, 46). No such inscriptions
can be seen today but they may have been the usual copperplate inscriptions on the
mounts.

Kathleen Raine has suggested that Blake took the symbolism of the rainbow in
the two companion watercolours from Jacob Boehme's *Mysterium Magnum* (ch. 33,
paras.28–31) as 'a Figure of the last Judgment, showing how the inward spiritual
World will again manifest itself and swallow up into itself this outward World of
four elements'. In this connection John Gage's suggestion that Blake deliberately
reversed the Newtonian order of the colours of the rainbow in his works of 1804
onwards may perhaps be significant.

49

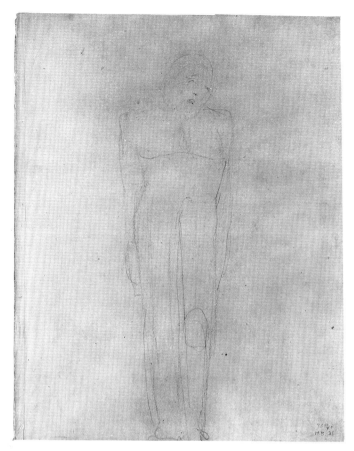

50(recto)   50(verso)

50   **Sketch for 'The Four and Twenty Elders casting their Crowns before the Divine Throne'** *c.*1803 (recto)

Standing Figure with Arms at his Side *c.*1805–10(?) (verso)

A 00033 / B 516
Pencil 488 × 389 (19¼ × 15⁵⁄₁₆); the drawing on the verso is upside down
Inscribed on recto by Frederick Tatham 'William Blake – First design. sketch, Frederick Tatham' b.r.
Presented by Mrs John Richmond 1922

PROVENANCE
Mrs Blake; Frederick Tatham; his brother-in-law George Richmond, sold Christie's 29 April 1897 (in 147 with 22 other items: see no.2) £2.10.0 bt Dr Richard Sisley; his daughter Mrs John Richmond

LITERATURE
Butlin 1981, pp.367–8 no.516, pls.612 and 614

The recto is a sketch for no.51. The verso could be for some such subject as a 'Raising of Lazarus', though it is nothing like the figure in the watercolour painted for Thomas Butts (see no.46). It is similar in character to the versi of nos.43, 53 and 54.

    This work was formerly inventoried as no.3694 i.

51

51 **The Four and Twenty Elders Casting their Crowns before the Divine Throne** *c*.1803–5

N 05897 / B 515
Pencil and watercolour 354 × 293 ($13\frac{15}{16}$ × $11\frac{1}{2}$)
Signed 'wB inv' in monogram b.r.
Presented by the Executors of W. Graham Robertson through the National Art-Collections Fund 1949

PROVENANCE
Thomas Butts; Thomas Butts jun.; Capt. F.J. Butts; his widow, sold April 1906 through Carfax to W. Graham Robertson, offered Christie's 22 July 1949 (48, repr.) £6,720 bought his executors

EXHIBITED
BFAC 1876 (210); Carfax 1904 (19); Carfax 1906 (47); Tate Gallery (34), Manchester (34), Nottingham (22) and Edinburgh (26) 1913–14; BFAC 1927 (31, pl.24); Paris, Antwerp, Zurich and Tate Gallery 1947 (22); Bournemouth, Southampton and Brighton 1949 (39)

LITERATURE
Rossetti 1863, p.202 no.63, and 1880, p.216 no.69; Preston 1952, pp.68–9 no.17, pl.17; Keynes *Bible* 1957, p.46 no.160 repr.; Keynes *Letters* 1968, p.117; Raine 1968, II, pp.210–11, pl.177; Bentley *Blake Records* 1969, pp.571–2; Gage in *Warburg Journal*, XXXIV, 1971, p.375 n.26a; Mellor 1974, p.197, pl.57; Rosenblum 1975, p.45, pl.50; Bindman 1977, pp.143, 165; Paley 1978, p.56, pl.82; Butlin 1981, p.367 no.515, colour pl.577. *Also repr*: *Mizue*, no.816, 1973, 2/3, p.20 in colour

This is an illustration to Revelation, iv, 2–11. It is listed in Blake's account with Thomas Butts of 3 March 1806, apparently as having been delivered on 12 May 1805. However, for stylistic reasons it appears to have been begun rather earlier, say c.1803; one reason for suggesting this is the less than precise technique and the use of pencil rather than pen as well as watercolour. For a preliminary sketch see no.50.

The old matt, now removed, was inscribed in pencil in the copperplate hand with traces of a title above and text below, and with the reference 'Rev^{ns} ch$^{:th}$ v. 2nd ... [erased] & ...' b.r. In the roughly contemporary 'Night the Ninth' of *The Four Zoas*, written c.1796–1807, Blake incorporated St. John's vision of the Divine Throne into his own account of the Last Judgment (Keynes *Writings* 1957, p.364).

52 **The River of Life** *c.*1805

N 05887/B 525
Pen and watercolour 305 × 336 (12 × 13$\frac{1}{4}$)
Signed 'WB inv' in monogram b.l. and inscr.
'Rev:cxxii v 1 & 2' b.r.
Bequeathed by W. Graham Robertson 1949

PROVENANCE
Thomas Butts; Thomas Butts jun.; Capt. F.J. Butts; his widow, sold April 1906 through Carfax to W. Graham Robertson

EXHIBITED
BFAC 1876 (94); Carfax 1904 (21); Carfax 1906 (48); *Century of Art* Grafton Galleries 1911 (127); Tate Gallery (36), Manchester (35), Nottingham (24) and Edinburgh (31) 1913–14; *British Empire Exhibition* Palace of Arts, Wembley 1924 (N.8, repr. *Illustrated Souvenir* p.59); BFAC 1927 (33, colour pl.1); *British Art* RA 1934 (787; 706); Whitechapel 1934 (54); *Two Centuries of English Art* Amsterdam 1936 (187); *British Painting* Paris 1938 (161); Paris, Antwerp, Zurich and Tate Gallery 1947 (23); Bournemouth, Southampton and Brighton 1949 (40)

LITERATURE
Rossetti 1863, p.237 no.215, and 1880, pp.251–2 no.245; Joseph Wicksteed *Blake's River of Life: Its Poetic Undertones* n.d. [1949]; Preston 1952, pp.70–1 no.18, pl.18; Roe 1953, p.185 n.; Keynes *Bible* 1957, p.50 no.170 repr.; Blunt 1959, pp.72–3, pl.38b; Raine 1968, I, p.98, pl.40; Roe in Rosenfeld 1969, p.453 n.53; Tolley in *Blake Newsletter*, VI, 1972–3, p.30; Bindman 1977, pp.143, 165; Klonsky 1977, p.106, repr. in colour; Butlin 1981, pp.371–2, colour pl.586; Warner 1984, pp.147–9, pl.85

This is an illustration to Revelation, xxii, 1–2. In the text only the River of Life proceeding from the Throne of God is mentioned, together with the Tree of Life with its twelve different fruits. The figures were added by Blake. Wicksteed identifies these figures as Christ leading two children through the Stream of Time towards the Divine Sun. To the right the Bride (the New Jerusalem) hovers in a stooping position in order to scoop up water from the River of Life. The river runs between and divides the two banks of Innocence on the left and Experience; each side has its own musician, clad in white and pink respectively. Seen above the figure of Christ is St John the Divine, haloed by the divine sun which is surrounded by figures symbolising eternal marriage.

William Rossetti, in an annotation to his lists in his own copy of Gilchrist's *Life* now in the Houghton Library, equates this watercolour with the 'finished picture from the *Metamorphoses* [of Ovid], after Giulio Romano', which Samuel Palmer, in a letter to Alexander Gilchrist of 23 August 1855 (Gilchrist 1863, I, p.301), said hung in Blake's room. This is clearly a mistake, particularly as the watercolour shares a common provenance with the other biblical watercolours painted for Thomas Butts, and William Rossetti did not include this insertion in the 1880 edition of his lists.

A strip of blue along the bottom edge, which was formerly covered by an old mount, indicates that much colour has been lost by fading over the rest of the watercolour.

52

53(recto)

53(verso)

53 **Composition Sketch for 'The Fall of the Rebel Angels'(?)** *c.*1805–10 (recto)

Standing Figure with Flaming Hair *c.*1805–10(?) (verso)

A 00049/B 588
Pencil approx. 375 × 290 ($14\frac{3}{4} × 11\frac{1}{2}$) on paper 502 × 425 ($19\frac{3}{4} × 16\frac{3}{4}$)
Inscribed on verso by Frederick Tatham 'William Blake Frederick Tatham' b.r.
Presented by Mrs John Richmond 1922

PROVENANCE
Mrs Blake; Frederick Tatham; his brother-in-law George Richmond, sold Christie's 29 April 1897 (in 147 with 22 other items; see no.2) £2.10.0 bt Dr Richard Sisley; his daughter Mrs John Richmond

LITERATURE
Butlin 1981, p.447 no.588, pls.823 and 824

As in the case of no.54, the drawings on both recto and verso are similar in style to those on nos.43 and 50 but the only known works related to the apparent subject on the recto are the two versions of 'The Rout of the Rebel Angels' in the 1807 and 1808 series of illustrations to *Paradise Lost* (Huntington Library and Boston Museum, Butlin 1981, nos.529 7 and 536 7, colour pls.638 and 651); the compositions are fairly dissimilar however.

The dating of the figure on the verso is difficult to establish as is the case with all the drawings of this type. The stiffness of the figure suggests that it could have been executed some time before the drawing on the recto.

This work was formerly inventoried by the Tate Gallery as no.3694 xxii.

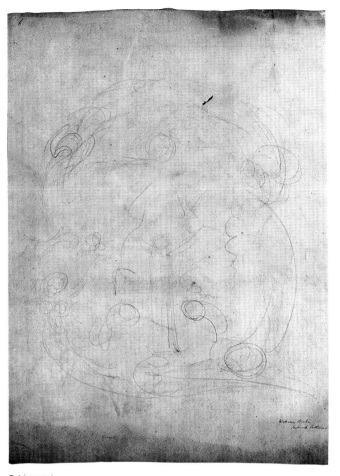

54(recto)

54(verso)

54 **Composition Sketch** *c.*1805–10 (recto)

Standing Figure Holding a Spear *c.*1805–10(?) (verso)

A 00048 / B 587
Pencil 405 × 340 (16 × 13½) on paper 508 × 370
(20 × 14 9/16); the drawing on the verso is upside down
Inscribed on recto by Frederick Tatham
'William Blake Frederick Tatham' b.r.
Presented by Mrs John Richmond 1922

PROVENANCE
Mrs Blake; Frederick Tatham; his brother-in-law George Richmond, sold Christie's 29 April 1897 (in 147 with 22 other items; see no.2) £2.10.0 bt Dr Richard Sisley; his daughter Mrs John Richmond

LITERATURE
Butlin 1981, pp.446–7 no.587, pls.821 and 822

In style the two drawings on this sheet resemble those on nos.43, 50 and 53. This suggests that the recto could be a study for one of the biblical watercolours painted for Thomas Butts, but it is difficult to identify the subject. The small figure with arms outstretched is shown standing before a larger figure, both being seen within an oval frame of swooping angels similar to those in 'Christ Offers to Redeem Man' in both the 1807 and 1808 series of illustrations to *Paradise Lost* (Huntington Library and Boston Museum respectively, Butlin 1981, nos.529 *3* and 536 *3*, colour pls.634 and 647).

This work was formerly inventoried by the Tate Gallery as no.3694 xxi.

[139]

55 **Landscape near Felpham** *c.*1800

A 00041 / B 368
Pencil and watercolour 237 × 343 ($9\frac{3}{8}$ × $13\frac{1}{2}$) on paper, trimmed irregularly 300 × 412 ($11\frac{13}{16}$ × $16\frac{3}{16}$)
Inscribed by Frederick Tatham 'William Blake vouched by Frederick Tatham. subject not known. perhaps near Felpham' b.r.
Presented by Mrs John Richmond 1922

PROVENANCE
Mrs Blake; Frederick Tatham; his brother-in-law George Richmond, sold Christie's 29 April 1897 (in 147 with 22 other items; see no.2) £2.10.0 bt Dr Richard Sisley; his daughter Mrs John Richmond

EXHIBITED
Tate Gallery 1947 (67); *Landscape in Britain c.1750–1850* Tate Gallery, November 1973–February 1974 (286, repr.); Tate Gallery 1978 (144, repr.)

LITERATURE
Wright 1929, I, at pl.36, repr.; Blunt 1959, p.68; Bindman 1977, p.139; Butlin 1981, pp.312–13 no.368, colour pl.346

From September 1800 until September 1803 Blake lived in a cottage at Felpham near Chichester, Sussex, under the patronage of the poet, biographer and man of letters William Hayley (1745–1820), to whom he had been recommended by John Flaxman. Although he was able to continue his work for Thomas Butts and other patrons, and to write much of the text of *Milton*, a lot of his time was taken up with increasingly uncongenial projects given him by the well-meaning but uncomprehending Hayley. These included decorating Hayley's library, painting miniature portraits and illustrating Hayley's poems and biographies of Cowper and Romney.

This watercolour shows the Church of St Mary and, in the centre, Hayley's house 'The Turret'. Blake's cottage was once identified as that shown between the two towers, but has now been established as that lit up by the perhaps visionary beams of sunlight breaking through the clouds on the right; it is similar in its general shape, with a lower annex on the right, though not in details of fenestration, to the illustration of 'Blake's Cottage at Felpham' on plate 36 of *Milton* (repr. Morchard Bishop, *Blake's Hayley*, 1951, between pp.160 and 161; Bishop also reproduces photographs of the cottage and of 'The Turret', and George Engleheart's drawing of *c.*1810 of the latter, showing the original appearance of the tower). The large mill on the left was a prominent feature in Felpham at the time but has since been destroyed.

It is tempting to see this watercolour as Blake's first reaction to the prospect that opened up with the move to Felpham. As he wrote to John Flaxman on 21 September 1800, three days after his arrival, 'Felpham is a sweet place for Study, because it is more Spiritual than London. Heaven opens here on all sides her Golden Gates; her windows are not obstructed by vapours; voices of Celestial inhabitants are more distinctly heard, & their forms more distinctly seen, & my Cottage is also a Shadow of their houses' (Keynes *Writings* 1957, p.802).

This work was formerly inventoried by the Tate Gallery as no.3694 xii.

55

56(recto)

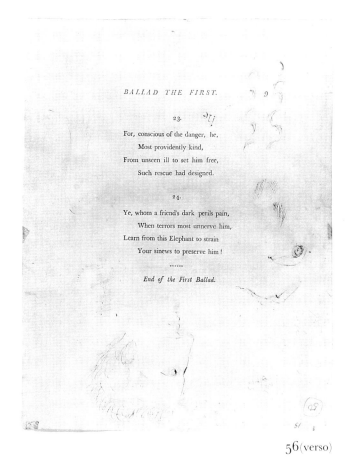

BALLAD THE FIRST.   9

23.

For, conscious of the danger, he,
    Most providently kind,
From unseen ill to set him free,
    Such rescue had designed.

24.

Ye, whom a friend's dark perils pain,
    When terrors most unnerve him,
Learn from this Elephant to strain
    Your sinews to preserve him!
    ......
    End of the First Ballad.

56(verso)

56 **Catherine Blake** *c.*1805 (recto)

A Man's Head and other Drawings (verso)

N 05188/B 683
Recto: pencil; Verso: pen; on paper 286 × 221
($11\frac{1}{4} \times 18\frac{11}{16}$)
Inscribed on recto, possibly by John Varley,
'Catherine Blake' b.r. and 'Mrs Blake drawn
by Blake' b.c.; for verso see below
Bequeathed by Miss Alice G.E. Carthew 1940

PROVENANCE
?John Varley; ...; Mrs Alexander Gilchrist by
1863; H.H. Gilchrist, sold Sotheby's 24 June
1903 (31) £6.10.0. bt Edwards; Miss Alice
G.E. Carthew by 1913

EXHIBITED
BFAC 1876 (110); *Examples of the English Pre-*
Raphaelite School of Painters ... together with a
Collection of the Works of William Blake,
Academy of the Fine Arts, Philadelphia,
December 1892 (165 or 170); Tate Gallery
(112), Manchester (171), Nottingham (133)

and Edinburgh (123) 1913–14; BFAC 1927
(65); Paris and Vienna 1937 (16); *Wartime*
Acquisitions 2nd Exhibition CEMA tour 1944–5
(3); Tate Gallery 1947 (82); Edinburgh 1969
(12); Cambridge 1971 (67); Tate Gallery
1978 (149, recto repr.)

LITERATURE
Rossetti 1863, p.250 list 2 no.105, and 1880,
p.268 list 2 no.133; Keynes *Bibliography* 1921,
p.485; Keynes *Drawings*, II, 1956, no.10, recto
repr.; G.E. Bentley Jr, 'The Date of Blake's
Pickering Manuscript *or* The Way of a Poet
with Paper', *Studies in Bibliography*, XIX, 1966,
pp.237–9; Keynes *Drawings* 1970, no.37, recto
repr.; Bentley *Blake Books* 1977, p.574 no.6;
Geoffrey Keynes, *The Complete Portraiture of*
William and Catherine Blake, 1979, pp.28, 151–2,
recto repr. pl. iv; Butlin 1981, p.491 no.683,
pls.900 and 901

The recto bears a drawing of Blake's wife Catherine. She was born at Battersea on
25 April 1762. Her full name was Catherine Sophia Boucher, also spelt Butcher.
They were married on 18 August 1782. According to J.T. Smith and Allan
Cunningham she helped Blake in printing and colouring his illuminated books,
and after Blake's death, according to Gilchrist, she even finished some of his
drawings, 'rather against Mr. Linnell's Judgment'; William Rossetti held her

responsible for the colouring of Blake's illustrations to Bunyan's *The Pilgrim's Progress* (Butlin 1981, no.829, colour pl.976 and pls.1093–1120). After Blake's death she went to live first with John Linnell as his housekeeper; in September 1828 she moved to perform the same office for Frederick Tatham, who thus came to inherit much of the contents of Blake's studio. She died at 17 Upper Charlton Street, Fitzroy Square on 18 October 1831. Three independent works attributed to her hand are catalogued in Butlin 1981, nos.C1, 2 and 3, repr. pls.1191, 348 in colour, and 1192 respectively.

This drawing was made on the back of p.9 of the quarto edition of William Hayley's *Ballads*, published in 1802 with illustrations by Blake. Bentley has demonstrated that Blake used spare sheets from the *Ballads* from 1805 onwards. On the printed side of the sheet there are slight sketches of a man's head in profile, an eye, a lip, a wing and some doodles, possibly not by Blake; also two simple mathematical sums and the numbers '13' and '50'.

The Blake exhibition held in Philadelphia in 1892 contained two so-called portrait drawings of Mrs Blake, both lent by H.H. Gilchrist, the first being described as being in pencil. The other exhibit has been tentatively identified with the drawing, also in pencil, of a full-face head of a young woman now in McGill University Library, Montreal (Butlin no.686, pl.902).

57   **The Soul Hovering over the Body Reluctantly Parting with Life** *c*.1805

N 05300 / B 625
Pencil on paper 272 × 456 ($10\frac{3}{4}$ × $17\frac{7}{8}$)
Bequeathed by Sir Hugh Walpole 1941

PROVENANCE
?Mrs Blake; ?Frederick Tatham; ?Joseph Hogarth, sold Southgate's 7–23 June 1854, 12th evening (in 5082 with 21 other works) 16/– bt Edsall; ...; Richard Johnson, sold Platt's 25 April 1912 (in 702 with 16 other works) purchaser unknown; sold Sotheby's 28–30 May 1934, 1st day (167) £22 bt Bain for Sir Hugh Walpole

EXHIBITED
Tate Gallery 1947 (81); Tate Gallery 1978 (155, repr.)

LITERATURE
Robert T. Stothard, 'Stothard and Blake', *Athenaeum*, 19 December 1863, p.838; Keynes *Drawings*, II, 1956, no.17 repr.; Keynes *Writings* 1957, pp.861–2; Keynes *Letters* 1968, pp.120–3, pl.20; Keynes *Drawings* 1970, no.40 repr.; Erdman *Notebook* 1973, p.18 and at N29; G.E. Bentley jun., 'Blake and Cromek: The Wheat and the Tares', *Journal of Modern Philology*, LXXI, 1974, pp.366–9; Helmstadter 1978, p.50 n.23; Butlin 1981, p.461 no.625, pl.861; Robert N. Essick and Morton D. Paley, *Robert Blair's The Grave illustrated by William Blake*, 1982, p.61 and *passim*, fig.8

This is a sketch for plate 6 of Robert Blair's *The Grave*, commissioned by Robert Hartley Cromek in 1805 and published in 1808. Originally it was intended that Blake, as well as providing the designs, should do the more renumerative job of engraving them himself, but the task was eventually entrusted to the more fashionable Luigi Schiavonetti. This book, like Edward Young's *Night Thoughts*, for a deluxe edition of which Blake had executed no fewer than 537 watercolours *c*.1795–7 (Butlin 1981, no.330), was an example of the contemporary taste for 'graveyard poetry' and had been first published in 1743.

Schiavonetti's engraving is entitled as above with a quotation from Blair's lines describing the death of a voluptuary:

> ... How wishfully she looks
> On all she's leaving, now no longer her's!

In the engraving the figure of the soul hovering above is the same but the dead voluptuary is shown lying on his back without the lyre and wreath shown in this drawing. An earlier stage in the evolution of the design appears to have been the

untraced indian ink drawing listed by William Rossetti as being in the collection of F.T. Palgrave, 'The Death of a Voluptuary' (Butlin no.626). The reclining figure has some affinity with that in Emblem 11 on p.29 of Blake's *Notebook* (Butlin no.201 *29*, repr.; Erdman and Moore *Notebook* 1973); Erdman seems however to overstress the closeness of this relationship while unjustifiably questioning Keynes's interpretation and dating.

The commisssion to illustrate Blair's *The Grave* is first recorded in a letter of 18 October 1805 from John Flaxman to William Hayley: 'Mͬ Cromek has employed Blake to make a set of drawings from Blair's poem of the Grave 20 of which he proposes [to] have engraved by the Designer'. On 27 November 1805 Blake himself wrote to Hayley, repeating much the same information and continuing 'In consequence of this I produced about twenty Designs which pleasd so well that he with the same liberality with which he set me about the drawings has now set me to Engrave them'. However the first version of Cromek's prospectus, dated November 1805, speaks of only 'fifteen prints from designs invented and to be engraved by William Blake', adding that 'The original Drawings, and Specimen of the Stile of Engraving, may be seen at the Proprietor's Mr. Cromek'. What happened next was later described by Thomas Stothard's son Robert: 'Cromek found, and explained to my father, that he [Blake] had etched one of the subjects, but so indifferently and so carelessly . . . that he employed Schrovenetti [*sic*] to engrave them'. This change of plan was reflected in a second version of Cromek's Prospectus also but perhaps incorrectly (the type was only partly reset) dated November 1805, which announced, reducing the number of plates again, 'twelve very spirited engravings by Louis Schiavonetti, from designs invented by William Blake' (a copy of Cromek's first prospectus annotated to bring it into line with the second version was sold with the Townley Papers by Lord O'Hagen at Sotheby's on 22–23 July 1985 (550, repr.); the words 'and to be engraved [by William Blake;]' have been deleted and a new line has been inserted after 'William Blake;' reading 'and to be engraved by L. Schiavonetti'). Blake was still unaware of this change when he wrote to Hayley on 11 December 1805. Paradoxically these designs of Blake, despite having been engraved by someone else, were to become his best known works for nearly half a century, although contemporary reviews ridiculed his contribution.

In view of the common provenance from the Joseph Hogarth sale shared by a number of drawings later sold from the Richard Johnson collection the history of this work as given above is the most likely, but the position is confused by the number of drawings that have been sold with similar titles.

BLAKE'S EXHIBITION 1809

Blake held his only one-man exhibition at his brother James's house, 28 Broad Street, Golden Square. It opened in mid-May 1809 and was scheduled to close on 29 September. However, the pictures still seem to have been at Broad Street well into 1810; Crabb Robinson saw the exhibition on 23 April and took Charles Lamb and his sister there on 11 June. Its scope is summed up in the title of Blake's catalogue: *A Descriptive Catalogue of Pictures, Poetical and Historical Inventions, Painted by William Blake, in Water Colours, Being the Ancient Method of Fresco Painting Restored: and Drawings, For Public Inspection, and for Sale by Private Contract*. In addition to an analysis of the exhibits, the catalogue contains an attack on those artists who had sacrificed form or outline to colour; the true method of Raphael, Michelangelo, Giulio Romano and Dürer is opposed to the false example of Titian, Correggio, Rubens and Rembrandt. The exhibition was a complete failure. No works appear to have been sold except to the ever-faithful Thomas Butts and only one, hostile, review has been traced.

The exhibition contained nine tempera paintings and seven 'Drawings', that is watercolours. Besides the three works catalogued here, the temperas included the famous 'Canterbury Pilgrims' (Pollok House, Glasgow; Butlin 1981 no.653, pl.878). The watercolours included what was almost certainly the Tate Gallery's version of 'The Penance of Jane Shore' (no.14) and a version of 'The Body of Abel found by Adam and Eve' (no.69).

LITERATURE
Keynes *Writings* 1957, pp.560–86; Bentley *Blake Records* 1969, pp.215–20, 225–6; Macmillan in *Blake Newsletter*, v, 1971–2, pp.203–6; Bindman 1977, pp.154–64; Paley 1978, pp.47–9, 51–3, 66

58 The Spiritual Form of Nelson Guiding Leviathan *c.*1805–9

N 03006/B 649
Tempera on canvas 762 × 625 (30 × 24⅝)
Purchased (National Loan Exhibitions Fund)
1914

PROVENANCE
Thomas Butts; Thomas Butts jun., sold
Foster's 29 June 1853 (70) £1.2.0 bt
Robinson; T. W. Jackson by 1876, by whose
executors sold to the Tate Gallery

EXHIBITED
Blake's exhibition 1809(1); Associated
Painters in Water-Colours 1812 (280); BFAC
1876 (126); Carfax 1906 (24); Tate Gallery
(65) and Manchester (44) 1913–14; Tate
Gallery 1947 (44); Tate Gallery 1978 (205,
repr.)

LITERATURE
Blake *Descriptive Catalogue* 1809, pp.1–7
(reprinted in Keynes *Writings* 1957,
pp.564–6); Rossetti 1863, p.211 no.79, and
1880, p.221 no.94; M.A., 'William Blake's
"Nelson"', *Burlington Magazine*, XXVI,
1914–15, pp.139–40, repr. p.138; Binyon
1922, pp.20–1, pl.52; Damon 1924, p.95;
Wright 1929, I, pp.110–11, pl.34; Edgar
Wind, 'The Revolution in History Painting',
Warburg Journal, VI, 1943, p.202, pl.59a;
Schorer 1946, pp.174–5, 478 n., pl.3;
Bronowski 1947, p.80; Frye 1947, pp.139–40;
Blunt 1959, pp.37, 78, 97–103, pl.46d;
Damon 1965, pp.39, 239–40; Beer 1968,
pp.189–90; Raine 1968, I, p.359; Erdman
1969, pp.449–53, 463 n.4, pl.8; Grant in
Rosenfeld 1969, pp.479–80 n.41; Paley 1970,
pp.171–99; Macmillan in *Blake Newsletter*, V,
1971–2, pp.204–5; John E. Grant, review of
Paley 1970 in *English Language Notes*, IX, 1972,
pp.212–16; Lindberg *Job* 1973, pp.19 no.xvii,
300–2 no.15F, 304–11, pl.54, a reconstruction
repr. pl.56a; Wittreich 1975, pp.68–9; Tayler
in *Blake Newsletter*, X, 1976–7, pp.80–1;
Bindman 1977, pp.155, 160–1, 163–4, pl.121;
Erdman 1977, pp.521–2; Paley 1978, pp.53,
66, 178–9, pl.47; Paley in Essick and Pearce
1978, p.176; Butlin 1981, pp.472–3 no.649,
pl.876; Warner 1984, pp.196 n.1, 197 n.16;
Baine 1986, p.132, pl.59; Boime 1987,
pp.345–9, pl.4.40. *Also repr: Studio*, CVII, 1957,
p.97 in colour

The picture was restored by W.G. Littlejohn and W. Graham Robertson *c.*1906 but was subsequently badly damaged when the Thames flooded the lower ground floor of the Tate Gallery in 1928. Only about half of Blake's original paint remains.

In Blake's *Descriptive Catalogue*, the title continues '. . . in whose wreathings are infolded the Nations of the Earth'. Lord Nelson died in 1805 and Blake may have been in part inspired (if only to contradiction rather than emulation) by Flaxman's monument in St Paul's, begun in 1808 though not completed until 1811 (repr. Margaret Whinney, *Sculpture in Britain 1530 to 1830*, 1964, pls.147–8), and by Benjamin West's 'Apotheosis of Nelson', exhibited at his house in 1806 (National Maritime Museum, Greenwich; repr. *Blake Newsletter*, V, 1971–2, p.205, and Bindman 1977, pl.122). Blake had indeed, in his advertisement for his exhibition, called the 'Nelson' and the companion 'Spiritual Form of Pitt', 'grand Apotheoses of NELSON and PITT' (Keynes *Writings* 1957, p.560). For a further discussion of the significance of this work see under no.59.

The sale of works from Samuel Palmer's collection at Christie's on 20 March 1882 included as lot 110 a 'Spiritual Form of Nelson guiding Leviathan' but there is no other record of this version and the title was almost certainly a mistake for the lost 'Spiritual Form of Napoleon' (Butlin 1981, no.652) which, together with 'The Spiritual Form of Pitt', did belong to Palmer. This identification is strengthened by the fact that the entry in the sale catalogue gives a reference to p.254 no.266 of Rossetti's 1880 list which in fact applies to 'The Spiritual Form of Napoleon'.

There is a preliminary sketch for 'The Spiritual Form of Nelson' in the British Museum (Butlin no.650, pl.875). The disposition of the figures and the serpent is much as in the painting though the exact poses, where they are clearly visible, were slightly modified. In the drawing itself Nelson's head was originally bent further over to the right but was altered by Blake to a position close to that in the painting.

58

59 The Spiritual Form of Pitt Guiding Behemoth 1805(?)

N 01110/B 651
Tempera heightened with gold on canvas
740 × 627 (29⅛ × 24¾)
Signed 'WBlake 1805 [? – the last digit is
obscure]' b.r.
Purchased by the National Gallery 1882;
transferred to the Tate Gallery 1931

PROVENANCE
Samuel Palmer; A.H. Palmer, offered
Christie's 20 March 1882 (108) £100 bt in and
sold 1882 to the National Gallery

EXHIBITED
Blake's exhibition 1809 (2); Associated
Painters in Water-Colours 1812 (279); *Old
Masters* RA 1871 (285, as 'Rt. Hon. William
Pitt'); BFAC 1876 (201); Tate Gallery (64),
Manchester (43), Nottingham (30) and
Edinburgh (1) 1913–14; *Two Centuries of
English Art* Amsterdam 1936 (2); Tate Gallery
1947 (43); Tate Gallery 1978 (206, repr.)

LITERATURE
Blake *Descriptive Catalogue* 1809, pp.2–7
(reprinted in Keynes *Writings* 1957,
pp.565–6); Rossetti 1880, p.221 no.95;
Robertson in Gilchrist 1907, p.493 no.14;
Damon 1924, p.95; Blunt in *Warburg Journal*,
VI, 1943, p.206, pl.59b; Schorer 1946,
pp.174–5, 478 n.; Bronowski 1947, pp.52, 80;
Frye 1947, p.139; Blunt 1959, pp.38, 78,
97–103, pl.46c; Damon 1965, pp.39, 239–40;
Beer 1968, pp.189–90; Raine 1968, I, p.359,
pl.116; Taylor in *Blake Studies*, I, 1968,
pp.72–8, pl.75; Erdman 1969, p.449; Paley
1970, pp.171–99; Macmillan in *Blake
Newsletter*, V, 1971–2, p.204; Lindberg *Job*
1973, pp.18–19 no.xv, 302–11 no.15G, pl.55,
a reconstruction repr. pl.56b; Raymond
Lister, *The Letters of Samuel Palmer*, 1974, I,
pp.475–6 n., II, pp.896–7; Wittreich 1975,
pp.68–9; Tayler in *Blake Newsletter*, x, 1976–7,
pp.80–1; Bindman 1977, pp.155, 160–1,
163–4; Erdman 1977, pp.521–2; Paley 1978,
pp.53, 66, 179, pl.48; Butlin 1981, pp.473–4
no.651, pl.877; Raymond Lister, 'The
National Gallery & Blake's "Spiritual Form of
Pitt Guiding Behemoth"', *Blake*, XVII,
1983–4, pp.105–6; Baine 1986, p.35; Boime
1987, pp.345–9, pl.4.41. *Also repr*: *Mizue*,
no.882, 1978, 9, pp.30–31 in colour

An old label on the back of the painting, seemingly inscribed by Samuel Palmer, supplies the date 1805; the date inscribed by Blake on the picture is obscure. The painting was restored by George Richmond in Palmer's studio and again at the Tate Gallery in 1977.

In the catalogue of Blake's exhibition the title continues '...; he is that Angel who, pleased to perform the Almighty's orders, rides on the whirlwind, directing the storms of war: He is ordering the Reaper to reap the Vine of the Earth, and the Plowman to plow up the Cities and Towers'.

The painting was exhibited as a companion to 'The Spiritual Form of Nelson guiding Leviathan' (no.58) and Blake goes on to explain that these two works 'are compositions of a mythological cast, similar to those Apotheoses of Persian, Hindoo, and Egyptian Antiquity, which are still preserved on rude monuments, being copies from some stupendous originals now lost or perhaps buried till some happier age ... The Artist wishes it was now the fashion to make such monuments, and then he should not doubt of having a national commission to execute these two Pictures on a scale that is suitable to the grandeur of the nation, who is the parent of his heroes, in high finished fresco, where the colours would be as pure and as permanent as precious stones though the figures were one hundred feet in height'.

In the light of Blake's reference to Eastern Antiquities it is particularly interesting that the form of Pitt's halo is similar to that used in Buddhist art; this was probably known to him through engravings. In more general terms the composition is probably indebted, as Lindberg has suggested, to Frans Floris's 'Charlemagne as Victory', engraved in 1552 by Hieronymous Cock (repr. *op. cit.* pl.130).

William Pitt (1759–1806) was a near contemporary of Nelson (1758–1805) and Blunt, followed by Lindberg, has shown that this work and 'The Spiritual Form of Nelson' are apocalyptic visions of war paralleled in Blake's writings of the same period. In these writings war appears as a perversion of energy (in itself a virtue) and as a prelude to the Last Judgment. The reaper and plowman who accompany Pitt are derived from Amos, ix, 13, and are the angels who, in Revelation, xiv,

59

14–19, prepare 'the great winepress of the wrath of God', introduced by Blake into *Milton*, written *c.*1800–10, as the 'Wine-press of Los ... call'd War on Earth' (Keynes *Writings* 1957, p.513). The biblical monsters Leviathan and Behemoth, from Job, xxxvii, 9, 12–13, appear in *Jerusalem*, *c.*1804–20, as 'the War by Sea enormous & the War By Land astounding' (Keynes *Writings* 1957, p.738).

Raine and Lindberg also see a secondary meaning in the two paintings as expressions of Blake's belief in the righteousness of the war then being waged against Napoleon, their protagonists being shown as victors as opposed to their apparently tethered and powerless opponent in the lost 'Spiritual Form of Napoleon' (Butlin 1981, no.652). They also point to the allusion in Blake's title to Addison's lines on Marlborough:

> Pleas'd the Almighty's order to perform
> He rides the whirlwind and directs the storm.

Later in his *Descriptive Catalogue* Blake adapts Nelson's famous message: 'England expects that every man should do his duty, in the Arts as well as in Arms, or in the Senate' (Keynes *Writings* 1957, p.584).

Raymond Lister has published some letters between George Richmond and Sir William Boxall RA, Director of the National Gallery 1865–74. From these it appears that the painting was offered to the National Gallery in 1870 through Richmond at 500 guineas, subsequently reduced by Palmer himself to 300 guineas, though renewed by Richmond at 350 guineas; the Trustees of the National Gallery refused it at this price. The picture was offered to them again in 1874 but nothing came of this and the picture was eventually acquired by the National Gallery in 1882 at the price, £100, at which it had been bought in at Christie's the same year.

60 The Bard, from Gray 1809(?)

N 03551 / B $\frac{6}{655}$
Tempera heightened with gold on canvas
600×441 $(23\frac{5}{8} \times 17\frac{3}{8})$
Signed 'WBlake [with traces of a date]' b.c.
Purchased (Clarke Fund) 1920

PROVENANCE
Samuel Palmer, given between 1873 and 1876 to George Richmond, given 1887 to his son William Blake Richmond, by whom sold to the Tate Gallery

EXHIBITED
Blake's exhibition 1809 (4); *Old Masters* RA 1873 (196); BFAC 1876 (45); *Century of British Art* Grosvenor Gallery 1887–8 (232); Carfax 1904 (35); Carfax 1906 (23); *Century of Art*

Grafton Galleries 1911 (57); Tate Gallery (54) and Manchester (49) 1913–14; Tate Gallery 1947 (45); Tate Gallery 1978 (207, repr.)

LITERATURE
Blake *Descriptive Catalogue* 1809, pp.35–8 (reprinted in Keynes *Writings* 1957, pp.576–7); Rossetti 1863, p.202 no.6, and 1880, p.221 no.100; Robertson in Gilchrist 1907, p.416 under no.6; F.I. McCarthy, '*The Bard* of Thomas Gray, Its Composition and its use by Painters', *The National Library of Wales Journal*, XIV, 1965, p.111, pl.11; Bentley *Blake Records* 1969, pp.178–9; Erdman 1969, pp.47–9, 453; Tayler in *Blake Newsletter*, X, 1976–7, p.81; Butlin 1981, pp.476–7, pl.885

A label on the back 'contributed by Sam! Palmer' gives the information 'Signed "*W.Blake* 1809"'; only the signature is now legible. Another inscription on the back records the gift by George Richmond of the picture to his son William Blake Richmond on 11 May 1887. The picture was restored at the Tate Gallery in 1977.

There are two sketches for the composition in the Philadelphia Museum of Art (Butlin 1981, no.656, recto and verso, pls.886 and 887). Blake had previously exhibited a watercolour of the same subject, now lost, at the Royal Academy in 1785 (Butlin no.160) and had also painted a series of 116 watercolour illustrations to Gray's poems, including 14 to 'The Bard', *c.*1797–8 (Butlin nos.335 *53–66*, the

whole series repr. Geoffrey Keynes, *William Blake Water-colour Designs for the Poems of Thomas Gray*, 1971 and Blake Trust colour facsimile 1972, and Irene Tayler *Blake's Illustrations to the Poems of Gray* 1971). William Rossetti, in his 1863 list, mistakenly associated the tempera in the Tate Gallery with the watercolour exhibited in 1785; he corrected this in his 1888 list.

Gray's poem recounts how Edward I, who on invading Wales condemned all the bards to death, was confronted by a lone survivor who prophesied the doom of the king and the successors of his blood. The surviving bard stands on a rock above the river Conway, accompanied by the ghosts of his fellows. In his *Descriptive Catalogue* Blake defends his 'mode of representing spirits with real bodies' by citing the example of Greek statues of the gods, 'all of them representations of spiritual existences'; moreover the Prophets and Apostles 'described what they saw in Vision as real and existing men whom they saw with their imaginative and immortal organs ... He who does not imagine in stronger and better lineaments, and in stronger and better light than his perishing mortal eye can see does not imagine at all'.

Blake goes on to describe the rest of this much darkened picture: 'King Edward and his Queen Elenor are prostrated, with their horses, at the foot of a rock on which the Bard stands; prostrated by the terrors of his harp on the margin of the river Conway, whose waves bear up a corse of a slaughtered bard at the foot of the rock. The armies of Edward are seen winding away among the mountains.... Mortimer and Gloucester lie spell bound behind their king'. He adds, somewhat confusingly, 'The execution of this picture is also in Water Colours, or Fresco'.

The picture is a proclamation of the enduring power of art against the force of arms. Blake chose a similar subject for the next picture in his exhibition, the lost 'Ancient Britons' (Butlin no.657).

VISIONARY HEADS *c.*1819–1825

Blake's 'Visionary Heads' are perhaps the most extraordinary of Blake's works, and somewhat apart from the other products of his visionary imagination. The term covers his portrayals of the heads or complete figures of supposed manifestations of historical and other personages seen at the home of John Varley (1788–1842), the landscape watercolourist and would-be astrologer (a drawing of Varley by Blake is in the National Portrait Gallery; Butlin 1981, no.689, pl.906). Some of the Visionary Heads were given dates in October 1819 (e.g. nos.61 and 65). Two were dated 1820 and one 1825 (Butlin nos.711 and 748, pls.923 and 960, and no.707, now lost). Blake seems to a considerable extent to have been humouring the credulous Varley's belief in the material presence of the visions; a drawing by John Linnell of a somewhat sceptical Blake in conversation with an enthusiastic John Varley, dated 1821, is in the Fitzwilliam Museum, Cambridge (see Butlin 1969, p.8, pl.1). On the other hand Joseph Burke has suggested the possibility that they could have been genuine eidetic images of physiological origin, and a number of other Blake scholars have been reluctant to see these works solely as jokes made by Blake at Varley's expense.

Most of the drawings seem to have been done at Varley's house in the evenings, but a tracing of 'The Egyptian Task Master Killed by Moses' in the Douglas Library, Queen's University, Kingston, Ontario bears an inscription by Varley saying that he was present when Blake saw the vision and drew it in his own front room, 'first floor No.3 Fountain Court near Exeter Change' (Butlin no.696A, pl.911). The tempera painting of 'The Ghost of a Flea' (no.64) presumably originated from one of these seances but could have been done independently at a later date.

Some of the drawings were engraved by John Linnell for the first, and only, part of Varley's projected four-part *Treatise on Zodiacal Physiognomy*, published in 1828 (in this connection it is perhaps interesting that Blake had engraved four plates for the 1789 English edition of Lavater's *Essays on Physiognomy*). A note by Varley criticising the first state of the plate of 'The Ghost of a Flea' (see no.63) mentions the existence of tracings and it seems likely that replicas of some of the drawings, whether counterproofs, copies or tracings, perhaps drawn with the aid of John Varley's brother Cornelius's invention, the Graphic Telescope (see no.67), were made as aids to the engravings, both executed and projected. While some of these replicas may have been made by Blake himself, it seems more likely that they were done by Linnell (see nos.65 and 67) and Varley; Varley's own drawings for his *Treatise*, in so far as they have been traced, were much smaller and more summary in execution. The Tate Gallery owns both originals and near-contemporary replicas; in many cases the closeness of the versions and the rather impersonal and laboured quality of Blake's draughtsmanship in this particular group of drawings makes it difficult to assess their authorship.

LITERATURE
Merlinus Anglicus, Jun. 'Nativity of Mr. Blake, The Mystical Artist', *Urania or The Astrologer's Chronicle, and Mystical Magazine* no.1, 1825, pp.70–2 (reprinted in Bentley *Blake Records* 1969, pp.296–7; Wilson 1971, pp.380–1); Cunningham *Lives*, II, 2nd ed. 1830, pp.170–5 (reprinted in Bentley *ibid.*, pp.496–9); Anon. 'Bits of Biography. No.1. Blake, the Vision Seer, and Martin, the York Minster Incendiary', *The Monthly Magazine*, XV, 1833, pp.244–5 (reprinted in Bentley *ibid.*, pp.298–9); Burke in Philipp and Stewart 1964, pp.112–15 (reprinted in Essick 1973, pp.258–66); Bentley *Blake Records* 1969, pp.259–65; Martin Butlin *The Blake–Varley Sketchbook of 1819*, 1969; Martin Butlin 'Blake, the Varleys, and the Patent Graphic Telescope', Paley and Phillips 1973, pp.294–304; Lindberg *Job* 1973, pp.152–4; Bindman 1977, pp.202–3; Anne K. Mellor 'Physiognomy, Phrenology, and Blake's Visionary Heads', Essick and Pearce 1978, pp.53–74; G. Ingli James 'Some Not-So-Familiar Visionary Heads', *Blake*, XII, 1978–9, pp.244–9.

61–63 **Drawings from the Small Blake–Varley Sketchbook** c.1819

The Tate Gallery owns three pages from the smaller Blake–Varley Sketchbook, first used by John Varley for landscape sketches and then by Blake for recording the visions he saw at Varley's house in 1819, the date inscribed on a number of the pages from the Sketchbook including no.61. The Sketchbook seems originally to have contained sixty-six leaves, sixteen of which are now lost. After a number of pages, including no.63, had been removed, the Sketchbook probably passed to Varley's friend the musician William Christian Selle, whose daughter married H. Buxton Forman, who definitely gave it to William Bell Scott in 1870. It remained at Penkhill Castle, the home of Scott's friend Miss Alice Boyd, until it was rediscovered there in 1967 by Mr M.D.E. Clayton-Stamm. It was subsequently broken up and reproduced in facsimile (Martin Butlin, *The Blake–Varley Sketchbook of 1819*, 1969; the Sketchbook is also fully described and catalogued, but not reproduced, in Butlin 1981, pp.495–506 no.692) and sold page by page at Christie's on 15 June 1971 (141–172, most of the Blakes repr.). On 21 March 1989 a second, larger Blake–Varley sketchbook was sold at Christie's (184, repr. in separate catalogue); this sketchbook had belonged to William Mulready, Varley's brother-in-law, and it was sold with his collection at Christie's 28–30 April 1864 (86).

61 **A Figure Standing in a Gothic Apse, perhaps the Empress Maud** c.1819 (recto)

Detailed Drawings for 'The Empress Maud in Bed' 1819 (verso)

T 01334/B 692 *23–4*
Pencil on paper 115 × 205 (6½ × 8)
Inscribed by John Varley on verso, 'the Empress Maud said rose water/ was in the vessel under the table/ octr. 29 friday. 11 PM. 1819./& said there were closets which/ contained all the conveniences for the bedchamber'
Watermarked '1806'
Purchased (Grant-in-Aid) 1971

PROVENANCE
John Varley; ? William Christian Selle, whose daughter married Henry Buxton Forman; Henry Buxton Forman, given 1870 to William Bell Scott; Miss Alice Boyd, bequeathed 1897 to her niece Miss Eleanor Margaret Courtney-Boyd, bequeathed 1946 to her niece Miss Evelyn May Courtney-Boyd, sold 1967 to M.D.E. Clayton-Stamm, sold Christie's 15 June 1971 (in 161 with no.62, recto repr.) 800 gns. bt Agnew's for the Tate Gallery

EXHIBITED
Burlington Fine Arts Club 1876 (in 318, the Blake–Varley Sketchbook); Tate Gallery 1969–71 (with the rest of the Blake–Varley Sketchbook; no catalogue issued)

LITERATURE
William B. Scott, 'A Varley-and-Blake Sketchbook', *The Portfolio*, II, 1871, pp.103–5; Rossetti 1880, p.263 list 2 in no.82; Butlin 1969, pp.1–4, 21–2, repr.; Butlin 1981, p.498 nos.692 *23* and *24*

This sheet was pages 23–4 of the Blake–Varley Sketchook. It was removed when the book was finally dismembered in 1969. The drawings on the verso are related to the finished composition on what was the facing page 25, which shows 'The Empress Maud in Bed' (coll. Mrs Edward Croft-Murray; Butlin 1981, no.692 *25*, repr. sale cat., Christie's 15 June 1971, lot 163). This shows a woman lying in a canopied bed in a room with Gothic arches and furnishings, some of which are referred to in the inscription on no.62, the drawings on which show the octagonal plan of the room and a detail of the vault and two hanging candelabra concealed behind the bed-curtains in the finished composition.

61 (recto)

61 (verso)

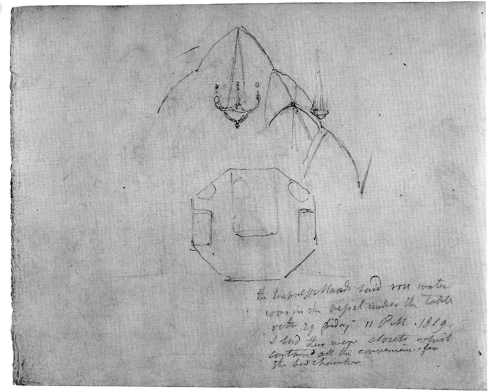

The woman is presumably intended as the Empress Maud of the inscription, more usually known as Matilda (1102–1167), daughter of Henry I of England, widow of the German Emperor Henry V, and contestant with her cousin Stephen for the English throne; her son by her second husband Geoffrey of Anjou became Henry II. She appears again on p. 27 of the sketchbook and is also the subject of a drawing in an American private collection (Butlin no. 725, pl. 941).

The recto shows the possible Empress Maud standing in a Gothic apse richly decorated with a ribbed vault, stained glass, blind Gothic tracery and a tall panel carved in relief in an elaborate pattern. On each side of the window are paintings of female saints, that on the left being the subject of the enlarged drawing on the once facing page 22, now also in the Tate Gallery, no.62, which also contains drawings of the base of one of the columns, what appears to be another architectural detail, and a detail of the stained glass window with the colour notes 'pl' (plum), 'M' (?), 'Lt. Blue' (light blue) and 'crimson'.

The second, larger sketchbook containing landscape drawings by John Varley and Visionary Heads by Blake, sold at Christie's on 21 March 1989, is clearly the 'volume containing 49 heads, in pencil, from visions which appeared to him [Blake] and remained while he completed them; at the other end of the book are 16 landscapes by Varley', described in the catalogue of the Mulready sale at Christie's, 28–30 April 1864 (86). The provenance given for the smaller Blake–Varley Sketchbook, as given above, is based on the statement made by William Bell Scott in his *Portfolio* article, according to which he had obtained the sketchbook from 'A young friend who had married the daughter of a companion of Varley, a fellow-artist, a musician who taught at the same seminary, as very many artists at the time eked out their incomes by teaching'. William Christian Selle was a musician and a friend of Varley. His daughter married Henry Buxton Forman, and Scott wrote inside the back cover of the smaller sketchbook, 'This sketchbook was presented to me by H. Buxton Forman. 1870'.

62

62 Detailed Drawings for 'A Figure Standing in a Gothic Apse' 1819

T 01335 / B 692 *22*
Pencil on paper 155 × 205 (6⅛ × 8)
Inscribed by John Varley with colour notes,
'pl', 'M', 'Lt. Blue' and 'crimson'
Purchased (Grant-in-Aid) 1971

PROVENANCE
As for no.61

EXHIBITED
As for no.61

LITERATURE
As for no.61

This sheet was originally pages 21 and 22 of the Blake–Varley sketchbook; the other side, the original page 21, is blank. The drawings show details of the composition shown on the original facing page 23, the recto of no.61, *q.v.*

63 The Head of the Ghost of a Flea *c.*1819 (recto)

A Profile and a Reduced Drawing of Milton's First Wife *c.*1819 (verso)

N 05184 / B 692 *97–8*
Pencil on paper 189 × 153 (7 7/16 × 6)
Inscribed by Varley on recto 'Original [? –
now practically invisible] W.Blake' b.l., and
on verso with colour-notes on the drawing of
Milton's First Wife, 'Gn velvet', 'Bk' and 'Eyes
Bn'
Watermarked '1806'
Bequeathed by Miss Alice G.E. Carthew 1940

PROVENANCE
John Linnell, sold Christie's 15 March 1918
(in 164 with nos.65, 66 and 67) £54.12.0 bt
Miss Carthew

EXHIBITED
Tate Gallery (69a), Manchester (74),
Nottingham (57) and Edinburgh (78)
1913–14; *British Drawings from the Tate Gallery*
CEMA tour 1944 (6); Tate Gallery 1947
(83); Hamburg and Frankfurt 1975 (163,
recto repr.); Tate Gallery 1978 (282, recto
repr.)

LITERATURE
Varley *Treatise on Zodiacal Physiognomy* 1828,
pp.54–5 (reprinted in Bentley 1969,
pp.372–3, and Butlin 1969, p.11); Gilchrist
1863, I, pp.255–6; Rossetti 1863, p.245 list 2
no.56, and 1880, p.262 list 2 no.65; Richard
C. Jackson, 'William Blake: An unlooked for
Discovery', *South London Observer* 22 June 1912
(see G.E. Bentley Jr, 'All the Evidence that's
fit to print', *Blake Newsletter*, II, 1968–9, p.12);
Keynes *Bibliography* 1921, p.318; Keynes
Drawings 1927, no.49, recto repr.; Blunt in
Warburg Journal, VI, 1943, p.203, recto pl.59d;
Frye 1947, pp.123–4; Charles Singer, 'The first
English microscopist: Robert Hooke
(1635–1703)', *Endeavour*, XIV, 1955, p.14;
Blunt 1959, p.82; Keynes in *Bulletin of the New
York Public Library*, LXIV, 1960, pp.570–1,
recto repr. facing p.567; Butlin 1969, pp.9–11,
28–9, repr.; Erdman 1969, p.106; Roe in
Rosenfeld 1969, p.175; Bindman 1977, p.202,
recto pl.165; Klonsky 1977, p.124, recto repr.;
Paley 1978, p.181, recto pl.87; Butlin 1981,
pp.495–6, 503 nos.692 *98* and *97*.

Unlike the other pages from the Small Blake–Varley sketchbook in the Tate Gallery, this leaf and three others that can be identified were removed from the book early on and were until recently regarded as separate entities (for the others see Butlin nos.692 *35–6* and *a–d*). In the original sketchbook the profile and reduced drawing of 'Milton's First Wife', which is here regarded as the verso, in fact came first, as page 97. The watermark '1806' is found on a number of pages in the Blake–Varley Sketchbook. The book itself is oblong in format.

The drawing of the head of a flea, accompanied by a larger sketch of its mouth alone, now open, is the subject of a well-known anecdote in Varley's *Treatise on Zodiacal Physiognomy*: 'I felt convinced by his [Blake's] mode of proceeding, that he had a real image before him, for he left off, and began on another part of the paper,

63(recto)   63(verso)

to make a separate drawing of the mouth of the Flea, which the spirit having opened, he was prevented from proceeding with the first sketch, till he had closed it. During the time occupied in completing the drawing, the Flea told him that all fleas were inhabited by the souls of such men, as were by nature blood-thirsty to excess . . .'

Linnell engraved two complete heads, one with mouth shut, one open, for Varley's *Treatise*. A note written by Varley to Linnell criticizes his engraving of the latter, adding 'it has been compared with a tracing & these remarks made' (coll. M. Butlin, repr. Butlin 1969, pl.6); no such tracing is known in this case. According to Gilchrist, Linnell also made a copy in colour; this could be a reference in the tempera painting, no. 64.

Blake's drawing may have been influenced by Robert Hooke's *Micrographia, or some Physiological Descriptions of Minute Bodies made by Magnifying Glasses, with Observations and Inquiries thereupon*, 1665, in which there is a greatly enlarged engraving of a flea on plate 32 (repr. Singer *op. cit.*, p.15, and Keynes 1960, facing p.567).

What is now regarded as the verso of this sheet originally faced page 96 in the Blake–Varley Sketchbook, a drawing of 'Milton's First Wife' now in a private collection in Great Britain (repr. Butlin *op. cit.* 1969 and sale cat., Christie's 1971, lot 145). This shows Milton's wife Mary Powell (b.1615) whom he married in 1643. From a Royalist, anti-Puritan family, she left him after a month and Milton declared that he would never take her back. The incident coincided with, and may have led to, Milton's pamphlet on divorce. In 1645, however, after the ruin of the Royalist cause, Milton did take her back, together with her family, and they had four children before her death in 1652. The reduced-scale drawing in the Tate Gallery, with its various colour-notes, was presumably done so that Varley could record observations without fear of spoiling the original drawing on the facing page. It is accompanied by a crude profile of a thick-lipped figure and also by traces of what may be another head in the lower left-hand corner.

64

64   **The Ghost of a Flea** *c.*1819–20

N 05889 / B 750
Tempera heightened with gold on mahogany
214 × 162 ($8\frac{7}{16} × 6\frac{3}{8}$)
Signed 'WBlake Fresco' b.r.
Bequeathed by W. Graham Robertson 1949

PROVENANCE
John Varley; his son Albert Varley, sold
February 1878 to William Bell Scott, sold
Sotheby's 14 July 1892 (235) £10.5.0., bt
Quaritch, by whom offered *rough list 127*
August 1892 £18, and sold 1892 to W.
Graham Robertson

EXHIBITED
International Exhibition of Industry, Science and Art
Edinburgh 1886 (Pictures and Works of Art
1444, as 'A Vampire'); Carfax 1906 (22);
Century of Art Grafton Galleries 1911 (59, as 'A
Vampire'); Tate Gallery 1913 (69); BFAC
1927 (57); Tate Gallery 1947 (48);
Bournemouth, Southampton and Brighton
1949 (17); *Romantic Movement* Tate Gallery
1959 (24); Tate Gallery 1978 (283, repr.)

LITERATURE
Smith *Nollekens and his Times* 1828, II,

pp.471–2, 480–1 (reprinted in Bentley 1969, pp.467, 472); Varley *Treatise on Zodiacal Physiognomy* 1828, p.55 (reprinted Bentley 1969, p.373, and Butlin 1969, p.11); Allan Cunningham, *Lives of the Most Eminent British Painters, Sculptors and Architects*, II, 2nd ed. 1830, pp.169–70 (reprinted Bentley 1969, pp.497–8, and Butlin 1969, p.16); Rossetti 1880, p.222 no.109; Robertson in Gilchrist 1907, p.494 no.19, repr. facing p.274; G.K. Chesterton, *William Blake*, 1910, p.153; Frye 1947, pp.123–4; Preston 1952, pp.77–82 no.21,

pl.21; Keynes in *Bulletin of the New York Public Library*, LXIV, 1960, pp.568–72, repr. facing p.566; Burke 1964, pp.122–3 (reprinted in Essick 1973, pp.281–4); Bentley *Blake Records*, 1969, pp.264, 352–3, 372–3, 467, 472, 497–8; Butlin 1969, pp.15–16, 28, pl.5; Keynes *Blake Studies* 1971, pp.131–2, 134, pl.31; Todd 1971, pp.113–7, repr.; Klonsky 1977, p.125, repr.; Butlin 1981, pp.524–5 no.750, colour pl.966. *Also repr.*: Eugenie de Keyser, *The Romantic West 1789–1850*, 1965, p.105 in colour; *Mizue*, no.882, 1978, 9, p.29 in colour

A label on the back, written by William Bell Scott, states that the panel was bought from John Varley's son Albert in February 1878. This is confirmed by an inscription by Scott of the same date, written inside the back cover of the Small Blake–Varley Sketchbook (see nos.61–3), saying that, 'I have since getting this book [in 1870], bought the *painting* of the "Ghost" of the Flea, from Mr Varley of Oakley St. Chelsea, son of John Varley'.

Another label, written in the same hand, supplies a copy of an inscription by John Varley on an earlier label, now nearly illegible. The original seems to have read, 'The Vision of the Spirit which inhabits the body of a Flea & which appeared to the Late Mr. Blake, the designer of the Vignettes for Blair's Grave & the Book of Job. The Vision first appeared to him in my presence & afterwards till he had finished this picture. A flea he said drew blood on this …, [the rest is illegible on both labels] J Varley'. In his *Treatise on Zodiacal Physiognomy* of 1828 Varley describes how, after Blake had drawn the head of the flea (no.63), it 'afforded him a view of his whole figure; an engraving of which I shall give in this work.' The engraving, which was never published, was presumably to have been based on the full-length drawing of the flea on page 94 of the Blake–Varley sketchbook. This shows the flea standing more erect than in the tempera, touching his tongue with the forefinger of his left hand (Butlin 1981, no.692 *94*, sold at Christie's 15 June 1971 (in 141, repr.) bought by Martin Breslauer and sold in 1977 to a British private collection; also repr. Butlin 1969).

When Alan Cunningham visited Varley in connection with the chapter on Blake for his *Lives*, published in 1830, he was shown the tempera, which Varley suggested was the product of a second visitation. '"I'll tell you all about it sir"', reports Cunningham. '"I called upon him one evening and found Blake more than usually excited. He told me he had seen a wonderful thing – the ghost of a flea! 'And did you make a drawing of him?' I inquired. 'No indeed' said he, 'I wish I had, but I shall, if he appears again!' He looked earnestly into a corner of the room, and then said, 'here he is – reach me my things – I shall keep my eye on him. There he comes! his eager tongue whisking out of his mouth, a cup in his hands to hold blood and covered with a scaly skin of gold and green;' – as he described him so he drew him."' Varley's account, though an accurate description of the painting, may be a fanciful one; Blake could well have worked up the painting from the drawing. Another locale for the execution of one of the versions of 'The Ghost of a Flea' is suggested by Walter Thornbury in his *British Artists from Hogarth to Turner*, 1861, I, p.28: 'the house of the father of my old friend, Leigh, the artist' (Samuel Leigh, father of James Mathews Leigh, where 'Blake was a frequent visitor'), but this seems unlikely both for the two drawings in the sketchbook, which seem to have been done at Varley's (see no.63), and for the tempera, according to Varley painted at Blake's own house.

The technique of this tempera is closer to the temperas of *c*.1800–10 than to Blake's late, very different temperas of *c*.1821–6 (see nos.35–39 and 58–60 as opposed to nos.68–70).

65

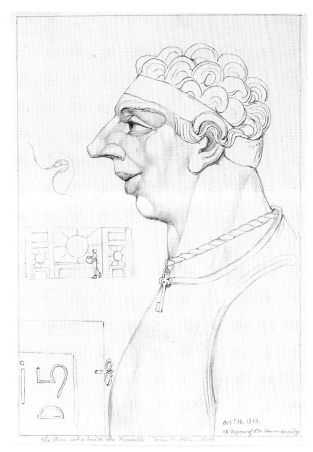

REPLICA AFTER BLAKE, PROBABLY BY JOHN LINNELL

65 **The Man who Built the Pyramids**

N 05185 / B 752
Pencil, framing line 287 × 197 ($11\frac{5}{16} × 7\frac{3}{4}$), on
paper 298 × 214 ($11\frac{3}{4} × 8\frac{7}{16}$)
Inscribed by John Linnell 'Oct! 18.1819. 15
Degrees of ♋ Cancer ascending' b.r. and 'The
Man who built the Pyramids drawn by
William Blake' below design, and, on back,
'JL'
Bequeathed by Miss Alice G.E. Carthew 1940

PROVENANCE
John Linnell, sold Christie's 15 March 1918
(in 164 with nos.63, 66 and 67) £54.12.0
bought Miss Carthew

EXHIBITED
BFAC 1927 (60); Paris and Vienna 1937 (15);
Wartime Acquisitions, 2nd Exhibition CEMA tour
1944–5 (5)

LITERATURE
Gilchrist 1863, I, p.252, repr.; Rossetti 1863,
p.243 list 2 no.32, and 1880, p.259 list 2 no.
31; Keynes *Drawings* 1927, no.41 repr.;
Bentley *Blake Records* 1969, p.259; Butlin 1969,
pp.14–15, 29–30, pl.4; Roe in Rosenfeld 1969,
pp.175, 194; Keynes *Drawings* 1970, no.62
repr.; Wilson 1971, p.68 n.; Klonsky 1977,
p.123, repr.; Mellor in Essick and Pearce
1978, pp.69–71, pl.79; Butlin 1981, pp.525–6
no.752, pl.979

The inscription on nos.65, 66 and 67 were formerly attributed to John Varley but
are similar to those on Linnell's drawings of Blake in the Fitzwilliam Museum,
Cambridge (repr. Keynes *Portraiture* 1977, pls.29–33) and Blake's drawing of
Linnell in the Lessing J. Rosenwald collection, National Gallery of Art,
Washington (Butlin 1981, no.688, repr. pl.905). Linnell's monogram on the
reverse may only be a mark of ownership but could well be a signature implying
authorship of the drawing.

  This drawing appears to be a replica of a missing page from the Small
Blake–Varley Sketchbook, page 103 of which (Butlin no.692 *103*, repr. Butlin

1969) contains a number of drawings and colour notes mainly if not wholly related to this composition, both to the main figure and to such details as the portfolio shown in the lower left-hand corner and the 'Egyptian' interior above this. The facing page 102 is missing but, by analogy with other drawings of details in the sketchbook which face the complete compositions to which they refer (see, for instance, no.61 verso), can be assumed to have contained Blake's original drawing of the whole composition. Although both Linnell and Varley probably made replicas or copies of Blake's Visionary Heads, and Blake himself may have done so as well, the relatively high degree of precision and finish, coupled with a certain feeling of deadness, point to Linnell as the artist.

As well as the main figure the sheet contains a drawing of his mouth open instead of shut (as in 'The Head of the Ghost of a Flea', no.63), 'the Place where Blake saw this Personage' (as Rossetti described it in his title) and the architect's portfolio. This last, it appears from the annotated drawing in the sketchbook, was 'Black' surrounding 'White Satinwood', contained '8 tablets' and was tied with 'Blue Catgut'. The architect had a 'Blue Ribbon' round his hair, a 'Black Shiny face', and a 'gold cord' on which hung a 'gold' key. The reference to '15 Degrees of Cancer ascending' reflects Varley's interest in Zodiacal physiognomy; Roe suggests that the pseudo-hieroglyphics on the portfolio repeat this inscription.

For Blake 'The Man who Built the Pyramids' would have represented materialistic oppression. In *Jerusalem* he wrote, '& souls are bak'd In bricks to build the pyramids of Heber & Terah' (plate 45 (31); Keynes *Writings* 1957, p.657).

COUNTERPROOF OF DRAWING BY BLAKE

66   The Man who Taught Blake Painting in his Dreams

N 05187/B 754
Approx. 240 × 230 ($9\frac{3}{8}$ × 9) on paper 296 × 235 ($11\frac{5}{8}$ × $9\frac{1}{4}$)
Inscribed by John Linnell 'Imagination of A man who Mr Blake has rec^d instruct[ion] &c from' b.r.
Bequeathed by Miss Alice G.E. Carthew 1940

PROVENANCE
John Linnell, sold Christie's 15 March 1918

(in 164 with nos.63, 65 and 67) £54.12.0 bt Miss Carthew

LITERATURE
Keynes *Drawings* 1927, no.48 repr.; Butlin 1969, p.12; Keynes *Drawings* 1970, no.63 repr.; Butlin in Paley and Phillips 1973, pp.296–9, pl.72; Keynes *Portraiture* 1977, pp.24–5, 131–3, pl.22b; Butlin 1981, p.527 no.754, pl.982

The paper has been trimmed along the edges, cutting off the last letters of 'instruction'; the last four words of the inscription are squeezed in above the rest.

This is apparently a counterproof of Blake's original, uninscribed drawing of this subject of c.1819–20 formerly in the collection of Sir Geoffrey Keynes and now in the Fitzwilliam Museum, Cambridge (Butlin 1981, no.753, pl.981). This was included by William Rossetti in his 1880 lists (p.263 list 2 no.81) as 'Lois' meaning 'Lais', the courtesan of Corinth who is in fact the subject of another of the Visionary Heads (Butlin no.712, pl.924); this mistake was followed until the 1950s. When the Keynes drawing was exhibited at the Tate Gallery in 1913 (71) Archibald G.B. Russell said of it that 'The drawing appears to be a duplicate taken by means of blackened paper with a hard pencil from the original sketch, and afterward touched up with pencil', in other words a counterproof, and indeed it seems to be in reverse to both of the examples in the Tate Gallery. However, it appears to this compiler that the Keynes drawing is the most sensitive of the three versions and that it must therefore be Blake's original. (It should perhaps be stressed that, although in reproduction these three drawings often look to be of different sizes, this is

66

67

because of the different sizes of the sheets of paper on which they have been executed. In fact the heads on each drawing measure 14.4 ($5\frac{11}{16}$) from the top of the hair to the point of the chin.)

Keynes (1977) saw this drawing as a visionary self-portrait, partly on account of its resemblance to the full-face highly finished drawing in pencil and grey wash attributed to John Linnell and now in the collection of Robert N. Essick (Keynes 1977, pl.35). As a portrayal of Blake's inspiration this could certainly be so. Keynes also interprets the strange form on the figure's forehead as the Menorah, the symbol of spiritual enlightenment derived from the seven-branched candlestick of the Jews, but in fact it appears to have eight branches and may rather be a more general allusion to the flames of inspiration.

See also no.67.

REPLICA AFTER BLAKE, PROBABLY BY JOHN LINNELL

67 **The Man who taught Blake Painting in his Dreams**

N 05186/B 755
Approx. 230 × 220 ($9\frac{1}{8} × 8\frac{5}{8}$) on paper
260 × 206 ($10\frac{1}{4} × 8\frac{1}{8}$)
Inscribed by John Linnell 'The Portrait of a Man who instructed M? Blake in Painting &c. in his Dreams' b.l. and 'Imagination of a Man whom Mr Blake has recd instruction in Painting &c from' b.r.
Bequeathed by Miss Alice G.E. Carthew 1940

PROVENANCE
John Linnell, sold Christie's 15 March 1918 (in 164 with nos.63, 65 and 66) £54.12.0 bt Miss Carthew

EXHIBITED
Paris and Vienna 1937 (14); Port Sunlight 1950 (29)

LITERATURE
Gilchrist 1863, I, p.254; Rossetti 1863, p.244 list 2 no.39, and 1880, p.262 list 2 no.64; Keynes *Drawings* 1927, under no.48; Butlin 1969, p.12; Butlin in Paley and Phillips 1973, pp.296–9, pl.73; Keynes *Portraiture* 1977, pp.24–5, 131–3, pl.22c; Klonsky 1977, p.122, repr.; Butlin 1981, p.527 no.755, pl.983

Of the two versions of this head in the Tate Gallery one is listed by Rossetti as 'Portrait of a Man who instructed Mr Blake in Painting, in his Dreams', which corresponds more or less to the first title written on this drawing. The other version, no.66, is almost certainly a counterproof of the work formerly in the Keynes collection while this drawing is a replica of no.66. Except for the fact that the probable original is in the reverse direction to the other two, the three versions are very close to each other, even to the placing of the individual hairs and lines of shading. The two drawings in the Tate Gallery do not coincide precisely enough to be the result of direct tracing but rather suggest the use of an optical aid to copying such as Cornelius Varley's Graphic Telescope (the portrait drawings done with the Graphic Telescope by both Cornelius and John Varley in the Victoria and Albert Museum and the British Museum show the same deadness of line and shading as the replicas of Blake's Visionary Heads: for a brief account of the Telescope see John Gage, exh. cat., *A Decade of English Naturalism 1810–1820*, Norwich and Victoria and Albert Museum 1969, pp.16, 40 nn. 18, 19, and Butlin 1973, *loc. cit.*). The two drawings in the Tate Gallery, with their varied inscriptions, were probably try-outs for a projected engraving for one of the unpublished parts of John Varley's *Treatise on Zodiacal Physiognomy*.

This section reflects the richness of Blake's work later in his life; versions of his series of illustrations to the Book of Job and his illustrations to Dante, which also date from this period, are the subject of separate sections. The three works in tempera (nos.68–70) show Blake experimenting in new and more effective techniques compared to that of his works of *c*.1799–1800 (nos.35–9) and *c*.1805–9 (nos. 58–60). The watercolour 'Epitome of James Hervey's "Meditations among the Tombs"' (no.71) shares the high finish and relatively graceful forms of the two later temperas though it may date from a few years earlier. The copy after 'The Parable of the Wise and Foolish Virgins' (no.72) represents the last stage in the evolution of one of Blake's most repeated compositions. The illustrations to Thornton's *Pastorals of Virgil* (nos.73–106) show one aspect of Blake's late accomplishment in engraving, in this case on wood, an accomplishment that resulted in a series of exquisite miniatures that were among the most admired, and the most influential, of the works known to the group of young artists including Samuel Palmer, George Richmond and Edward Calvert that gathered round Blake in his last years. Finally, there is a late, quavery drawing of 'The Crucifixion' (no.107) that one likes to think of as one of Blake's very last works.

68 **Winter** *c*.1820–5

T 02387 / B 808
Tempera on pine 902 × 297 ($35\frac{1}{2}$ × $11\frac{11}{16}$)
Purchased (Grant-in-Aid) 1979

PROVENANCE
Rev. John Johnson; Canon Cowper Johnson; Bertram Vaughan-Johnson; his widow; the Rev. B. Talbot Vaughan Johnson; the Vaughan Johnson Trust, sold Sotheby's 18 July 1979 (58, repr. in colour) £30,000 bt Agnew's for the Tate Gallery

EXHIBITED
Carfax 1906 (19); Tate Gallery 1913 (55);
BFAC 1927 (51, pl.38); on loan to Tate Gallery 1933–4; *The Lyrical Trend in English Painting*, Roland, Browse and Delbanco, March–April 1946 (17, repr. on cover); Paris, Antwerp (repr. pl.23), Zurich and Tate Gallery (repr.) 1947 (33); Port Sunlight 1950 (27); Arts Council 1951 (3, pl.2); Cambridge 1957; on loan to Tate Gallery 1972–9; Tate Gallery 1978 (308, repr.)

LITERATURE
Robertson in Gilchrist 1907, p.492 no.4; Wright 1929, I, p.131; Butlin 1981, p.551 no.809, pl.1049

The panels of 'Winter' and the companion 'Evening' (now in an American private collection; Butlin 1981, no.809, pl.1050) were painted for the Rev. Johnson for the sides of the fireplace in his rectory at Yaxham, Norfolk. They illustrate the lines by Johnson's cousin William Cowper from *The Task*, Book IV, lines 120–9 and 243–6 respectively. The lines describing Winter read:

> O Winter! ruler of the inverted year,
> Thy scattered hair with sleet like ashes filled,
> Thy breath congealed upon thy lips, thy cheeks
> Fringed with a beard made white with other snows
> Than those of age, thy forehead wrapt in clouds.
> A leafless branch thy sceptre, and thy throne
> A sliding car, indebted to no wheels,
> But urged by storms along its slippery way;
> I love thee, all unlovely as thou seemest,
> And dreaded as thou art.

68

A third picture, of 'Olney Bridge', apparently ran along the top of the same fireplace (Butlin no.810). According to family tradition it was last seen in a damaged condition in 1905 and was subsequently thrown away.

Although Johnson had got to know Blake through William Hayley and had had his miniature portrait painted by him in 1802 (Butlin no.347, pl.455) 'Winter' and 'Evening' are stylistically, and in their technique, characteristic of Blake's late works. It has been suggested that they were painted following Johnson's rebuilding of Yaxham Rectory in 1820–1, which seems much more likely than that they were painted in the early years of the century.

That the fireplace was not yet set up, or had already been dismantled, in 1834, is suggested by a shopping-list of wines dated 'March 6 1834' on the back of 'Evening'. Both panels were framed for some time with part of their surfaces covered by mounts, under which the blues remained considerably stronger than elsewhere, suggesting that the pictures have faded and that the paint is closer to watercolour than to Blake's earlier form of tempera, which tends to have darkened with time. It is likely that originally there was considerably more of the gold of which only traces remain on the two pictures.

69   The Body of Abel Found by Adam and Eve   c.1826

N 05888 / B 806
Pen and tempera, in places over gold, on mahogany 325 × 433 ($12\frac{13}{16}$ × $17\frac{1}{16}$)
Signed 'fresco W.BLAKE ... [damaged – ?'fecit' missing]' incised b.r.
Bequeathed by W. Graham Robertson 1949

PROVENANCE
?Thomas Butts; ?Thomas Butts jun.; ?his daughter Mrs Graham Foster Piggot; ?Capt. F.J. Butts by 1863; ...; ?Rev. Thomas Buchanan, Archdeacon of Wiltshire; ?B.F.C. Costeloe by 1890; Mr Fitzmaurice of the Close, Salisbury; Carfax, sold January 1906 to W. Graham Robertson

EXHIBITED
?Whitechapel Fine Art Exhibition St Jude's School-House, March–April 1890 (81, as 'The Death of Abel'); Carfax 1906 (17); Bournemouth, Southampton and Brighton 1949 (4); Tate Gallery 1978 (312, repr.)

LITERATURE
?Rossetti 1863, p.221 no.102, and 1880, p.221 no.102; Robertson in Gilchrist 1907, p.492 no.9, repr. facing p.248; Preston 1952, pp.72–3 no.19, pl.19; Wicksteed Jerusalem 1953, p.65; Keynes Bible 1957, p.2 no.15a, repr.; H.M. Margoliouth, 'William Blake, Historical Painter', Studio, CLIII, 1957, pp.98–100, repr.; Blunt 1959, pp.40–1, pl.57c; Taylor and Grant in Blake Studies, I, 1968–9, pp.68–71, 200, repr. p.69; Keynes Blake Studies, 1971, pp.145–6, 217; Todd 1971, pp.124–5, repr.; Lindberg Job 1973, p.228; Schiff Füssli 1973, I, pp.289, 605; Geoffrey Keynes William Blake's Laocoön, a last Testament, with Related Works, 1976, pp.40–5, 61–2, pl.11; Bindman 1977, p.252 n.14; Klonsky 1977, p.108, repr. in colour; Leslie Tannenbaum, 'Blake and the Iconography of Cain', Essick and Pearce 1978, pp.23–4, pl.42; Butlin 1981, pp.550–1 no.806, colour pl.971; Warner 1984, p.68

This work and 'Satan Smiting Job with Sore Boils' (no.70) are similar in size, technique, support and form of signature to the version of 'Count Ugolino in Prison' formerly in the collection of Sir Geoffrey Keynes and now in the Fitzwilliam Museum, Cambridge (Butlin 1981 no.805, colour pl.970); this last work is painted in tempera on panel, 327 × 430 ($12\frac{7}{8}$ × $16\frac{15}{16}$) and is signed 'W. BLAKE fec.' incised b.r. In comparison with Blake's earlier temperas (see nos.35–9) the technique consists of a much thinner paint film, akin to watercolour, on a gesso ground laid on panel. These late temperas have survived in a much better condition than the earlier examples and they also seem to show an advance on 'Winter' (no.68). Both examples, in the Tate Gallery were cleaned 1977–8.

The 'Ugolino' panel seems to be the work mentioned in Blake's letter to John Linnell of 25 April 1827: 'as to Ugolino &c I never supposed that I should sell them[;] my wife alone is answerable for their having Existed in any finishd state – I am too much attachd to Dante to think much of anything else' (Keynes *Writings* 1957, p.879; Keynes *Letters* 1968, p.164). The reference to Dante is to the series of illustrations begun in 1824 but left incomplete at Blake's death in August 1827 (see nos.131–65) and of the several other versions of the composition of 'Ugolino' that closest to the panel is the pencil drawing from this series (British Museum; Butlin no.812 *68*, repr. Roe 1963, pl.64). There are further reasons for dating 'Satan Smiting Job with Sore Boils' to 1825 or later, so the probable date for all three panels is *c*.1826.

This painting in tempera of 'The Body of Abel Found by Adam and Eve' is a later version of the watercolour shown in Blake's exhibition of 1809 as 'The Body of Abel found by Adam and Eve; Cain, who was about to bury it, fleeing from the face of his Parents'; this was one of four watercolours in the exhibition that 'the Artist wishes were in Fresco, on an enlarged scale to ornament the altars of churches, and to make England like Italy, respected by respectable men of other countries on account of Art' (Blake *Descriptive Catalogue* 1809, pp.60–1, Keynes *Writings* 1957, p.584); for what seems to be this watercolour, a work from the Linnell collection now in the Fogg Museum, see Butlin 1981 no.664, repr. in colour pl.596. There is a drawing related to this watercolour in the British Museum (Butlin no.665 recto, repr. pl.882). A small replica of the watercolour in Indian ink, with squaring lines apparently made in preparation for an engraving, was formerly in the collection of Sir Geoffrey Keynes; this may be the drawing sold by Mrs Blake through Haviland Burke to Dr John Jebb, Bishop of Limerick, in 1830 or alternatively a copy done by John Linnell on 12 September 1821 and finished two days later (for these two works see Butlin no.666, the Keynes drawing repr. pl.884). Blake treated the subject again as one of the illustrations to his manuscript copy of Genesis now in the Henry E. Huntington Library and Art Gallery, San Marino (Butlin no.828 *10*, pl.1091).

The history of this panel is uncertain. Rossetti lists a painting of this subject as in the collection of Captain Butts but relates it to the 1809 exhibition, the work shown at which seems to have been the watercolour that later belonged to John Linnell. Preston quotes a note of W. Graham Robertson that the panel passed to Captain Butt's sister together with sixteen further works which perished in an attic, apart from this solitary exception which seems to have been previously acquired by her brother. In addition Graham Robertson wrote on a label on the back of the picture that it came from a Mr Fitzmaurice of the Close, Salisbury, but told Ruthven Todd, in a letter of 18 May 1942, that Robert Ross of Carfax said it came from a house in the Close but would not say whose. Ruthven Todd has suggested that the picture at one time belonged to Archdeacon Thomas Buchanan, canon of Salisbury and husband of Laura, a daughter of George Richmond, Blake's friend and owner of the companion picture no.70. The Salisbury association may therefore reflect a Richmond provenance rather than a Butts one. To add to the complications a work entitled 'The Death of Abel' was lent by B.F.C. Costelloe to an exhibition at Whitechapel in 1890. This could also be the tempera or the missing Jebb drawing, if it is missing, referred to above.

The incident shown in this picture is not in the Bible but appears in Blake's *The Ghost of Abel* of 1822. In this short dramatic piece the Ghost of Abel, seconded by Satan, cries for vengeance while Jehovah, supported by angels, upholds the 'Covenant of the Forgiveness of Sin' (Keynes *Writings* 1957, pp.779–81). William Vaughan has pointed out that the inclusion of Adam and Eve in the scene must derive from Solomon Gessner's *Death of Abel*, first published in an English translation in 1761 and again with illustrations by Henry Richter in 1795 and Stothard in 1797. Twelve depictions of this subject were exhibited in London between 1790 and 1830, some with actual references to Gessner, and five indeed between 1819 and 1826, the date of Blake's tempera (see William Vaughan, *German Romanticism and English Art*, 1979, pp.107–9, 259).

69

70

70 **Satan Smiting Job with Sore Boils** *c.*1826

N 03340/B 807
Pen and tempera on mahogany 326 × 432
($12\frac{7}{8}$ × 17)
Signed 'w.BLAKE fecit' incised b.r.
Presented by Miss Mary H. Dodge through
the National Art-Collections Fund 1918

PROVENANCE
George Richmond; Frederick Locker; Sir
Charles Wentworth Dilke, Bt., by 1876; his
son, sold Christie's 10 April 1911 (128)
£157.10.0 bt Carfax; Miss Mary H. Dodge

EXHIBITED
BFAC 1876 (150, as a watercolour); Carfax
1906 (18); Tate Gallery (10), Manchester
(17), Nottingham (11) and Edinburgh (13)
1913–14; *English Painting* Paris 1938 (160);
Paris, Antwerp (pl.6), Zurich (repr.) and Tate
Gallery (repr.) 1947 (7); Arts Council 1951
(15); *The Devil in Figurative Art*, Stedelijk
Museum, Amsterdam, June–September 1952;
Tate Gallery 1978 (313, repr.)

LITERATURE
Robertson in Gilchrist 1907, p.491 no.8 (as a
varnished watercolour); *National Art-Collections
Fund Report for 1918*, 1919, p.36 no.248, repr.;
Binyon 1922, p.17, colour pl.95; Wicksteed
Job 1924, p.122 n.3; Binyon and Keynes *Job*
1935, I, pp.6–8, 28, repr. p.6; Collins Baker in
Huntington Library Bulletin, X, 1936, p.144;
Blunt in *Warburg Journal*, VI, 1943, p.199;
Keynes *Faber Gallery* 1946, pp.5, 14, 24, colour
pl.6; Keynes *Bible* 1957, p.22 no.69, repr.;
Blunt 1959, pp.31, 36–7, 83, pl.55b; Damon
1965, pp.49–50; Lindberg 1973, pp.33
no.XXXI, 227–8 no.6e, pl.20; Bindman 1977,
p.252 n.14; Klonsky 1977, p.109, repr. in
colour; Butlin 1981, pp.551–2 no.807, colour
pl.972; Warner 1984, pp.22, 91, 107, 113, 118,
120–1

This picture is a development of the composition of plate 6 of Blake's Illustrations to the Book of Job, published in March 1826 but probably engraved the previous year (see no.115). Unlike the engraving, and unlike the related compositions in the two preceding series of watercolours, that painted for Thomas Butts in about 1805–6 and that painted for John Linnel in 1821, and unlike the reduced scale drawing made in preparation for the engravings in 1823–5, Satan is shown with wings and the clouds framing the sun are more schematic; the general effect is more monumental and, although the borders of the engraving add further subtleties of meaning, the painting seems to represent the final stage of the composition (for the preceding versions see Butlin 1981 nos.550 *6*, 551 *6* and 557 *17*, colour pl.702 and pls.738 and 766 respectively).

An inscription on the back of the panel reads, 'This drawing by Blake belonged to George Richmond RA Frederick Locker'.

71 Epitome of James Hervey's *Meditations among the Tombs* *c*.1820–5

N 02231 / B 770
Pen and watercolour 431 × 292 (16$\frac{15}{16}$ × 11$\frac{1}{2}$)
Signed 'WBlake inv & [?] ...' b.l. with traces of at least two further characters and the possibility that more were lost when the lower edge of the drawing was trimmed; for other inscriptions see text below
Given by G.T. Saul to the National Gallery 1878; transferred to the Tate Gallery 1909

PROVENANCE
Thomas Butts; Thomas Butts jun., sold Foster's 29 June 1853 (135, as 'One from Hervey's Meditations') £2.10.0 bt Money; G.T. Saul

EXHIBITED
BFAC 1876 (69); Tate Gallery (58), Manchester (54), Nottingham (35) and Edinburgh (27) 1913–14; *Opening Exhibition* Graves Art Gallery, Sheffield 1934 (633); *British Painting* Hamburg, Oslo, Stockholm and Copenhagen 1945–50 (4); *English Water-Colours* Norwich 1955 (29); *Masters of British Painting* New York, St Louis and San Francisco 1956–7 (7, repr. p.55); Tate Gallery 1978 (314, repr. in colour)

LITERATURE
Rossetti 1863, p.255 list 3 no.19, and 1880, p.245 no.229; Robertson in Gilchrist 1907, p.494 no.17; Figgis 1925, at pl.89, repr.; Blunt in *Warburg Journal*, VI, 1943, p.201; Damon 1965, pp.3, 65, 126, 183–5, 409, pl.11; Tolley in *Blake Newsletter*, VI, 1972–3, p.30; Mellor 1974, pp.243–6, pl.64; Bindman 1977, pp.118, 120–1, 169–70, 242 n.20, pl.98; Mitchell 1978, pp.64–6, 69, 73; Paley 1978, p.181, pl.88; Butlin in *Blake*, XIII, 1979–80, p.21; Butlin 1981, p.536 no.770, colour pl.967. *Also repr: Blake Studies*, VI, no.2, 1975, insert in colour; *Mizue*, no.882, 1978, 9, p.37 in colour

James Hervey (1714–58) was a Calvinist and a popular devotional writer. His *Meditations among the Tombs* was first published in 1746 but reappeared frequently in new editions well into the nineteenth century. Blake knew it as early as 1784–5, when he mentioned it together with Edward Young's *Night Thoughts* in *An Island in the Moon* (Keynes *Writings* 1957, p.52), but the watercolour is considerably later. Stylistically it follows, probably by a number of years, his various paintings of the 'Last Judgment' and similar subjects of 1806–8 (see, for example, Butlin 1981 nos.639 and 642, pls.868 and 870); in its smooth finish and dark glowing colouring it resembles Blake's reworkings for Linnell and Lawrence of 'The Wise and Foolish Virgins' in the 1820s (see no.72). Like Blake's other complex compositions of many figures both the general composition and certain individual motifs are derived from Michelangelo's 'Last Judgment' in the Sistine Chapel, a work known to Blake through engravings and greatly admired by him.

Hervey appears in *Jerusalem*, *c*.1804–15, as one of the guards of 'the Four-fold Gate Towards Beulah ... with all the gentle Souls Who guide the great Wine-press of Love' (plate 72; Keynes *Writings* 1957, p.712). His book consists mainly of reflections on mortality and the Resurrection and particularly on the pathos of the

71

separations caused by early deaths. The ecclesiastical setting of Blake's watercolour and the identification of the resurrected figures are largely based on Hervey's text, but the central vision and the presence of Hervey himself between two angels were introduced by Blake.

Practically every figure is identified by an inscription (Damon gives a key facing pl.11 but this is not completely accurate). In the foreground 'Hervey' is seen from behind between an 'Angel of Providence' and a 'Guardian Angel', standing before an altar which bears the Eucharistic bread and wine. Above he sees a sequence of incidents from the Old Testament arranged on a spiral staircase. At the top of this vision appears God the Father with a scroll; then 'Adam', 'Eve' and the 'Serpent'; 'Cain' and 'Abel' as children; 'Enoch'; 'Noah' with his Ark; the 'Mother of Leah & Rachel' and the 'Mother of Rebecca'; 'Abraham believed God', with Isaac; 'Aaron'; 'David'; and 'Solomon'. The sequence culminates in the Transfiguration group, 'Jesus' flanked by 'Moses' and 'Elias', directly over the altar.

Above God the Father is the source of the fire that fills much of the upper part of the picture, with the inscription 'God out of Christ is a Consuming Fire', a variant of Hebrews, xii, 29, quoted by Calvinists to prove the existence of Hell. In the two upper corners appear 'MERCY' and 'WRATH'.

On the left of the picture a number of figures rise towards Mercy, assisted by 'Ministering Angels'. Starting at the bottom, where there is a font labelled 'Baptism', they are accompanied by the words 'Old Age', 'Babe', 'Wife', 'Husband', 'Infancy', 'Where is your Father' and 'These died for Love'.

On the right two 'Angel[s] of Death', two 'Protecting Angel[s]' and a group of 'Recording Angels' escort the resurrected 'Virgin', 'Widow', 'Father', 'Mother', 'The Lost Child', 'Sophronia Died in Childbed', 'Orphan', 'She died on the Wedding Day' and 'orphans'.

As Mellor points out, Blake's representation of God the Father now represents righteous anger, dispensing Wrath but tempered by Mercy, and in this respect can be distinguished from representations in earlier works by Blake when He was seen as the embodiment of negative religion. He appears above Christ, who stands between Moses, representing the Law, and Elias, representing Divine Vision. On the staircase that links them the Old Testament figures demonstrate ways in which we can, and cannot, achieve salvation.

There are two possible sketches for this composition on a sheet in the National Gallery of Art, Washington, D.C. (Lessing J. Rosenwald Collection) (Butlin no.771, pls.997 and 998). The recto shows an ascending spiral of figures, as in the centre of the Tate Gallery's watercolour. On the back there is a drawing of a seated figure shown full-face which could well be a sketch for God the Father enthroned above the spiral, though the figure here is younger and more Christ-like than in the watercolour, with only a short beard clinging to his chin; his hands are held open by his knees as if to display the Stigmata, and there is an open book rather than a scroll across his knees. The style of both drawings supports a dating in the 1820s.

COPY AFTER BLAKE

72 **The Parable of the Wise and Foolish Virgins**

N 05196/–
Pen and watercolour 400 × 332 (15¾ × 13⅛)
Bequeathed by Miss Alice G.E. Carthew 1940

PROVENANCE
…; Lord Coleridge; Lady Coleridge, sold
anonymously Christie's 12 December 1898
(61) £23.2.0 bt Messrs Dunthorne, sold 1899
to Miss Carthew

EXHIBITED
Carfax 1904 (not in catalogue; letter in Tate
Gallery files); Bradford 1904 (399); Tate
Gallery (25), Manchester (24), Nottingham
(17) and Edinburgh (21) 1913–14; BFAC
1927 (22, pl.17); *English Painting* Brussels 1929
(3, pl.25); *British Art* RA 1934 (783, pl.86;

710, pl.164); Paris and Vienna 1937 (8);
Wartime Acquisitions National Gallery 1942
(16); *British Drawings from the Tate Gallery*
CEMA tour 1944 (5); Paris (repr. in colour
facing p.18), Antwerp (repr. in colour as
frontispiece), Zurich and Tate Gallery 1947
(14); *Masters of British Painting* New York, St
Louis and San Francisco 1956–7 (8, repr.
p.56)

LITERATURE
Keynes *Faber Gallery* 1946, pp.5–6, colour
pl.2; Keynes *Bible* 1957, p.38 no.130d repr.;
Blunt 1959, p.73; Butlin 1981, p.355, under
no.481. *Also repr*: Binyon 1922, pl.1922, pl.85
in colour

The subject is from Matthew xxv, 1–9. Although this watercolour was long
accepted as a genuine work by William Blake, and indeed was much reproduced
and exhibited (as listed above, with many further reproductions), it was recognized
in the second edition of this catalogue (1971, p.54 no.44 repr.) as a copy after a
version of this subject painted for Sir Thomas Lawrence in about 1825 (Butlin 1981
no.481, colour pl.569). According to Gilchrist (1863, I, p.357) the original was one
of two replicas after earlier compositions commissioned by Lawrence for 15 guineas
each, the other being 'The Vision of Queen Katherine' (Butlin no.549, pl.589); he
states that they were among 'the last drawings executed, or at least finished by
Blake'. There is evidence that Blake was at the same dinner party as Lawrence at
Lady Caroline Lamb's on either 20 January 1818 or 20 June 1820, and visited him
with John Linnell on 13 July 1822 (Bentley *Blake Records* 1969, pp.249–50, 277).
Lawrence was also among those who defended Blake's illustrations to Thornton's
Virgil (see nos.73–89). The replicas painted for Lawrence presumably date from
this period or, bearing in mind Gilchrist's suggestion of a very late date, later, say
c.1825. Lawrence's watercolours are now in a private collection and the National
Gallery of Art, Washington, respectively.

Blake seems to have painted no fewer than three other versions of 'The Parable of
the Wise and Foolish Virgins' before that commissioned by Lawrence. The first was
one of the series of biblical subjects painted for Thomas Butts and was apparently
delivered to him on 12 May 1805; it is now in the Metropolitan Museum of Art,
New York (Butlin no.478, colour pl.566). The second was painted for John
Linnell, according to William Rossetti in 1822, and is now in the Fitzwilliam
Museum, Cambridge (Butlin no.479, colour pl.567). A close variation of this was
painted for William Haines a year or two later and is now in the Yale Center for
British Art, Paul Mellon Collection, New Haven (Butlin no.480, colour pl.568).

As well as this copy after the Lawrence version there is a copy seemingly in the
same hand of the second version, that painted for John Linnell, in the Santa
Barbara Museum of Art (see Alfred Moir, ed., *European Drawings in the Collection of*

72

the Santa Barbara Museum of Art, 1976, p.126, repr.; also repr. Keynes *Bible* 1957 no.130e in mistake for the Yale Center version). Both can be attributed, for stylistic reasons, to John Linnell or one of his family or pupils; Linnell is known to have trained his pupils, who included a number of his sons, by setting them to copy works by Blake.

The reference by Bentley (1961, p.400 n.2) to Miss Carthew as being the granddaughter of John Poynder is a result of a misreading of the Tate Gallery exhibition catalogue of 1913, which refers to the Lawrence watercolour, then in the collection of the Poynder family, as another version of that lent to the exhibition by Miss Carthew.

73–89 Illustrations to Thornton's *Pastorals of Virgil* 1821/*c*.1830

A 01111–27/–
Seventeen wood-engravings on commercial
thin wove paper
Presented by Herbert Linnell 1924

PROVENANCE
John Linnell: by descent to Herbert Linnell

LITERATURE
[Henry Cole] 'Fine Arts, *The Vicar of Wakefield,
With thirty-two Illustrations*. By W. Mulready,
R.A. van Voorst', *Athenaeum* 21 January 1843,
p.165; Gilchrist 1863, I, pp.270–5; A.H.
Palmer *Life and Letters of Samuel Palmer* 1892,
p.15; Russell *Engravings* 1912, pp.97–101
no.30; Keynes *Bibliography* 1921, pp.211–14
no.778; Geoffrey Keynes *Illustrations of William*
Blake for Thornton's Virgil 1937; Keynes
Engravings 1950, pp.15–16, series repr.
pls.I–XVII; Raine 1968, II, pp.279–80; Bentley
Blake Records 1969, pp.266–8, 271–3, 582;
Keynes *Blake Studies* 1971, pp.136–42, 215–16;
Easson and Essick, I, 1972, pp.48–50 no.X,
series repr.; Bentley *Blake Books* 1977,
pp.627–30 no.504; Iain Bain, David
Chambers and Andrew Wilton *The Wood
Engravings of William Blake for Thornton's Virgil*
1977, published with restrikes (see
nos.90–106); Bindman 1977, pp.204–5;
Bindman *Graphic Works* 1978, p.485,
nos.602–18, series repr.; Paley 1978, p.69;
Essick *Printmaker* 1980, pp.224–33; Butlin
1981, pp.532–5

These are separate impressions from Blake's original wood-blocks, probably made by Edward Calvert (1799–1883), one of the Ancients who gathered round Blake in his later years and also a friend of John Linnell, for Linnell who actually owned the blocks. For a more recent set of impressions see nos.90–106.

Blake's wood-engravings were commissioned by Dr Robert John Thornton through John Linnell, whose doctor he was. Blake first met Thornton in September 1818 and by September 1820 Blake was actually working on the engravings which were commissioned for the third edition of Dr Thornton's *The Pastorals of Virgil . . . adapted for Schools*, published in 1821; the first unillustrated edition had been published in 1812. Beside these seventeen engravings after his own designs for Ambrose Philips's 'Imitation of Virgil's First Eclogue', Blake engraved on copper five busts of Theocritus, Virgil, Caesar Augustus, Julius Caesar and Epicurus, and a group of five medallion heads 'From Antique Coins'. In addition, he is credited with the drawing of 'The Giant Polypheme' after Poussin that was engraved by Byfield; however, Linnell wrote in his Journal on 18 October 1820 that he himself 'Began a small Drawing on a wood Block of Polypheme (from N. Poussin) for Dr Thornton' and that he was 'to receive a guinea for it' (Bentley 1977, p.629). The *Pastorals* contain 232 illustrations in all.

The existence, if not the present location, of twenty of Blake's original drawings for the illustrations to Philips's 'Imitation' is known (see Butlin 1981 no.769; nos.1–4, 6–11, 13–17 and 19–20 are repr. pls.999, 999A, 1000–1014). Of Blake's designs no.4, 'Colinet and Thenot stand together conversing, their sheep behind' (Pierpont Morgan Library, New York) was not engraved. No drawing for the frontispiece, which is larger in format and shows Thenot and Colinet, has been recorded. Some of Blake's other engravings where lost as a result of Dr Thornton's dissatisfaction; indeed, only a chance conversation between Sir Thomas Lawrence, James Ward, Linnell and others at Mr Ader's prevented all of them from being recut by a commercial engraver. Three, corresponding to the drawings Butlin nos.769 *14–16*, did suffer this fate (repr. Bentley 1969, pl.41). The design no.769 *2* was also recut (repr. *Athenaeum* 21 January 1843, p.165, and Keynes 1971, pl.35) but in this case Blake's original engraving was retained. In the end Thornton published Blake's engravings with the disclaimer that 'they display less of art than genius, and are much admired by some eminent painters'.

Apart from the frontispiece, Blake cut his designs four on a block and proofs of eight of the designs from two blocks are in the British Museum and elsewhere. When they came to be printed in the book they were indeed printed four to a page but simple captions were placed under each design; this entailed cutting each design by about $\frac{3}{16} \times \frac{3}{8}$ (4×9).

On 16 September 1825 John Linnell bought the blocks from Dr Thornton for two guineas and, according to a manuscript 'List' of Linnell's 'Letters and Papers' by John Linnell jr (in the Ivimy MSS), 'E. Calvert printed them for J.L. & self, &c (certain number of imprints of the set) (J.L. jnr & brother printed a few of the blocks, but did not finish the set)'. Calvert's printings were apparently done soon after Blake's death, both for Calvert himself and Linnell. As the set of impressions presented to the Tate Gallery by Henry Linnell in 1924 is complete, it was presumably one of those printed by Calvert.

The blocks themselves were rediscovered in 1937, still in the possession of Linnell's descendants, by Sir Geoffrey Keynes, who had electrotypes made from them and printed from these electrotypes for his edition of *The Illustrations of William Blake for Thornton's Virgil* published that year. The blocks were sold from the Linnell estate at Christie's on 2 December 1938 and presented by the National Art-Collections Fund to the British Museum (accession nos. 1939–14–1–2 to 18).

These tiny woodcut illustrations, though untypical of Blake's art as a whole, were the most influential of all his works on other artists by way of the work of the Ancients, particularly Calvert and Samuel Palmer. As Samuel Palmer wrote (A.H. Palmer 1892): 'I sat down with Mr. Blake's Thornton's *Virgil* woodcuts before me, thinking to give their merits my feeble testimony. I happened first to think of their sentiment. They are visions of little dells, and nooks, and corners of Paradise; models of the exquisitest pitch of intense poetry. I thought of their light and shade, and looking upon them I found no word to describe it. Intense depth, solemnity, and vivid brilliancy only coldly and partially describe them. There is in all such a mystic and dreamy glimmer as penetrates and kindles the innermost soul, and gives complete and unreserved delight, unlike the gaudy daylight of this world. They are like all that wonderful artist's works the drawing aside of the fleshy curtain, and the glimpse which all the most holy, studious saints and sages have enjoyed, of that rest which remaineth to the people of God'. The influence of the designs extended well into the twentieth century, for instance in the early etchings of Graham Sutherland.

These works were formerly inventoried as nos. 3866 i–xvii.

73 Frontispiece: Thenot and Colinet

Wood-engraving 62×84 ($2\frac{7}{16} \times 3\frac{5}{16}$) on paper
65×87 ($2\frac{9}{16} \times 3\frac{3}{8}$)

As Dr Thornton wrote in his introduction to Philips's 'Imitation of Virgil's First Eclogue', 'THENOT is the *happy* and COLINET the unhappy *shepherd*'. Thenot addresses the younger Colinet with the experience of age.

Unlike the other designs, there is no record of a preliminary drawing for this composition in the Linnell collection.

74 Plate 2: Thenot Remonstrates with Colinet

Wood-engraving 38×74 ($1\frac{1}{2} \times 2\frac{7}{8}$) on paper
40×76 ($1\frac{9}{16} \times 2\frac{9}{16}$)

Thenot chides Colinet for being so mournful 'when all things smile around', to which Colinet replies that it is his sad lot, unlike the lark and the linnet, to mourn.

The drawing for this design was in the collection of Sir Geoffrey Keynes (Butlin no. 769 *1*, pl. 999).

75 **Plate 3: Thenot and Colinet Converse Seated between Two Trees**

Wood-engraving 33 × 75 ($1\frac{5}{16}$ × $2\frac{9}{16}$) on paper
35 × 77 ($1\frac{3}{8}$ × 3)

Thenot describes his own body bowing down as 'trees beneath their fruit in autumn bend', and this is illustrated literally by Blake.

The drawing cannot be traced since it was exhibited in Philadelphia in 1939 (132) (Butlin no. 769 2, pl. 999A). This was one of the designs that Thornton had re-engraved, in reverse, but in this case Blake's own engraving was in fact used in the book.

76 **Plate 4: Thenot Remonstrates with Colinet; Lightfoot in the Distance.**

Wood-engraving 33 × 73 ($1\frac{5}{16}$ × $2\frac{7}{8}$) on paper
35 × 75 ($1\frac{3}{8}$ × $2\frac{15}{16}$)

Colinet declares that it will take all day to recite his woes and that as a result Thenot's flocks will be neglected. Thenot replies that his man Lightfoot can guard them while 'I 'tween whiles, across the plain will glance mine eyes'.

The drawing for this design belongs to Mr and Mrs Arthur Vershbow, Newport, Massachusetts (Butlin no. 769 3, pl. 1000). The small figure of Lightfoot in the distance recalls those of the messengers in the illustration to Job, 'And I only am escaped alone to tell thee' (no. 113).

77 **Plate 5: Thenot, with Colinet Waving his Arms in Sorrow**

Wood-engraving 36 × 73 ($1\frac{7}{16}$ × $2\frac{15}{16}$) on paper
39 × 76 ($1\frac{9}{16}$ × 3)

Colinet begins the recital of his griefs by comparing his plight with 'Yonder naked tree, which bears the thunder-scar too plain, I see'.

The drawing for this design has not been traced since it was bought at the American Art Association on 22 April 1924 (69) by the Brick Row Bookshop, New York (Butlin no. 769 5).

78 **Plate 6: The Blighted Corn**

Wood-engraving 34 × 73 ($1\frac{3}{8}$ × $2\frac{7}{8}$) on paper
36 × 74 ($1\frac{7}{16}$ × $2\frac{15}{16}$)

Thenot agrees with Colinet that he was born in a 'hapless hour of time... when blightning mildews spoil the rising corn, or blasting winds o'er blossom'd hedge-rows pass, to kill the promis'd fruits...'.

The drawing was in the collection of Sir Geoffrey Keynes (Butlin no. 769 6, pl. 1002).

79 **Plate 7: 'Nor Fox, nor Wolf, nor Rat among our Sheep'**

Wood-engraving 35×73 ($1\frac{3}{8} \times 2\frac{7}{8}$) on paper
37×76 ($1\frac{7}{16} \times 3$)

Thenot continues in his comforting of Colinet by saying that not even a good shepherd can preserve his flock against fox or wolf.

The drawing is in the Beinecke Rare Book and Manuscript Library, Yale University, New Haven, Connecticut (Butlin no. 769 7, pl. 1003).

80 **Plate 8: Sabrina's Silvery Flood**

Wood-engraving 33×72 ($1\frac{5}{6} \times 2\frac{7}{8}$) on paper
35×75 ($2\frac{3}{8} \times 2\frac{15}{16}$)

Colinet regrets that he 'left, Sabrina fair, thy silvery flood', a reference to the naiad associated with the River Severn.

The drawing, formerly in the collection of Mr and Mrs Anton G. Hardy, U.S.A., is now in the Department of Printing and Graphic Arts of the Houghton Library, Harvard University (Butlin no. 769 *8*, pl. 1004).

81 **Plate 9: Colinet's 'Fond Desire Strange Lands to Know'**

Wood-engraving 37×74 ($1\frac{7}{16} \times 2\frac{7}{8}$) on paper
37×74 ($1\frac{7}{16} \times 2\frac{7}{8}$)

Colinet is shown passing a milestone marked 'LXII miles to London', following his 'fond desire strange lands and swains to know'.

The drawing is in the Houghton Library, Harvard University, Cambridge, Massachusetts (Butlin no. 769 *9*, pl. 1005).

82 **Plate 10: 'A Rolling Stone is ever Bare of Moss'**

Wood-engraving 33×77 ($1\frac{1}{4} \times 3$) on paper
34×78 ($1\frac{5}{16} \times 3\frac{1}{16}$).

Thenot points to the moral in the previous design, 'A rolling stone is ever bare of moss', a chance for Blake to show some unfortunate rolling a path contrary to nature in front of a rationally designed classical house.

The drawing is in the Pierpont Morgan Library, New York (Butlin no. 769 *10*, pl. 1006).

83 **Plate 11: Colinet Rests by a Stream at Night**

Wood-engraving 33×75 ($1\frac{5}{16} \times 2\frac{15}{16}$) on paper
35×77 ($1\frac{3}{8} \times 3$)

Colinet's wanderings have taken him to Cambridge, where Blake shows King's College Chapel rising above the trees on the left.

The drawing has not been traced since it was reproduced in Keynes *Drawings* in 1927 (Butlin no. 769 *11*, pl. 1007).

84 **Plate 12: Colinet with his Shepherd's Pipe, Mocked by Two Boys**

Wood-engraving 36×77 ($1\frac{3}{8} \times 3$) on paper
39×78 ($1\frac{9}{16} \times 3\frac{1}{16}$)

Worse still, Colinet complains, no 'pinching cold' was as bad as the 'blasting storms of calumny', or 'Untoward lads' making 'mock of all the ditties I endite'.

The drawing has not been traced since its purchase by the Brick Row Bookshop in 1924 (Butlin no. 769 *12*).

85 **Plate 13: 'For him Our Yearly Wakes and Feasts We Hold'**

Wood-engraving 35×75 ($1\frac{3}{8} \times 2\frac{15}{16}$) on paper
38×78 ($1\frac{1}{2} \times 3\frac{1}{16}$)

Unlike the mocking boys, Menalcas, 'Lord of these fair fertile plains...seems to like my simple strain', and Blake shows one of the 'yearly wakes and feasts' held for Menalcas by his shepherds.

The drawing is untraced since it was exhibited at Philadelphia in 1939 (*134*) (Butlin no. 769 *13*, pl. 1008).

Plates 14, 15 and 16, though based on drawings by Blake (Butlin nos. 769 *14–16*, pls. 1009–11), were the designs that Thornton had engraved by another hand.

86 **Plate 17: Thenot and Colinet Folding their Flocks together at Sunset**

Wood-engraving 36×76 ($1\frac{7}{16} \times 3$) on paper
38×78 ($1\frac{9}{16} \times 3\frac{1}{16}$)

After their discussion Thenot proposes to Colinet, as consolation, to 'fold thy flock with mine'.

The drawing is untraced since its reproduction in Keynes *Drawings* 1927 (Butlin no. 769 *17*, pl. 1012).

87 **Plate 18: Thenot and Colinet at Supper**

Wood-engraving 35×76 ($1\frac{3}{8} \times 3$) on paper
37×78 ($1\frac{7}{16} \times 3\frac{1}{16}$)

Thenot, in addition to inviting Colinet to fold his flocks with his own, invites him to share 'New milk and clouted cream, mild cheese and curd, with some remaining fruit of last year's hoard'.

The drawing has not been traced since it was acquired by the Brick Row Bookshop in 1924 (Butlin no. 769 *18*).

88 **Plate 19: 'With Songs the Jovial Hinds Return from Plow'**

Wood-engraving 35×75 ($1\frac{3}{8} \times 3$) on paper
37×77 ($1\frac{7}{16} \times 3\frac{1}{16}$)

Thenot bids Colinet to 'now behold the sun's departing ray, o'er yonder hill, the sign of ebbing day; with songs the jovial hinds return from plow'.

The drawing for this design belongs to Edmund Astley Prentis, U.S.A. (Butlin no. 769 *19*, pl. 1013).

89 **Plate 20: 'And Unyok'd Heifers, Loitering Homeward, Low'**

Wood-engraving 33×77 ($1\frac{5}{16} \times 3$) on paper
34×78 ($1\frac{5}{16} \times 3\frac{1}{16}$)

This illustrates the line following the verses quoted under the last entry, 'And unyok'd heifers, loitering homeward, low'.

The drawing is in the Art Museum, Princeton University, Princeton, New Jersey (Butlin no. 769 *20*, pl. 1014).

90–106 **Illustrations to Thorton's *Pastorals of Virgil*: Restrikes** 1821/1977

T 02115–31 /–.
Seventeen wood-engravings on Japanese
Hosho paper, each sheet approx. 121×153
($4\frac{3}{4} \times 6$)
Presented by British Museum Publications
Ltd through Iain Bain and David Chambers
1977

PROVENANCE
Printed for the donors 1977

EXHIBITED
Tate Gallery 1978 (287–303, repr.)

LITERATURE
As for Nos. 73–89

Blake's woodblocks for his illustrations to Ambrose Philip's 'Imitation of Virgil's First Eclogue' in Dr Thornton's *Pastorals of Virgil...Adapted for Schools* were acquired by the British Museum in 1939 (1939–14–1–2 to 18). In 1977 one hundred and fifty sets of the seventeen engravings, together with an additional fifty impressions of the larger frontispiece, were printed for the British Museum by Iain Bain and David Chambers. The efforts taken to produce the optimum results are described in their introduction to the publication that goes with the restrikes. Despite some damages and warping certain details and gradations of tone were revealed which had not been picked out either in the early printings or in those from the electrotypes.

90 **Frontispiece: Thenot and Colinet**

Wood-engraving 61×83 ($2\frac{7}{16} \times 3\frac{1}{4}$)

91 **Plate 2: Thenot Remonstrates with Colinet**

Wood-engraving 38×74 ($1\frac{1}{2} \times 2\frac{7}{8}$)

92 **Plate 3: Thenot and Colinet Converse Seated between Two Trees**

Wood-engraving 33×75 ($1\frac{5}{16} \times 2\frac{9}{16}$)

93 **Plate 4: Thenot Remonstrates with Colinet; Lightfoot in the Distance**

Wood-engraving 33×73 ($1\frac{5}{16} \times 2\frac{7}{8}$)

94 **Plate 5: Thenot, with Colinet Waving his Arms in Sorrow**

Wood-engraving 36 × 73 ($1\frac{7}{16}$ × $2\frac{15}{16}$)

95 **Plate 6: The Blighted Corn**

Wood-engraving 34 × 73 ($1\frac{3}{8}$ × $2\frac{7}{8}$)

96 **Plate 7: 'Nor Fox, nor Wolf, nor Rat among our Sheep'**

Wood-engraving 35 × 73 ($1\frac{3}{8}$ × $2\frac{7}{8}$)

97 **Plate 8: Sabrina's Silvery Flood**

Wood engraving 33 × 73 ($1\frac{5}{16}$ × $2\frac{7}{8}$)

98 **Plate 9: Colinet's 'Fond Desire Strange Lands to Know'**

Wood-engraving 36 × 73 ($1\frac{7}{16}$ × $2\frac{7}{8}$)

99 **Plate 10: 'A Rolling Stone is ever Bare of Moss'**

Wood-engraving 32 × 76 ($1\frac{1}{4}$ × 3)

100 **Plate 11: Colinet Rests by a Stream at Night**

Wood-engraving 32 × 75 ($1\frac{1}{4}$ × $2\frac{15}{16}$)

101 **Plate 12: Colinet with his Shepherd's Pipe, Mocked by Two Boys**

Wood-engraving 36 × 77 ($1\frac{3}{8}$ × 3)

102 **Plate 13: 'For him Our Yearly Wakes and Feasts We Hold'**

Wood-engraving 35 × 75 ($1\frac{3}{8}$ × $2\frac{15}{16}$)

103 **Plate 17: Thenot and Colinet Folding their Flocks together at Sunset**

Wood-engraving 36 × 76 ($1\frac{7}{16}$ × 3)

104 **Plate 18: Thenot and Colinet at Supper**

Wood-engraving 35 × 76 ($1\frac{3}{8}$ × 3)

105 **Plate 19: 'With Songs the Jovial Hinds Return from Plow'**

Wood-engraving 33 × 77 ($1\frac{5}{16}$ × 3)

106 **Plate 20: 'And Unyok'd Heifers, Loitering Homeward, Low'**

Wood-engraving 33 × 77 ($1\frac{5}{16}$ × 3)

90

91

92

93

94

95

101

96

102

97

103

98

104

99

105

100

106

107

107 **The Crucifixion** *c*.1825–7

A 00046/B 798
Pencil, approx. 415 × 245 (16¼ × 9¾), on paper
432 × 276 (17 × 10⅞)
Inscribed by Frederick Tatham 'First design
William Blake./ Crucifixion – very curious
shewing how he/ began/Frederick Tatham'
b.r.
Presented by Mr John Richmond 1922

PROVENANCE
Mrs Blake; Frederick Tatham; his brother-in-
law George Richmond, sold Christie's 29 April
1897 (in 147 with 22 other items; see no. 2)
£2.10.0 bt Dr Richard Sisley; his daughter
Mrs John Richmond

LITERATURE
Butlin 1981, p.546 no.798, pl.1033

This rough pencil sketch is not related to any other known depiction of the
Crucifixion by Blake. The nervous lines suggest that this is a late work. It can be
related to some of the more sketchy of the illustrations to Dante such as no.149 and
to the drawings illustrating the Book of Enoch done at about the same time (Butlin
1981, no.827, pls.1079–83).

Above the figure of the Crucified there is another figure with arms upraised with
a very roughly sketched form rising from one hand, and on each side the sun and
moon, shaded and, in the case of the moon, apparently dripping with blood. Some
Apocalyptic interpretation of the subject is presumably involved. There are the
usual mourning figures below.

This work was formerly inventoried by the Tate Gallery as no.3694 xix.

ILLUSTRATIONS TO THE BOOK OF JOB

c.1821–1826

In all Blake executed three more or less finished series of illustrations to the Book of Job, together with a number of related works. First there was a set of watercolour illustrations, painted for Thomas Butts, apart from two later additions to the series, c.1805–6 (Butlin 1981, no.550, colour pls.697–717). In 1821 John Linnell commissioned a duplicate set, painted by Blake over outlines copied from the Butts series by Linnell (Butlin no.551, pls733–753). The Linnell set consists of 21 illustrations and it seems that it was at this time, or even slightly later, that the Butts series was increased from an original total of 19 compositions to the same number. In 1823 Linnell commissioned a set of engravings which, though dated 1825, were not in fact completed until 1826. This consists of the same 21 subjects plus a title-page, though among the works executed in connection with this scheme there are studies for an alternative composition for the subject of 'Every Man also Gave him a Piece of Money'. These related works are a group of watercolours of the early 1820s done either in connection with those compositions that were added or most varied in the Linnell series of watercolours or in connection with the engravings (Butlin nos.552–556, pls.718, 754–7), and a sketchbook containing 27 drawings for the engraved illustrations (together with other drawings) done in 1823 (Butlin no.557, pls.758–86); in addition there is a separate sketch for the engraved title-page (Butlin no.558, pl.787) and a group of proof engravings with rough drawings suggesting the marginal decorations added round the main compositions for the engravings (Butlin no.559, pls.788–93). The Tate Gallery owns one of the watercolour sketches of the early 1820s, for the alternative composition of 'Every Man also Gave him a Piece of Money', and a posthumous set of the engravings. The collection also includes a tempera painting of c.1826 based on the composition 'Satan Smiting Job with Sore Boils' (no.70).

Blake re-interpreted the Biblical story of Job to give a less arbitrary reason for Job's sufferings. For Blake these were explained and justified as the result of Job's concentration on the observance rather than the inspiration of religion. The contrasted details of the first and last designs, which are given particular emphasis by the otherwise similar compositions of the two works, clearly express this: in the first design musical instruments hang unplayed on the tree as the sun sets behind a large church representing established religion, while in the final design Job and his family stand playing the musical instruments as the sun rises behind them. In the last stage of the evolution of the designs, the engravings, Blake added the marginal designs with texts which stress and add further subtleties to his own personal interpretation.

A recent article by Robert N. Essick, analysing for the first time a group of pre-publication proofs of the Job engravings sold in 1936 but now untraced, has shown that the earliest border texts to the first design, later deleted, showed it in a far more positive light, in particular the words 'Prayer to God is the Study of Imaginative Art', parallelling an early text for the last design reading 'Praise to God is the Exercise of Imaginative Art'. It seems therefore that Blake only evolved the final development of his theme, given above, as he worked on the engravings.

LITERATURE
Joseph H. Wicksteed *Blake's Vision of the Book of Job* 1910, revised edition 1924; Damon 1924, pp.223–38; Laurence Binyon and Geoffrey Keynes *Illustrations of the Book of Job* 1935; Blunt 1959, pp.83–7; Damon 1965, pp.217–23; S. Foster Damon *Blake's Job* 1966;

Raine 1968, II, pp.258–61; Beer 1969, pp.269–74; Bentley *Blake Records* 1969, pp.273–4, 277–8, 300, 305–6, 321, 326–9, 332–3, 335–7, 395; Northrop Frye, 'Blake's Reading of the Book of Job', Rosenfeld 1969, pp.221–34; Ben F. Nelms, 'Text and Design in *Illustrations of the Book of Job*', Erdman and

Grant 1970, pp.336–58; Keynes *Blake Studies* 1971, pp.176–86, 206–12, 217–19; Andrew Wright *Blake's Job: A Commentary* 1972; Jenijoy LaBelle, 'Words graven with an Iron Pen: The Marginal Texts in Blake's *Job*', Essick 1973, pp.527–50; Bo Lindberg *William Blake's Illustrations to the Book of Job* 1973; Mellor 1974, pp.249–54; Bentley *Blake Books* 1977, pp.517–24; Bindman 1977, pp.208–14; Bindman *Graphic Works* 1978, pp.486–7; Paley 1978, pp.69–71; Butlin 1981, pp.410–35; Kathleen Raine, *The Human Face of God: William Blake and the Book of Job*, 1982; Robert N. Essick, 'Blake's *Job*: Some Unrecorded Proofs and their Inscriptions', *Blake*, XIX, 1985–6, pp.96–102; David Bindman, ed., *William Blake's Illustrations of the Book of Job* 1987.

108   'Every Man also Gave him a Piece of Money' *c.*1821–3 (recto)

God the Father with Attendant Angels *c.*1821–3 (verso)

T 03233 / B 553

Recto: pencil, pen and watercolour, framing line 228 × 178 (9 × 7); Verso: pencil, approx. 95 × 150 ($3\frac{1}{4}$ × 6); on paper 242 × 190 ($9\frac{1}{2}$ × $7\frac{1}{2}$) Presented by the Friends of the Tate Gallery 1981.

PROVENANCE

?Mrs Blake; ?Frederick Tatham, sold Sotheby's 29 April 1862 (in 176, '"Job Sacrificing for his Friends", three different designs in colours') 15/- bt Col.Gould Weston; Alexander Anderdon Weston by 1876; his widow, sold anonymously Christie's 28 June 1904 (in 8 with another as 'Job surrounded by his family') £11.11.0 bt E. Parsons, sold 1904 to W. Graham Robertson, sold Christie's 22 July 1949 (20) £315 bt Agnew's for Kerrison Preston, sold Sotheby's 21 March 1974 (16, recto repr.) £9,500 bt Colnaghi's, from whom stolen 1976; recovered and offered Sotheby's 19 July 1979 (62, recto repr. in colour) bt in and sold 1981 to the Friends of the Tate Gallery

EXHIBITED

BFAC 1876 (in 188, as 'Job surrounded by his Family'); Bournemouth, Southampton and Brighton 1949 (27); *77th Annual Exhibition of Water Colour Drawings*, Agnew's, January – March 1950 (78); Port Sunlight 1950 (19); Whitworth 1969 (30); Edinburgh 1969 (116); Hamburg and Frankfurt 1975 (204, recto repr.); *English Drawings, Watercolours and Paintings*, Colnaghi's, September – October 1976 (83, recto pl.6).

LITERATURE

Rossetti 1880, p.226 in no.120 as of '1825 (?) – Job surrounded by his Family', framed with another work; Robertson in Gilchrist 1907, p.491 no.6; Russell 1912, p.113; Binyon and Keynes 1935, I, p.42; Preston 1952, pp.138–9 no.50, recto pl.46; Keynes *Drawings*, II, 1956, no.43, recto repr.; Keynes *Bible* 1957, p.22 no.73, recto repr.; Keynes *Drawings* 1970, no.79, recto repr. as frontispiece; Lindberg 1973, pp.22 no.xxiv, 338–9 no.19F; Butlin 1981, pp.423–4 no.553, recto colour pl.718; Martin Butlin, 'A New Acquisition for the Tate and a New Addition to the Catalogue', *Blake*, XV, 1981–2, pp.132–3, recto and verso repr.

The recto is an illustration to the Book of Job, xlii, 11, and is one of three sketches in pencil and watercolour painted by Blake in the early 1820s when he returned to the theme at the instigation of John Linnell who commissioned a second set of watercolours in 1821 (Fogg Art Museum, Harvard University, and elsewhere; Butlin no.551, pls.733–53), and in 1823 engravings of the twenty-one designs plus a title-page; see nos.109–130. Most of the Linnell watercolours were finished by Blake on the basis of outlines copied by Linnell from the Butts set, but in certain cases there are considerable differences between the two series; the other two pencil and watercolour sketches, 'Job's Sacrifice' (City Art Gallery, Leeds; Butlin no.552, pl.754) and 'Job and his Daughters' (sold Christie's 10 July 1984 (225, repr. in colour); Butlin no.556, pl.757), seem to have been painted by Blake to help him in such cases.

The Tate watercolour, however, is a sketch for an alternative composition of the nineteenth design, an upright composition instead of an oblong one and with Job and his wife placed centrally, with people bringing them gifts from each side in a vaguely symmetrical composition, instead of being seated on the right with the gift-bearers on the left; above, Blake has added God the Father, soaring aloft in an

108(recto)

108(verso)

energetic circle of clouds and angels. Blake developed this upright composition in a pencil, pen and wash drawing (British Museum 1894–6–12–13; Butlin no.554, pl.755) and in the sketchbook containing rough, reduced-size pencil drawings for the engravings (Fitzwilliam Museum, Cambridge; Butlin no.557 *43*, pl.779); Job and his wife are now shown seated at the foot of a tree. However, in the end Blake reverted to the original oblong composition for the engraved plate.

Graham Robertson (as reported by Kerrison Preston, *loc.cit.*) states that, when he owned the drawing, 'behind the earthly group the sky glows faintly with tender gold and rose, till rising higher it frames the Angelic Vision in softest blue'. Now only the blue can be seen, and not even a trace of the 'tender gold and rose' can be detected by the Tate Gallery's Conservation Department. Graham Robertson described similar colours in 'Job and his Daughters' (*ibid.*, p.140 no.51), but again only the blue remains. However, in the case of 'Job's Sacrifice' most of the colours he describes (*ibid.*, p.136 no.49) can still be seen. Blue is usually the first colour to fade from a Blake watercolour, so the discrepancy between Graham Robertson's accounts and the present states of "Every Man also Gave him a Piece of Money" and 'Job and his Daughters' is difficult to explain.

The pencil sketch on the reverse seems to be an alternative idea for the group of God the Father with attendant angels on the recto; it is placed relatively low on the paper which precludes it from being the beginning of an alternative sketch of the whole composition. God the Father now holds a large scroll which forms an arc above His head, and there are fewer angels.

This work was sold in 1904 from the Gould Weston collection in the same lot as the pencil and watercolour sketch of 'Job and his Daughters' already referred to. It can therefore be presumed to be the work described by William Rossetti in 1880 as being framed with that work, and also the work exhibited with that work in 1876. Both works, together with the Leeds 'Job's Sacrifice', can therefore also be presumed to be the works sold by Frederick Tatham in 1862, and hence to have a provenance back to the artist's widow.

109–130 **Illustrations to *The Book of Job*: Engravings** 1823–6/1874

A 00012–32 /–
Twenty-two line engravings on india paper
laid on drawing paper approx. 510 × 345
(20 × 13½)
Purchased with the assistance of a special
grant from the National Gallery and
donations from the National Art-Collections
Fund, Lord Duveen and others, and presented
through the National Art-Collections Fund
1919

PROVENANCE
John Linnell; his heirs, sold Christie's 15
March 1918 (183) £33.12.0. bt Martin for the
donors

LITERATURE
Gilchrist 1863, I, pp.283–4, 297; Wicksteed
1910 and 1924; Russell *Engravings* 1912,
102–15 no.33: Keynes *Bibliography* 1921,
pp.179–82 no.55: Binyon and Keynes 1935,
series repr.vol.VI; Keynes *Engravings* 1950,
pp.16–17, series repr.pls. 42–68; Keynes
Writings 1957, pp.869–70, 872, 874, 876–7;
S. Foster Damon, *Blake's Job* 1966, series
repr.; Bentley *Blake Records* 1969, pp.234 n.i,
277–397 *passim*, 586–605; Andrew Wright
Blake's Job: A Commentary 1972, series repr.;
Lindberg 1973, pp.24–32, 40–52, 167–76,
183–352 nos.0A–21A, series repr.; Bentley
Blake Books 1977, pp.517–24 no.421; Bindman
Graphic Works 1978, pp.486–7 nos.625–46,
series repr.; Mitchell 1978, pp.41–2; Essick
Printmaker 1981, pp.92, 105, 220, 234–50, 252;
Robert N. Essick, 'Blake's Engravings to the
Book of Job; An Essay on their Graphic Form
with a Catalogue of their States and Printings'
in David Bindman, ed., *William Blake's
Illustrations of the Book of Job* 1987, pp.35–101.

John Linnell, who had commissioned the second set of watercolour illustrations to the Book of Job in 1821, entered into a formal agreement with Blake for the engravings on 25 March 1823: Linnell was to pay Blake £5 a plate or £100 for the set, and in addition he agreed to give Blake an extra £100 if the profits of the work made this possible. The agreement was for twenty engravings though in the event twenty-one subjects were engraved together with a title-page. On 5 March 1825 Linnell went with Blake to the printer J. Lahee to see proofs being taken. The series is dated 8 March 1825 but the final engravings do not seem actually to have been ready until the end of March 1826 (Bentley 1969, pp.277, 300 and 327). At this time 215 sets of engravings marked 'Proof' were issued; these should be distinguished from the working proofs, on some of which Blake tried out designs for the borders. The word 'Proof' was then deleted (traces can be seen on no.111) and a further 100 sets were printed on drawing paper. According to John Linnell Jr, writing to Bernard Quaritch on 6 May 1892, Linnell, after the 1826 printing, 'put the plates away, & they were never again used after this time until the year 1874. At this time my father...had one hundred copies printed from the plates upon India paper'. Although the distinctive cover is now missing, it seems that the Tate Gallery's copies of the engravings are from this 1874 printing. The original plates were given by Herbert Linnell to the British Museum Print Room on 28 May 1919.

Each engraving is inscribed 'W Blake inv. & sculp'. In addition each is inscribed in the lower margin with variations of the text 'London. Published as the Act directs March 8:1825 by William Blake Nº3 Fountain Court Strand'; the first actual design (no.110) is mistakenly dated with the year 1828 and 'Willm' is sometimes substituted for 'William', while the punctuation is also slightly varied.

More importantly, the borders of each design bear a number of inscriptions taken from the Bible or with variations of biblical texts. These add a verbal gloss to the designs which in themselves embody Blake's critical reaction to the original story as set out in the Old Testament. The fullest analysis is in Lindberg though Wicksteed, Damon 1966 and Wright also contain full commentaries. Blake's interpretation of his text is only given in summary form in this catalogue.

These engravings were formerly inventoried as nos.3372 i–xxii. The new inventory numbers omit the title-page.

109   **Title-Page**

109

Line engraving 191 × 147 ($7\frac{9}{16}$ × $5\frac{3}{4}$); platemark 217 × 169 ($8\frac{9}{16}$ × $6\frac{5}{8}$)
Inscribed 'Invented & Engraved by William Blake 1825' b.c. and 'London Published as the Act directs March 8:1825. by William Blake

N°3 Fountain Court Strand' below, and with title as given below

EXHIBITED
Tate Gallery 1978 (199, repr.)

The title-page was added to the series for the engravings and does not figure in either of the sets of watercolours. There is a pencil, pen and ink sketch in the Rosenwald Collection, National Gallery of Art, Washington (Butlin 1981, no. 558, pl. 787)

The title is given in ornate, somewhat Gothic lettering: 'ILLUSTRATIONS of The Book of JOB' with above, in Hebrew letters, 'The Book of Job'. On the sketch the title in Hebrew comes below the main title.

110   **Job and his Family**

110

Line engraving 184 × 150 ($7\frac{1}{4}$ × $5\frac{7}{8}$); platemark 198 × 164 ($7\frac{13}{16}$ × $6\frac{7}{16}$)
Inscribed 'WBlake inv & sculp' b.r., 'London.

Published as the Act directs. March 8:1828 [sic]. by Will Blake N3 Fountain Court Strand' below, '1' t.r., and with texts given below.

Illustration no. 1: Job, i, 1–3. Blake quotes as main title, 'Thus did Job continually' from Job, i, 5. What Job did was to pray the words inscribed above: 'Our Father which art in Heaven/hallowed be thy Name' (Matthew, vi, 9; Luke, xi, 2). Blake stresses the negative quality of this prayer by quoting below, 'The Letter Killeth/The Spirit giveth Life' (II Corinthians, iii, 6) followed by 'It is Spiritually Discerned' (I Corinthians, ii, 14). The scene is set for the whole series by the straightforward quotation from Job, i, 1–2, 'There was a Man in the/Land of Uz whose Name/was Job. & that Man/was perfect & upright/& one that feared God/& eschewed Evil & there/was born unto him Seven/Sons & Three Daughters'.

To add to the negative impact of this design Blake shows musical instruments hanging unplayed on the tree, the sun setting while the moon rises, and the sheep fast asleep. For a recent discovery that suggests, however, that even as late as the final state of this engraving the negative impact of the inscription was much less evident see the introduction to this section, p. 185.

111 **Satan before the Throne of God**

Line engraving 197 × 151 (7¾ × 5¹⁵⁄₁₆);
platemark 217 × 169 (8⁹⁄₁₆ × 6⅝)
Inscribed 'WBlake inv & sc' b.l., 'London
Published as the Act directs March 8: 1825. by

Willm Blake N3 Fountain Court Strand' below,
'2' t.r., and with texts given below; traces of
the former inscription 'Proof' can still be seen
b.r.

111

Illustration no. 2: Job, i, 6–12. Blake's main title applies to the lower part of the composition showing Job and his Family: 'When the Almighty was yet with me. When my Children/were about me' (Job, xxix, 5). Below this a subsidiary text describes what is happening in the upper half of the composition: 'There was a day when the Sons of God came to present themselves before the Lord & Satan came also among them/to present himself before the Lord' (Job, i, 6). Above there are further inscriptions: 'I beheld the Ancient of Days' (condensed from Daniel, vii, 9); 'Hast thou considered my Servant Job' (Job, i, 8; God the Father is pointing out Job as an example to Satan); 'The Angel of the Divine Presence' (Isaiah lxiii), and the Hebrew for 'The Lord is King' (Psalms, x, 16, xlvii, 7, and xcvii). These inscriptions are flanked by two more: 'I shall see God' (based on Job, xix, 26) and 'Thou art our Father' (Isaiah, lxiii, 16, and lxiv, 8). Flanking all these inscriptions, and broken by them, is the single sentence 'We shall awake up/in thy Likeness' (a rewording of Psalms, xvii, 15).

God the Father, apart from his somewhat spikey hair which anticipates the horrific vision of no. 120, is given the same likeness as Job. Satan, on the other hand, is shown as a physically ideal, young man, surrounded by flames in which appear images of the heads of Job and of his wife.

The lower part of the composition is developed, in reverse, from the large watercolour of 'Enoch walked with God (?)' of *c.*1780–5 in the Cincinnati Art Museum (Butlin 1981, no. 146, colour pl. 181). This drawing has also been identified as showing Job in prosperity.

112 **Job's Sons and Daughters Overwhelmed by Satan**

Line engraving 197 × 153 (7⅞ × 6); platemark
219 × 170 (8⅝ × 6¹¹⁄₁₆)
Inscribed 'WBlake inven: & : sculp' b.r.,
'London. Published as the Act directs

March 8: 1825 by Willm Blake N⁰ 3 Fountain
Court Strand' below, '3' t.r., and with texts
given below

112

Illustration no. 3: Job, i, 13, 18–19. Blake gives this design a long descriptive title from Job, i, 18–19: 'Thy Sons and thy Daughters were eating & drinking Wine in their eldest Brothers house & behold there came a great wind from the Wilderness & smote upon the four faces of the house & it fell upon the young Men and they are Dead'. At the top is written 'The Fire of God is fallen from Heaven' (Job, i, 16) and 'And the Lord said unto Satan Behold All that he hath is in thy Power' (Job, i, 12).

Here the figure of Satan, unlike the previous design, is shown in traditional horrific guise with large bat-like wings. The somewhat strange placing of Satan's feet is one of the stronger arguments for Wicksteed's theory of Blake's left- and right-hand symbolism; Satan's left-hand foot is placed forward denoting evil. The placing of the feet also relates to those of the central figure below, whose pose, as Lindberg has shown, is based on an Antique pathos formula, exemplified by the Laocoön, the subject of three drawings and a famous engraving by Blake (Butlin 1981, nos. 679–81, repr. pls. 898, 898A and 899, and, for the engraving, Bindman

Graphic Works 1978, no.623 repr. and Essick *Separate Plates* 1983, no.xix, pls.51–3). The upside-down figure in the pose of the crucified on the right may allude to Blake's comment that 'The Modern Church Crucifies Christ with the Head Downwards' (*A Vision of the Last Judgment* 1810; Keynes *Writings* 1957, p.615).

113 The Messengers Tell Job of his Misfortunes

113

Line engraving 200 × 152 (7⅞ × 6); platemark 217 × 170 (8 9/16 × 6 11/16)
Inscribed 'WBlake invent & sculp' b.r., 'London. Published as the Act directs

March 8: 1825. by Willm Blake N° 3 Fountain Court Strand' below, '4' t.r., and with texts given below

Illustration no.4: Job, i, 14–17. Blake's main title reads 'And I only am escaped alone to tell thee', the conclusion of the sentence given across the top of the engraving, 'And there came a Messenger unto Job & said The Oxen were plowing & the Sabeans came down & they have slain the Young Men with the Sword' (Job, i, 14–15). The account continues below the main title: 'While he was yet speaking there came also another & said/The Fire of God is fallen from heaven & hath burned up the flocks & the/Young Men & consumed them & I only am escaped alone to tell thee' (Job, i, 16). In the margin above the main design Satan is shown from behind with the words of his reply to God who asked him on his return to Heaven (as shown in the next design) where he had been: 'Going to & fro in the Earth/& walking up and down in it' (Job, ii, 2).

In the two preliminary watercolours only two messengers are shown. Here Blake has added another tiny figure, seen on the horizon between the legs of the foremost messenger.

114 Satan Going Forth from the Presence of the Lord, and Job's Charity

114

Line engraving 198 × 152 (7 13/16 × 6); platemark 218 × 170 (8⅝ × 6 11/16)
Inscribed 'WBlake inventor & sculp' b.r., 'London. Published as the Act directs

March 8: 1825. by Willm Blake N° 3 Fountain Court Strand' below, '5' t.r., and with texts given below

Illustration no.5: Job, ii, 3–7. Blake's main text refers to the upper part of the composition: 'Then went Satan forth from the presence of the Lord' (Job, ii, 7). Blake then describes the Lord's reactions: 'And it grieved him at his heart' (Genesis, vi, 6), 'Who maketh his Angels Spirits & his Ministers a Flaming Fire' (a misquotation from Psalms, civ, 4; as Lindberg points out this last quotation is, in the Bible, meant to celebrate God's omnipotence but Blake sees the Lord as the cause of his angels being scorched by Satan's phial). Above the main design Blake writes God's injunction to Satan, 'Behold he is in thy hand: but save his Life' (Job, ii, 6). Above is inscribed, 'Did I not weep for him who was in trouble Was not my Soul afflicted for the Poor', Job's defence later in the story (Job, xxx, 25).

Satan is shown in his 'ideal' form, being in heaven. However, he already holds the phial he uses against Job in the next design. The gothic cathedral that has been seen the background of nos.109 and 112 is here replaced by a druidical structure which reappears in the next two designs and also appears in no.120; Wicksteed and other commentators find this significant though Lindberg sees it as merely indicating that Job lived in very distant times.

115 **Satan Smiting Job with Sore Boils**

Line engraving 198 × 153 (7$\frac{13}{16}$ × 6); platemark
218 × 170 (8$\frac{9}{16}$ × 6$\frac{13}{16}$)
Inscribed 'WBlake inv &sc' b.l., 'London. as

Act directs Published March 8: 1825 by
William Blake No 3 Fountain Court Strand'
below, '6' t.r., and with texts given below

Illustration no.6: Job, ii, 7, the source of Blake's main title, 'And smote Job with sore Boils/from the sole of his foot to the crown of his head'. Blake stresses Job's submission by the quotation above the main design, 'Naked came I out of my/mothers womb & Naked shall I return thither/The Lord gave & the Lord hath taken away. Blessed by the Name of the Lord' (Job, i, 21).

Wicksteed relates Job's affliction to a passage on plate 21 of Blake's *Jerusalem*, *c.*1804–15 (Keynes *Writings* 1957, p.643):

> 'The disease of shame covers me from head to feet: I have no hope
> Every boil upon my body is a separate & deadly Sin.
> Doubt first assaild me, then Shame took possession of me
> Shame divides Families. Shame hath divided Albion in sunder!'

Doubt and Shame have led Job to doubt the bodily side of his love for his wife, who crouches in despair at his feet.

This design was developed still further in the tempera painting of *c.*1826, no.70. There Satan, already shown in his unidealised, scaley form, is given the large bat-like wings of nos.112 and 113 (in margin above main design).

116 **Job's Comforters**

Line engraving 198 × 153 (7$\frac{13}{16}$ × 6); platemark
218 × 170 (8$\frac{5}{8}$ × 6$\frac{11}{16}$)
Inscribed 'WBlake inven & sculpt' b.r.,
'London. Published as the Act directs

March 8: 1825 by William Blake N3 Fountain
Court Strand' below, '7' t.r., and with texts
given below

Illustration no.7: Job, ii, 9–12. Blake's main title is a quotation from Job, ii, 12 reflecting the reaction of the three comforters, Eliphaz, Bildad and Zophar: 'And when they lifted up their eyes afar off & knew him not they lifted up their voice & wept. & they rent every Man his mantle & sprinkled dust upon their heads towards heaven'. Above, Blake quotes Job's response to his wife, 'What! shall we recieve Good at the hand of God & shall we not also recieve Evil' (Job, ii, 10). At the foot of the page Blake quotes the comment from James, v, 11: 'Ye have heard of the Patience of Job and have seen the end of the Lord'.

Although the King James Bible states that Job is sitting on 'ashes' (Job, ii, 8) Blake follows traditional imagery, and the Septuaginta and Vulgate translations 'dunghill', though he makes it look more like a heap of straw. The pose of Job and his wife echoes that of 'A Lamentation over the Dead Christ' and Lindberg demonstrates the parallel with an engraving after Michelangelo's 'Pietà' in St Peter's (repr. Lindberg 1973, pl.107). That this was a conscious imitation is supported by the fact that the architectural form on the extreme right suggests the Cross. The three comforters on the left rush in left foot forward demonstrating, according to Wicksteed's theory, that they are the 'Corporeal Friends' who are 'our Spiritual Enemies' (*Milton* plate 4 and *Jerusalem* plate 44/30; Keynes *Writings* 1957, pp.484, 655).

117 Job's Despair

117

Line engraving 199 × 150 ($7\frac{13}{16}$ × $5\frac{7}{8}$);
platemark 217 × 168 ($8\frac{9}{16}$ × $6\frac{5}{8}$)
Inscribed 'WBlake inv & sculp' b.r., 'London.

Publish'd as the Act directs March 8: 1825 by
Willm Blake N° 3 Fountain Court Strand'
below, '8' t.r., and with texts given below

Illustration no.8: Job, iii, 1–7. Blake's main title consists of Job's words from Job, iii, 3: 'Let the Day perish wherein I was born'. Above there is a quotation from later in the same book: 'Lo let that night be solitary/& let no joyful voice come therein' (Job, iii, 7). The lines below the main title describe the action of the three comforters: 'And they sat down with him upon the ground seven days & seven/nights & none spake a word unto him for they saw that his grief/was very great' (Job, ii, 13).

Blake seems to be unique in the long line of artists who illustrated the Book of Job in showing this scene.

118 The Vision of Eliphaz

118

Line engraving 198 × 152 ($7\frac{3}{4}$ × 6); platemark
217 × 170 ($8\frac{9}{16}$ × $6\frac{11}{16}$)
Inscribed 'WBlake invenit & sculp' b.r.,
'London. Published as the Act directs

March 8: 1825 by William Blake N3 Fountain
Court Strand' below, '9' t.r., and with texts
given below

Illustration no.9: Job, iv, 13–17. Blake's main title is taken from the description by Eliphaz, one of Blake's comforters, of his vision: 'Then a Spirit passed before my Face/the hair of my flesh stood up' (Job, iv, 15). The scene above shows Eliphaz in bed seeing his vision of God the Father (in Job's likeness) who has told him, 'Shall mortal Man be more Just than God? Shall a Man be more Pure than his Maker? Behold he putteth no trust in his Saints & his Angels he chargeth with Folly' (Job, iv, 17–18).

For Blake, of course, man was immortal, not mortal, and the comforters stand for all that was most repugnant to him.

119 Job Rebuked by his Friends

119

Line engraving 198 × 152 ($7\frac{3}{4}$ × 6); platemark
219 × 171 ($8\frac{5}{8}$ × $6\frac{3}{4}$)
Inscribed 'WBlake invenit & sculp' b.r.,
'London Published as the Act directs

March 8: 1825. by William Blake N3 Fountain
Court Strand' below, '10' t.r., and with texts
given below

Illustration no. 10: Job, xii, 4, 'The Just Upright Man is laughed to scorn', Blake's main title, though the design sums up the whole encounter of Job and his friends (Job, iv-xxxi), whose rebuke is echoed more gently by his wife. The other inscriptions are taken from Job's statements to his God: 'Man that is born of a Woman is of few days & full of trouble/he cometh up like a flower & is cut down he fleeth also as a shadow/& continueth not And dost thou open thine eyes upon such a one/& bringest me into judgment with thee' (Job, xiv, 1–3); 'But he knoweth the way that I take when he hath tried me I shall come forth like gold' (Job, xxiii, 10); 'Have pity upon me! Have pity upon me! O ye my friends for the hand of God hath touched me' (Job, xix, 21); and 'Though he slay me yet will I trust in him' (Job, xiii, 15).

The composition of the main design is taken, in reverse, from an earlier engraving by Blake. This is known in two states, the later of which is dated 1793 though it was probably executed considerably later (for the preliminary drawings for this engraving, and the whole problem of the dating of that group of works, see no.6 above; the various works are repr. together in Essick *Separate Plates* 1983, figs. 7–11). Job's wife is however moved back to the other side of Job as in no.6 and the friends, or comforters, no longer sit passively but point accusingly at Job, each with both arms outstretched, a repeated gesture probably taken from Fuseli's 'Three Witches' from *Macbeth* (versions of 1783 onwards are repr. Blunt 1959, pl.51 b, Tomory *Fuseli* 1972, pl.72, and Schiff *Füssli* 1973, II, pp.176 nos.733, 734 and 735). Lindberg finds a common source in Agostino Veneziano's engraving after Giulio Romano's 'Adoration of the Shepherds', 1531 (repr. pl.109). Blake used a similar motif for the accusers of Socrates on plate 93 of *Jerusalem* (repr. Blunt 1959, pl.51c; Lindberg 1973, pl.111).

Lindberg draws attention to the fact that this scene was traditionally seen as a prefiguration of the mocking of Christ.

120 **Job's Evil Dreams**

Line engraving 197 × 152 ($7\frac{3}{4}$ × 6); platemark 217 × 170 ($8\frac{9}{16}$ × $6\frac{13}{16}$)
Inscribed 'WBlake invenit & sculp' b.l., 'London. Published as the Act directs

March 8: 1825 by Willm Blake N° 3 Fountain Court Strand' below, '11' t.r., and with texts given below·

Illustration no.11: Job, vii, 13–15, the source of Blake's main title, 'With Dreams upon my bed thou scarest me & affrightest me/with Visions'. At this point in the book the nature of Job's dreams and visions are not stated but Blake took some of his imagery, and his other quotations, from later in the book and elsewhere in the Bible: 'Why do you persecute me as God & are not satisfied with my flesh. Oh that my words/were printed in a Book that they were graven with an iron pen & lead in the rock for ever/For I know that my Redeemer liveth & that he shall stand in the latter days upon/the Earth & after my skin destroy thou This body yet in my flesh shall I see God/whom I shall see for Myself and mine eyes shall behold & not Another tho consumed be my wrought Image' (Job, xix, 22–7), and 'Who opposeth & exalteth himself above all that is called God or is Worshipped' (II Thessalonians, ii, 4); 'My bones are pierced in me in the/night season & my sinews/take no rest' (Job, xxx, 17); 'My skin is black upon me/& my bones are burned/with heat' (Job, xxx, 30); 'The triumphing of the wicked/is short, the joy of the hypocrite is/but for a moment' (Job, xx, 5); 'Satan himself is transformed into an Angel of Light & his Ministers into Ministers of Righteousness' (II Corinthians, xi, 14–15).

This design is a turning-point of the series, which perhaps explains why it falls out of sequence as an illustration to the Book of Job. Traditionally Job's dreams were identified with a vision of Hell but Blake expands this by making the flames and demons of hell, shown below, dependent upon the Tables of the Law above, the two being linked by the outstretched arms of the figure that hovers over Job; this figure is developed from the God of the second design (no.111) but is shown entwined by a serpent and with a cloven hoof: Job's God has become Satan. In recognizing that his idea of God is in fact Satan Job, in the depths of his despair, is now capable of spiritual salvation. This possibility is embodied in a number of the quotations inscribed by Blake, particularly 'For I know that my Redeemer liveth', which alludes, of course, to the God of the New Testament.

121 **The Wrath of Elihu**

121

Line engraving 200 × 151 ($7\frac{7}{8}$ × $5\frac{15}{16}$);
platemark 219 × 168 ($8\frac{5}{8}$ × $6\frac{5}{8}$)
Inscribed 'WBlake invenit & sculpt' b.c.,
'London Published as the Act directs

March 8: 1825 by Willm Blake N3 Fountain
Court Strand' below, '12' t.r., and with texts
given below

Illustration no.12: Job, xxxii–xxxvii. Blake's main title quotes from the opening of Elihu's speech: 'I am Young & ye are very Old wherefore I was afraid [and durst not shew you mine opinion]' (Job, xxxii, 6). The other marginal inscriptions are also taken from his speech: 'For God speaketh once yea twice/& Man percieveth it not In a Dream in a Vision of the Night/in deep Slumberings upon the bed/*sic* Then he openeth the ears of Men & sealeth their instruction/That he may withdraw Man from his purpose/& hide Pride from Man' (Job, i), and 'If there be with him an Interpreter One among a Thousand/then he is gracious unto him/& saith Deliver him from going down to the Pit/I have found a Ransom' (Job, xxxiii, 14–16, 23–4); 'For his eyes are upon/the ways of Man & he observeth/all his goings' (Job, xxxiv, 21); 'Lo all these things worketh God oftentimes with Man to bring/back his Soul from the pit to be enlightened/with the light of the living' (Job, xxxiii, 29–30); 'Look upon the heavens & behold the clouds/which are higher/than thou/If thou sinnest what doest thou against him or if thou be/righteous what givest thou unto him' (Job, xxxv, 5–7).

Blake's design makes clear the difference between Elihu's message (and Job's more positive response) and the earlier reproaches of Job's friends in nos.116 and 119. Lindberg has shown that Elihu's attitude and gestures are based on such traditional representations of inspired preachers as Raphael's St Paul in 'The Blinding of Elymas', one of the tapestry cartoons in the Royal Collection now on deposit at the Victoria and Albert Museum but which were at Windsor Castle until 1809 and subsequently at Hampton Court Palace. In addition the unrelieved gloom of the sky in nos.117–120 is now redeemed by the presence of stars unmentioned in the biblical text. The group of three friends is derived from the earlier Job print mentioned under no.119 (see also no.6); here their expressions are passive, not accusing.

The figures in the margins seem to contrast the Urizenic old man with the scroll, perhaps Job's former idea of the Law, lying quiescent with the young spirits full of energy rising up from his body. This would parallel the new inspiration brought into the discussion by Elihu.

122 **The Lord Answering Job out of the Whirlwind**

Line engraving 198 × 151 ($7\frac{3}{4}$ × $5\frac{7}{8}$); platemark
217 × 170 ($8\frac{9}{16}$ × $6\frac{13}{16}$)
Inscribed 'WBlake invenit & sculp' b.r.,
'London Published as the Act directs March
8: 1825 by William Blake N° 3 Fountain Court

Strand' below, '13' t.r., and with texts given
below

EXHIBITED
Tate Gallery 1958 (200, repr.)

Illustration no.13: Job, xxxviii, i, the source of Blake's main title, 'Then the Lord answered Job out of the Whirlwind'. This quotation is continued by a line from the Psalms, civ, 3, 'Who maketh the Clouds his Chariot & walketh on the Wings of the Wind'. The other quotations are from the Book of Job: 'Hath the Rain a Father &

who hath begotten the Drops of the Dew' (Job, xxxviii, 28), and 'Who is this that darkeneth counsel by words without knowledge' (Job, xxxviii, 2).

The Lord appears in a new, active guise, questioning Job's lack of illumination and asking rhetorical questions about the Creation. The whirlwind has flattened the trees in the margin but, though bowed, they are not broken, just as Job has remained unbroken under adversity. In an early state of the engraving Blake showed the whirlwind bursting out of the central design into the margin above to much greater effect, but in the end he reverted to the usual clearly defined rectangle for the main design (repr. Bindman 1978, pl.638b).

Blake had already treated this subject in his watercolour painted for Thomas Butts *c.*1803–5, 'Job confessing his Presumption to God who Answers from the Whirlwind', now in the National Gallery of Scotland, Edinburgh (Butlin 1981, no.461, colour pl.538). The composition is completely different and the Lord is accompanied by angels. Job's wife, like the friends, bows down to the ground in fear rather than sharing in Job's vision.

122

123 **When the Morning Stars Sang Together**

Line engraving 191 × 150 ($7\frac{1}{2}$ × $5\frac{7}{8}$); platemark 207 × 164 ($8\frac{3}{16}$ × $6\frac{7}{16}$)
Inscribed 'WBlake Invenit & Sc' b.l., 'London. Published as the Act directs March 8: 1825 by Willm Blake N3 Fountain Court

Strand' below, '14' t.r., and with texts given below

EXHIBITED
Tate Gallery 1958 (205, repr.)

123

Illustration no.14: Job, xxxviii, 4–7. Blake's main text is 'When the morning Stars sang together. & all the/Sons of God shouted for joy' (Job, xxxviii, 7); in the third state of the engraving these words were preceded, as in the Bible, by 'When I laid the Foundations of the Earth' with 'And' replacing the initial 'When', and Lindberg suggests that Blake deleted these words to indicate that this state of joy only related to the upper part of the composition, referring to the time of eternity before creation. In the upper margin Blake quotes the Lord's question 'Canst thou bind the sweet influences of Pleiades or loose the bands of Orion' (Job, xxxviii, 31). In each of the flanking margins there are little scenes of creation, each with its own inscription: 'Let there be/Light' (Genesis, i, 3); 'Let there be A/Firmament' (Genesis, i, 6); 'Let the Waters be gathered/together in one place & let the Dry Land appear' (Genesis i, 9); 'And God made Two Great/Lights/Sun Moon' (Genesis, i, 16); 'Let the Waters bring/forth abundantly' (Genesis, i, 20); 'Let the Earth bring forth/Cattle & Creeping thing/& Beast' (Genesis, i, 24).

This is the first of a sub-group of three compositions in which God reveals to Job the creation, the organisation and the annihilation of the natural world. The angels or 'morning stars' exist in eternity above, while Job, his wife and his friends are shown in a cave-like Earth below. In between, in a zone partly occupied by the Lord, are the Sun and Moon gods representing time, identified by Lindberg as Helios and Selene rather than Apollo and Diana.

The figures of Helios and Selene are probably derived from Antique gems, which Blake on his Laocoön print of *c.*1818–20 equated with 'The Gems of Aaron's Breast Plate' (Keynes *Writings* 1957, p.777; repr. Bindman 1978, pl.623, Essick *Separate Plates* 1983, pl.51). Indeed, Lindberg suggests that this whole design is a reconstruction by Blake of Aaron's breastplate, which was understood in the eighteenth century to represent the original map of the universe.

The motif of angels with upstretched arms crossing each other to form a frieze had already been used by Blake in one of his illustrations to Young's *Night Thoughts* of *c.*1795–7 (Butlin no.330 *437*; repr. Blunt 1959, pl.54b, and Grant, Rose and Tolley 1980). It is probably based on a relief from Persepolis engraved for Jacob Bryant's *New System of Ancient Mythology* in Basire's workshop 1775–6 when Blake was an apprentice there (repr. Blunt 1959, pl.54a). The motif reappears in the second illustration in Blake's two series of illustrations to Milton's *On the Morning of Christ's Nativity* of 1809 and *c.*1815 (Butlin nos.538 *2* and 542 *2*, repr. in colour pls.661 and 667). In the Job engraving, as opposed to the preceding watercolours, Blake added further arms cut by the edge of the composition, suggesting an infinitude of angels in eternity.

124 **Behemoth and Leviathan**

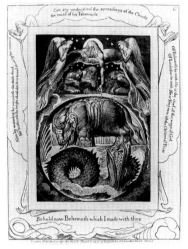

124

Line engraving 200 × 151 ($7\frac{7}{8}$ × $5\frac{15}{16}$); platemark 218 × 170 ($8\frac{5}{8}$ × $6\frac{11}{16}$)
Inscribed 'WBlake invenit & sculpt' b.r., 'London Published as the Act directs March 8:1825 by Willm Blake N3 Fountain Court Strand' below, '15' t.r., and with texts given below

EXHIBITED
Tate Gallery 1958 (202, repr.)

Illustration no.15: Job, xl, 15; xli, 34. Blake's main text only mentions Behemoth: 'Behold now Behemoth which I made with thee' (Job, xl, 15). However, the text in the right margin mentions both monsters: 'Of Behemoth he saith. He is the chief of the ways of God/Of Leviathan he saith, He is King of all the Children of Pride' (Job xl, 19; xli, 34). The other two quotations relate the monsters to natural phenomena: 'Can any understand the spreadings of the Clouds/the noise of his Tabernacle' (Job, xxxvi, 21), and 'Also by watering he wearyeth the thick cloud/He scattereth the bright cloud also it is turned about by his counsels' (Job, xxxvii, 11–12).

The Lord humbles Job by enumerating the extent and power of His creation. Leviathan is described in various places in the Bible as a sea-monster, while the representation of Behemoth as a hippopotamus is the traditional one. Blake shows them as presiding over land and sea respectively, perhaps, as Lindberg suggests, on the basis of the pseudo-epigraphical Fourth Book of Estras, vi, 47–52. In *Jerusalem* Blake makes the monsters the representatives of war by land and sea respectively (see nos.58 and 59), in a passage that describes the Spectre creating the material world and 'refusing to believe without demonstration' (Keynes *Writings* 1957, p.738). The monsters are therefore shown in a material, global world below that inhabited by Job and his companions. Lindberg suggests that this is Hell and that its global form is an attack on the scientific belief in the roundness of the earth; Blake was later to tell Crabb Robinson that 'I do not believe that the world is round. I believe it quite flat' (Bentley *Blake Records* 1969, pp.313, 541).

125 **The Fall of Satan**

Line engraving 186 × 150 ($7\frac{5}{16}$ × $5\frac{13}{16}$); platemark 201 × 164 ($7\frac{7}{8}$ × $6\frac{7}{16}$) Inscribed 'WBlake inv & sculp' b.r., 'London.

Published as the Act directs March 8: 1825 by William Blake № 3 Fountain Court Strand' below, '16' t.r., and with texts given below

125

Illustration no.16: Job, xxxvi, 17; xlii, 1–7. The main title quotes from Elihu's verdict on Job and his companions: 'Thou hast fulfilled the Judgment of the Wicked' (Job xxxvi, 17; this continues 'Judgment and justice take hold on thee'). The judgment of Job was traditionally seen as forshadowing the Last Judgment and the defeat of Satan, and Blake quotes various texts including some from the New Testament with this wider connotation: 'Hell is naked before him & Destruction has no covering' (Job, xxvi, 6); 'Even the Devils are Subject to Us thro thy Name. Jesus said unto them. I saw Satan as lightning fall from Heaven' (Luke, x, 17–18); 'God hath chosen the foolish things of the World to confound the wise/And God hath chosen the weak things of the World to confound the things that are mighty' (I Corinthians, i, 27); 'Canst thou by searching find out God/Canst thou find out the Almighty to perfection It is higher than Heaven what canst thou do/It is deeper than Hell what canst thou know' (Job, xi, 7–8); 'The Accuser of our Brethren is Cast down/which accused them before our God day & night' (Apocalypse, xii, 10); 'The Prince of this World shall be cast out' (John, xii, 31).

This is the third of the sub-group of designs showing the Lord instructing Job and his companions. Here Blake develops the traditional connection between the judgment of Job and that of the world as a whole. The composition echoes that of the second and fifth designs (nos.111 and 114), particularly the former. The two simulacra of Job and his wife that appear in no.111 in the flames surrounding Satan now accompany him in his fall, shown here in the solid form without which error cannot be cast out. At the same time Satan's fall splits the ground on which Job and his companions kneel, dividing Job and his wife in their calm acceptance of the Lord's judgment from the group of Eliphaz and his two companions. There are parallels with Blake's depiction of the Last Judgment (see Butlin 1981, nos.639–48, pls.868–74). In particular God is now shown not as the God of the Old Testament but as Christ with the Book of Life spread open on his knees.

126 **The Vision of Christ**

126

Line engraving 200 × 151 ($7\frac{7}{8}$ × $5\frac{13}{16}$); platemark 219 × 170($8\frac{5}{8}$ × $6\frac{11}{16}$) Inscribed 'WBlake' b.l. and 'inv & sculp' b.r., 'London Published as the Act directs

March 8: 1825 by William Blake № 3 Fountain Court Strand' below, '17' t.r., and with texts given below

Illustration no.17: Job, xlii, 5, the source of Blake's main title which significantly omits the word 'of' from the Authorised Version, following the Vulgate: 'I have heard [of] thee with the hearing of the Ear but now my Eye seeth thee'. Another of the lines quoted by Blake had already been used by St Gregory the Great as an interpretation of Job's revelation as being his apprehension of the unity of Christ and the Father: 'I & my Father are One' (John, x, 30), and this is accompanied by another quotation of similar import, 'He that hath seen me hath seen my Father also' (John, xiv, 9). The theme is developed in a selection of further sayings from

John, xiv, partly rearranged but forming a coherent whole: 'If you had known/me ye would/have known my/Father also and/from henceforth/ye know him &/have seen him/Believe me that/I am in the Father & the Father in me/He that loveth me/shall be loved of/my Father/For he dwelleth in/you & shall be with/you', 'At that day ye shall know that I am in/my Father & you in me & I in you/If ye loved me ye would rejoice/because I said I go unto the Father', 'He that loveth/me shall be loved/of my Father & I/will love him &/manifest myself/unto him/And my Father/will love him & we/will come unto him/& make our abode/with him/And the Father/shall give you/Another Comforter/that he may abide/with you for ever/Even the Spirit of/Truth whom the/World Cannot receive' (John, xiv, 7, 11, 16–17, 20, 21, 23, and 28). Further quotations continue this theme and the identification of Job's judgment with that of mankind as a whole: 'He bringeth down to/the Grave & bringeth up' (I Samuel, ii, 6); 'we know that when he shall appear we shall be like him for we shall see him as He Is' (John, iii, 2); 'When I behold the Heavens the work of thy hands the Moon & Stars which thou hast ordained. Then I say. What is Man that thou art mindful of him?/& the Son of Man that thou visitest him' (Psalms, viii, 3–4).

Blake stresses the difference between Job's finite world and the infinite world of his vision by placing God on a cloud rather than on the earth; however, the flames of inspiration spread beyond God to embrace the kneeling figures of Job and his wife though they only just touch the three friends. In the lower margin an angel is shown with a quill, accompanying the open books and scroll bearing the quotations from St John. Wicksteed identifies her as Jerusalem but Lindberg doubts this; as she is definitely female she cannot be St John herself but is presumably his muse.

127 Job's Sacrifice

127

Line engraving 198 × 150 ($7\frac{13}{16} \times 5\frac{7}{8}$); platemark 218 × 171 ($8\frac{5}{8} \times 6\frac{3}{4}$) Inscribed 'WBlake inv & sculpt' b.r., 'London Published as the Act directs

March 8: 1825 by Will Blake Nº 3 Fountain Court Strand' below, '18' t.r., and with texts given below

Illustration no.18: Job, xlii, 8–10. Blake's main text is 'And my Servant Job shall pray for you', that is, his friends (Job, lxii, 8). The consequences are given in the two other main quotations: 'Also the Lord accepted Job' (Job, lxii, 9) and 'And the Lord turned the captivity of Job when he prayed for his Friends' (Job, lxii, 10). The moral is pointed by a long quotation from Matthew, v, 44–5, 48: 'I say unto you/Love your Enemies bless them/that curse you/do good to them/that hate you & pray for them/that despitefull[y]/use you & perse/cute you/That you may be/the children of/your Father which/is in heaven, for he maketh his Sun to shine on the E/vil & the Good &/sendeth rain on/the Just & the Unjust/Be ye therefore/perfect as your Fa/ther which is in heaven is perfect'.

Job stands in front of the altar in the pose of the crucified. The composition is based on that of 'Noah and the Rainbow, "The Covenant"', painted *c.*1803–5 for Thomas Butts (Houghton Library, Harvard University, Cambridge, Mass.; Butlin 1981, no.437, pl.514). In this, as in the engraving and the preliminary Linnell watercolour and Fitzwilliam Museum pencil sketch, the main figure is seen from behind, though in the Butts watercolour he faces the viewer.

128 **Every Man also Gave him a Piece of Money**

Line engraving 197 × 150 (7¾ × 5⅞); platemark 218 × 170 (8⅝ × 6¹¹⁄₁₆) Inscribed 'WBlake inv & sculp' b.c., 'London.

Published as the Act directs March 8:1825. by William Blake N 3 Fountain Court Strand' below, '19' t.r., and with texts given below.

128

Illustration no.19: Job, xlii, 11, the source of Blake's main title, 'Every one also gave him a piece of Money'; Blake substitutes 'Every one' for the 'every man' of the Authorised Version. The other texts relate to charity: 'The Lord maketh Poor & maketh Rich He bringeth Low & Lifteth Up' (I Samuel, ii, 7); 'who provideth for the/Raven his Food/When his young ones cry unto God' (Job, xxxviii, 41); and 'Who remembered us in our low estate/For his Mercy endureth forever' (Psalms, cxxxvi, 23).

Blake had shown Job giving alms in his fifth design (no.114) but this design is less a counterpart to that than to the fourth design (no.113) in which Job receives the news of his misfortunes. Instead of sheep and a gothic cathedral the background is filled by a field of ripe corn, and it is early morning with the sun about to rise rather than evening.

For an alternative project for this subject see no.108.

129 **Job and his Daughters**

Line engraving 199 × 151 (7¹³⁄₁₆ × 5¹⁵⁄₁₆); platemark 217 × 170 (8⅝ × 6¹¹⁄₁₆) Inscribed 'WBlake invenit & Sc' b.r., 'London Published as the Act directs March 8:1825 by William Blake N⁰ 3 Fountain Court Strand' below, '20' t.r., and with texts given below

EXHIBITED
Tate Gallery 1958 (203, repr.)

129

Illustration no.20: Job, xlii, 13–15. The main text is 'There were not found Women fair as the Daughters of Job/in all the Land & their Father gave them Inheritance/among their Brethren' (Job, lxii, 15). The two other quotations are from the Psalms: 'How precious are thy thoughts/unto me O God/how great is the sum of them' (Psalms, cxxxix, 17), and 'If I ascend up into Heaven thou art there/If I make my bed in Hell behold Thou/art there' (Psalms, cxxxix, 8).

The Book of Job contains no more than a passing reference to Job's three daughters (and seven sons), to their beauty and to how Job gave them their inheritance; their names are also given, Jemima, Kezia and Keren-Happuch. Lindberg points out that Blake has drawn on the apocryphal Testament of Job in which Job, shortly before his death, tells his daughters of his afflictions and of his salvation. In the main design Job points out, on the walls of the room, depictions of incidents from his life. They are, on the left, the destruction of his servants by the Chaldeans (Job, i, 17) with Satan hovering overhead, on the right that of his ploughmen (by Satan himself, again shown hovering overhead, rather than by the Sabeans mentioned in Job, i, 15), and in the centre God appearing in the whirlwind (see design 13, no.122).

All the other versions of this composition among the various Job series and related sketches show the scene at least partially out of doors. However, in this, apparently the last version of the subject, Blake reverts to the interior setting of the small tempera painted *c.*1799–1800 for Thomas Butts (Butlin 1981, no.394, colour pl.500).

[200]

130 **Job and his Family Restored to Prosperity**

130

Line engraving 196 × 149 ($7\frac{11}{16} \times 5\frac{7}{8}$);
platemark 217 × 170 ($8\frac{9}{16} \times 6\frac{11}{16}$)
Inscribed 'WBlake inv & sculp' b.r., 'London
Published as the Act directs March 8:1825 by
William Blake Fountain Court Strand' below,
'21' t.r., and with texts given below.

EXHIBITED
Tate Gallery 1958 (204, repr.)

Illustration no.21: Job, xlii, 12–13. Blake's main title reads 'So the Lord blessed the latter end of Job/more than the beginning' (Job, xlii, 12). Below this is the text 'After this Job lived/an hundred & forty years/& saw his Sons & his/Sons Sons/even four Generations/So Job died/being old/& full of days' (Job, xlii, 16–17). The moral of the whole series is given in the inscription on the altar in the bottom margin, 'In burnt offerings for Sin/thou hast had no Pleasure' (Hebrews, x, 6; see also Psalms, xl, 6), with, as a final word in the upper margin, 'Great & Marvellous are thy Works/Lord God Almighty/Just & True are thy Ways/O thou King of Saints' (from the apocryphal *Testament of Job*, xiv, 3).

Blake again draws on the apocryphal Testament of Job in which Job tells his daughters to honour God with music and singing. The composition is designed as the counterpart to the first in the series (no.110) in which the musical instruments hang unused on the tree; here they are being used to praise God. Lindberg points to the tradition linking music and prophecy. In addition, whereas the sun is setting in the first design, here it is rising. The relationship with the first design is stressed by the fact that they have identical marginal designs though in reverse and with different inscriptions.

The figures of Job and his wife are close to the two central figures playing musical instruments in 'The Hymn of Christ and the Apostles' of *c.*1805 (Butlin 1981, no.490, colour pl.546). That of Job is also similar to the Ancient Bard in the illustration to 'The Voice of the Ancient Bard', an illustration to *Songs of Innocence and of Experience* (repr. Bindman 1978, pls.52 and 223).

ILLUSTRATIONS TO DANTE'S *DIVINE COMEDY* 1824-1827

These watercolours were commissioned by John Linnell, who had met Blake in 1818 and had already commissioned a duplicate set of Blake's watercolour illustrations to the Book of Job in 1821 and financed the engraving of them from 1823 onwards. Blake began working on the Dante drawings in the Autumn of 1824 and it was again planned to engrave the series, but this project was interrupted by Blake's death on 12 August 1827. The main series consists of one hundred and two watercolours of the same size in varying degrees of completion; the Tate Gallery owns twenty of these. There are also a number of related pencil sketches such as no.151 recto. The Tate Gallery also owns two sets of the seven engravings, one made in 1827, the other, also from the original plates, printed in 1968.

The drawings are first mentioned in a note by Samuel Palmer referring to a visit he paid Blake on 9 October 1824, when he found Blake at work in bed with a scalded foot: 'He designed them (100 I think) during a fortnight's illness in bed'. The engravings were presumably not begun until after Blake had finished those for the Book of Job early in 1826; they are first mentioned in a letter from Blake to Linnell on 2 July 1826. In another letter to Linnell on 25 April 1827 Blake says that he has taken proofs from six plates and is about to begin engraving the seventh; this last is particularly unfinished (see no.154). In January and February 1831 Linnell made copies of the drawings; these, omitting designs nos.12, 16 and 102, are now at Yale University. In March he offered the originals for sale to the Earl of Egremont.

Henry Crabb Robinson states that Blake was using J.F. Cary's translation of the *Divine Comedy* when he visited him on 17 December 1825. However Blake also learnt Italian in about 1824 in order to be able to read the work in the original. Gizzi 1983 gives the original Italian texts for each illustration, Roe 1953 and Klonsky 1980 English translations.

As in the case of the Book of Job, Blake's designs are not mere illustrations to the text but also act as a commentary on it, drawing parallels with Blake's own writings and in places criticizing Dante's more orthodox views on salvation. As Blake told Crabb Robinson on 10 December 1825, '*Dante* saw devils where I see none – I see only good' (Bentley *Blake Records* 1969, p.313; see also p.316). Blake's objections to Dante's basic ideas are contained in inscriptions on two of the drawings: 'Everything in Dantes Comedia shews That for Tyrannical Purposes he has made This World the Foundation of All & the Goddess Nature [inserted above is the word 'Memory'? and inserted below 'is his Inspirer'] & not ['Imagination'? seems to have been inserted] the Holy Ghost; and 'it [Dante's Hell] must have been originally Formed by the Devil Him self . . . Whatever Book is for Vengeance for Sin & whatever Book is Against the Forgiveness of Sins is not of the Father but of Satan the Accuser & Father of Hell'. (The full inscriptions on these drawings are given in Butlin 1981, pp.557–8 and 588 nos.8127 and *101*; repr. Roe 1953, pls.7 and 101).

The most detailed analysis of Blake's illustrations to Dante, and the most extreme interpretation of how he differs from the text of the *Divine Comedy*, is that given by Albert Roe in 1953. According to Roe, Blake replaced Dante's orthodox trilogy of Hell, Purgatory and Paradise by a more complex system in which the path of salavation led from Ulro through Generation to Beulah, which was a state of relaxation from which one might either pass on to Eden, the highest state, or fall back into Ulro. According to Roe, Blake felt that Dante, in his role as the character in the Divine Comedy, never reached Eden but chose a mistaken, materialist conception of Paradise (see no.148). Throughout the series of watercolours Dante is clothed in red and Virgil in blue. Roe associates these with Blake's own characters Luvah and Los, two of the four Zoas, who in Blake's writing represent the four basic 'humours' of Man; Luvah and Los stand for feeling and imagination, the two qualities necessary for the creative artist. As Raine has pointed out, Swedenborg associated red with love and blue with wisdom. For Blake the imagination was the chief means of salvation in a world founded on materialism, hence its association with Virgil who guides Dante through an Inferno that, according to Roe, Blake seems to equate with this world (see no. 132).

Anthony Blunt, in his review of 1954, made a few criticisms of detailed points in Roe's analysis but accepted his main thesis. However, David Fuller, in his article in *Art History* in 1988, is far more critical, accusing Roe of imposing on Blake a semi-private symbolism that in fact can be traced more to the systemization of Northrop Frye in his book of 1947 than to Blake himself. While Fuller accepts that there is some element of criticism in Blake's illustrations of Dante, he confines this to certain specific aspects, in particular Blake's attack on Dante for seeing Christianity as a continuation of much of the thought and ethics of Antiquity and for his acceptance of a god with a system of punishments rather than as the incarnation of selfless love. Much of Roe's detailed analysis is swept aside with the majority of the illustrations being seen as straightforward illustrations to the text. In particular Fuller attacks Roe's interpretation of one of the key watercolours in his theory of Blake's thorough-going criticism of Dante, 'Beatrice Addressing Dante from the Car' (no. 148). Further examples of the differences between Fuller and Roe are given in the individual entries below.

The drawings seem to have been executed in a large volume in which each whole sheet of paper, now divided in two, was watermarked 'W ELGAR 1796' and with a fleur-de-lys incorporating the initials 'WE'. Most if not all the drawings are inscribed on the back to give a system of cross references though the actual purpose of this is unclear. The notes like 'N...' or 'No 1 next at p 4' for example (no. 132) have been shown by Miss Mary Laing to embody a consistent system of cross-references to the page numbers such as the '3' written on the same watercolour, the sense being that this item, though on page 3, is number 1, with number 2 following on page 4. Similarly the inscriptions '14' and 'N 13 next at p 78' (no. 133) imply that this is number 13 drawn on page 14, and that number 14 is to be found on page 78. Howver, so far it has not been possible to find any logic in either series of numbers. These inscriptions are all written with the paper held upright. A similar inscription is found on one of the drawings Blake did to illustrate the *Book of Enoch* (Butlin no.827 *3*, pl.1081); and one of the Dante watercolours seems to have an Enoch subject on the back (Butlin no.812 *11* verso, pl.1052). Presumably Blake was working on both series of illustrations at the same time.

The order of the illustrations first given with some omissions by Rossetti, finally established in the National Art-Collections Fund portfolio of 1922, and used in Roe's monograph has been retained here, despite the fact that some drawings appear to be misplaced while others cannot be firmly tied to a particular passage in Dante's text; see for instance no. 150.

LITERATURE
'William Blake', Obituary in *The Literary Gazette* 18 August 1827, p.541; Gilchrist 1863, I, p.342; A.H. Palmer *The Life and Letters of Samuel Palmer* 1892, pp.9–10; Keynes *Bibliography* 1921, pp.182–5; Binyon 1922, pp.25–8; Damon 1924, pp.218–20; Albert S. Roe *Blake's Illustrations to the Divine Comedy* 1953; Anthony Blunt, review of Roe 1953 in *Burlington Magazine*, XCVI, 1954, p.389; Keynes *Writings* 1957, pp.785, 869, 873, 876–7, 879; Blunt 1959, pp.87–91; Burke 1964, pp.121–4; Keynes *Letters* 1968, pp.152, 156, 160–2, 164; Raine 1968, I, p.423 n.14; Beer 1969, pp.274–81; Bentley *Blake Records* 1969, pp.290, 313, 315–16, 333, 338–9, 349–50, 403–9, 414–15, 417, 475, 527, 543, 589–90, 604; Keynes *Blake Studies* 1971, pp.212, 224–8; Todd 1971, p.146; Bindman 1977, pp.216–19; Paley 1978, pp.71–3; Milton Klonsky *Blake's Dante* 1980; Bindman 1982, pp.178–85; Corrado Gizzi, ed., *Blake e Dante*, 1983; David Fuller 'Blake and Dante' in *Art History*, XI, 1988, pp.349–73; M. Butlin and T. Lott, *William Blake in the Collection of the National Gallery of Victoria*, 1989

131 **Dante and Virgil Penetrating the Forest** 1824–7

N 03351 / B 812 2
Pencil, pen and watercolour 371 × 527
($14\frac{9}{16} \times 20\frac{3}{4}$)
Inscribed 'HELL Canto 2 line 140' b.r. in
pencil, ?not by Blake, and, on reverse in
pencil, '92' t.r., 'N37 next at p 71' t.c. and
'Hell Canto 22' along right-hand edge as seen
with the paper turned through a right-angle
Watermarked 'WE'
Purchased with the assistance of a special
grant from the National Gallery and
donations from the National Art-Collections
Fund, Lord Duveen and others, and presented
through the National Art-Collections Fund
1919

PROVENANCE
John Linnell; his heirs, sold Christie's
15 March 1918 (in 148, the entire Dante
series) £7,665 bt Martin for the donors

EXHIBITED
Tate Gallery (41 i), Manchester (48 i),
Nottingham (42 vi) and Edinburgh (56)
1913–14, as 'Tu duca, tu signore, e tu maestro'

LITERATURE
Rossetti 1863, p.216 no.101b, and 1880, p.227
no.123b; Roe 1953, pp.50–1 no.2, repr.;
Klonsky 1980, p.137, pl.2; Butlin 1981, p.556
no.812 2; Gizzi 1983, p.80 repr. *Also repr.:*
Savoy, no.3, July 1896, p.43

This is an illustration to *Inferno* II, 139–42. Dante, in the midst of his mortal life, has
found himself lost in a great forest and pursued by three beasts. He encounters
Virgil who offers to lead Dante to safety, telling him that this entails a journey
through Hell and Purgatory to Paradise. In this design, the second of the series,
Virgil leads Dante on through the forest. The title under which the drawing has
sometimes been known is a line from the appropriate text, 'Tu duca, tu signore, e tu
maestro'. Blake shows the trees as oaks, perhaps to represent Druidical error.

131

132

132   **The Inscription over the Gate** 1824–7

N 03352 / B 812 *4*
Chalk, pencil, pen and watercolour 527 × 374
(20¾ × 14¾)
Signed 'WB' b.l. and inscribed 'HELL Canto 3'
b.r. in ink and 'Lasciate ogni speranza voi che
inentrate [?–the last word is obscure] Leave
every hope you who in enter' in pencil,
reinforced and ?over an erased inscription, at
top, and, on reverse in pencil, 'No 1 next at
p 4' t.c. and '3' t.r.
Watermarked 'WE'
Purchased with the assistance of a special
grant from the National Gallery and
donations from the National Art-Collections
Fund, Lord Duveen and others, and presented
through the National Art-Collections Fund
1919

PROVENANCE
As for no.131

EXHIBITED
RA 1893 (1); Tate (41 ii), Manchester (48 ii),
Nottingham (42 vii) and Edinburgh (59)

1913–14; Paris (repr.) and Vienna 1937 (18);
Paris, Antwerp (pl.16), Zurich and Tate
(repr.) 1947 (29 i); *National Art-Collections
Fund: Sixty Years of Patronage* Arts Council,
September–October 1965 (34); Tate Gallery
1978 (319, repr.); Pescara 1983 (1, repr. in
colour)

LITERATURE
Rossetti 1863, p.216 no.101d, and 1880, p.227
no.123d: Roe 1953, pp.53–4 no.4, repr.:
Blunt 1959, p.90, pl.58a; Bindman 1977,
pp.216–17, pl.176; Klonsky 1980, p.138,
colour pl.4; Butlin 1981, pp.556–7 no.812 4;
Gizzi 1983, p.82 repr., and in colour p.53;
Warner 1984, p.112; Fuller in *Art History*
1988, p.372 n.17

This is an illustration to *Inferno* III, 1–21. Virgil leads Dante over the threshold of
Hell. The inscription over the gate as written by Blake does not correspond exactly
with Dante's text, which reads 'Lasciate ogni speranza voi ch'entrate'; it was
presumably quoted from memory. The literal translation is Blake's own.

Roe suggests that Blake here equates Dante's Hell with the created world as
opposed to the world of the spirit. One sees the four continents together with the
submerged Atlantis. Fuller disputes this equation with the created world, pointing
out that in his later work Blake accepted material creation as a divine mercy and
also that the inscription over Hell-Gate would hardly be appropriate for this world.

133 Homer and the Ancient Poets 1824–7

N 03353 / B 812 8
Pencil, pen and watercolour 371 × 528
($14\frac{9}{16} × 20\frac{3}{4}$)
Inscribed 'HELL Canto 4' in ink over pencil
b.r. and, on reverse in pencil, 'N 13 next at
p 78' t.c. and '14' t.r., both turned through a
right-angle, and 'N 13 next at p 78' in centre
Watermarked 'WE'
Purchased with the assistance of a special
grant from the National Gallery and
donations from the National Art-Collections
Fund, Lord Duveen and others, and presented
through the National Art-Collections Fund
1919

PROVENANCE
As for no.131

EXHIBITED
Tate Gallery (41 iii), Manchester (48 iii),
Nottingham (42 viii) and Edinburgh (60)
1913–14; Tate Gallery 1947 (60)

LITERATURE
Rossetti 1863, p.227 no.101i, and 1880, p.228
no.123i; Roe 1953, pp.60–1 no.8, repr.; Blunt
1959, pp.89–90; Klonsky 1977, p.116, repr.;
Klonsky 1980, pp.138–9, colour pl.8; Gizzi
1983, p.86 repr.; Fuller in *Art History* 1988,
pp.360, 372 n.17

An illustration to *Inferno* IV, 8–12, 29–30 and 64–94, a scene in the first of the nine
circles of Hell, Limbo. Blake combines the incident of Virgil and Dante looking
down into the abyss thick with cloud with that of their first seeing the ancient poets
by the light of the fire.

Dante lists only four poets, Homer, Horace, Ovid and Lucan. Roe suggests that
Blake added the fifth figure to equate the poets with the five senses, holding them to
be embodiments of rational as opposed to divine inspiration. Blake's opinion of the
ancient poets is given in the inscription on the drawing preceding this one in the
series, in which Homer is the central figure: 'round Purgatory is Paradise & round
Paradise is Vacuum or Limbo, so that Homer is the Center of All [;] I mean the
Poetry of the Heathen Stolen & Perverted from the Bible not by Chance but by
design by the Kings of Persia & their Generals The Greek Heroes & lastly by the
Romans' (Fogg Museum; Butlin 1981, no.812 7, repr. Roe 1953, Klonsky 1980 and
Gizzi 1983, all as pl.7). Blake saw the Greek and Roman poets as 'Slaves of the
Sword', their art being subservient to war-like governments (preface to *Milton*

133

c. 1800–10, c.f. also *On Homer's Poetry* and *On Virgil*, c. 1820; Keynes *Writings* 1957, pp. 480, 778). Blake shows the poets in a Grove, a symbol of error which prevents them from seeing the flying Daughters of Imagination. Blake regards the pastoral figures making music in the Arcadian scene to the right in a more favourable light than he does the poets.

Fuller accepts that here Blake is attacking Dante's view that, although the classical poets are in Hell because they lacked the Christian faith, they are to be admired for their ethics and philosophy. He points out that, contrary to Roe's suggestion, the figures floating in the sky are derived from Dante's original text.

134 **Cerberus** 1824–7

N 03354 / B 812 *12*
Pencil, pen, and watercolour 372 × 528
($14\frac{5}{8} \times 20\frac{3}{4}$)
Inscribed 'HELL Canto 6' in ink b.l. and, on reverse, '29' t.r., turned through a right-angle
Watermarked 'WE'
Purchased with the assistance of a special grant from the National Gallery and donations from the National Art-Collections

Fund, Lord Duveen and others, and presented through the National Art-Collections Fund 1919

PROVENANCE
As for no. 131

EXHIBITED
?RA 1893 (5); Tate Gallery 1947 (61); Pescara 1983 (3, repr. in colour)

LITERATURE
Rossetti 1863, p.217 no.101l, and 1880, p.228 no.123l; Roe 1953, pp.66–7 no.12, repr.; Klonsky 1980, pp.139–40, colour pl.12; Butlin 1981, pp.559–60 no.812 *12*; Gizzi 1983, p.90 repr., and in colour p.55

This is an illustration to *Inferno* VI, 13–24. The three-headed monster Cerberus is shown guarding the entrance to the third circle of hell. There is a second version of this subject in the National Gallery of Victoria, Melbourne (Butlin, 1981 no.812 *13*, repr. Roe 1953, Klonsky 1980 and Gizzi 1983, all as pl.13). Roe suggests that the Melbourne version was done before that in the Tate and was abandoned because it failed to show Cerberus in a sufficiently formidable manner; the sketch formerly in the collection of Hugo Schwab (Butlin no.818 verso, pl.1068) is closer to the Melbourne version. However, the Melbourne version seems to illustrate a slightly later moment in the narrative, the pacification of the beast through being fed handfuls of earth by Virgil (*Inferno* VI, 22–33); in the Tate watercolour Virgil is shown as being less directly involved, just about to feed the first of Cerberus's three heads.

In both watercolours Blake shows Cerberus in a cave which is not in Dante's text, probably to suggest the weight of the material world.

The work exhibited at the Royal Academy in 1893 was entitled 'Cerberus – the Circle of the Gluttons'. This could be either of the two versions of 'Cerberus' already mentioned or 'The Circle of the Gluttons, with Cerberus' now in the Fogg Art Museum (Butlin no.812 *11*, repr. Roe 1953, Klonsky 1980 and Gizzi 1983, all as pl.11).

134

135

135 **Plutus** 1824–7

N 03355/B 812 *14*
Pencil, pen and watercolour 527 × 371
$(20\frac{3}{4} \times 14\frac{5}{8})$
Inscribed 'Money' in pencil on sack b.l. and,
on reverse in pencil, with page upside down,
'93' t.l.
Watermarked 'WE'
Purchased with the assistance of a special
grant from the National Gallery and
donations from the National Art-Collections
Fund, Lord Duveen and others, and presented

through the National Art-Collections Fund
1919

PROVENANCE
As for no. 131

EXHIBITED
Tate Gallery 1942 (62); *National Art-Collections
Fund: Sixty Years of Patronage*, Arts Council,
September–October 1965 (35)

LITERATURE
Rossetti 1863, p.217 no.101n, and 1880, p.228
no.123n; Roe 1953, pp.68–9 no.14, repr.;
Klonsky 1980, p.140, pl.14: Butlin 1981,
p.560 no.812 *14*; Gizzi 1983, p.92 repr.; Fuller
in *Art History* 1988, p.365

This is an illustration to *Inferno* VI, 113–15, and VII, 1–12. Plutus, the God of Wealth, guards the edge of the fourth Circle, that of the Avaricious, clutching his money-sack. Dante blurred the distinction between Plutus and Pluto, the God of the Underworld.

As Klonsky points out, Blake had attacked money in one of the inscriptions on his engraving of 'The Laocoön' of *c.*1820 (repr. Bindman *Graphic Works* 1978, pl.623, and Essick *Separate Plates* 1983, pl.51): 'Where any view of Money exists Art cannot be carried on, but War only'.

136 The Wood of the Self-Murderers: The Harpies and the Suicides 1824–7

N 03356/B 812 *24*
Pen and watercolour 372 × 527 ($14\frac{5}{8}$ × $20\frac{3}{4}$)
Inscribed 'HELL Canto 13' in ink b.r. and, on reverse in pencil, 'N21 next at p.86' t.c. and again in centre, turned through a right-angle, and 'Hell Canto 13' b.r.
Watermarked 'WELGAR 1796'
Purchased with the assistance of a special grant from the National Gallery and donations from the National Art-Collections Fund, Lord Duveen and others, and presented through the National Art-Collections Fund 1919

PROVENANCE
As for no.131

EXHIBITED
Pescara 1983 (5, repr.in colour)

LITERATURE
Rossetti 1863, p.217 no.101w, and 1880, p.229 no.123w; Roe 1953, pp.79–80 no.24, repr.; Klonsky 1977, p.115, repr.; Klonsky 1980, p.143, colour pl.25; Butlin 1981, pp.563–4 no.812 *24*; Gizzi 1983, p.103 repr., and repr. in colour p.57; Warner 1984, p.112

This is an illustration to *Inferno* XIII, 2–108, a scene in the second ring of the seventh circle of hell. Dante and Virgil are in a wood full of harpies, birds with human heads which feed upon the leaves of trees in which are encased people who have committed suicide. Dante has just torn a branch off the tree in which is embedded Pier delle Vigne, a minister of the Emperor Frederick II who committed suicide after losing favour. The upside-down female figure transformed into a tree on the left may have been suggested by Dante's reference to 'La Meretrice', Envy, to whom Pier delle Vigne attributes his disgrace; it also represents the vegetative existence seen at its lowest.

136

137 **The Simoniac Pope** 1824–7

N 03357 / B 812 *35*
Pen and watercolour 527 × 368 (20¾ × 14½)
Inscribed 'WB HELL Canto 19' in ink b.l. and,
on reverse, '8' t.r.
Watermarked 'WELGAR 1796'
Purchased with the assistance of a special
grant from the National Gallery and
donations from the National Art-Collections
Fund, Lord Duveen and others, and presented
through the National-Art Collections Fund
1919

PROVENANCE
As for no.131

EXHIBITED
RA 1893 (10); Paris, Antwerp (pl.17), Zurich
and Tate Gallery (repr.) 1947 (29iv); *Masters
of British Painting*, New York, St Louis and San
Francisco 1956–7 (10, repr. in colour p.58);
Tate Gallery 1978 (325, repr.); Pescara 1983
(8, repr. in colour)

LITERATURE
Rossetti 1863, p.218 no.101g[1] and 1880, p.229
no.123g[1]; Roe 1953, pp.91–2 no.35, repr.;
Blunt 1959, p.90, pl.58b; Burke 1964, p.124,
pl.106 (reprinted in Essick 1973, p.290,
pl.99); Klonsky 1977, p.112, repr. in colour;
Klonsky 1980, p.145, colour pl.36; Butlin
1981, p.567 no.812 *35*; Gizzi 1983, p.114
no.36 repr., also repr. in colour p.60; Fuller in
Art History 1988, p.365. *Also repr.: Mizue*,
no.882, 1978, p.44 in colour

This is an illustration to *Inferno* XIX, 31–126, showing the punishment of the
Simoniacs in the third trench of the eighth circle. Virgil clasps Dante to carry him
away from the wrath of Pope Nicolas III, whose punishment for simony was to be
suspended head downwards in a well of fire until replaced by another Pope guilty of
the same sin. Pope Nicolas has mistaken Dante for Boniface VIII whom he has
foreseen as his successor, but Boniface did not die until 1303, three years after the
date established by Dante for *The Divine Comedy*, hence Nicolas's anger; Nicolas is
also angry with Dante for upbraiding him for his wickedness.

Blake depicts the scene in a cave rather than on the open floor of the trench,
emphasizing that it is a place of spiritual darkness. Dante's placing of the Pope in an
upside down position to symbolise the subordination of spiritual to material values
would have been readily acceptable to Blake. Burke suggests that the form the
Pope's figure takes may derive from an engraving of an Egyptian acrobat (Burke
1964, pl.107; 1973, pl.100).

137

138

138   The Devils with Dante and Virgil by the Side of the Pool 1824–7

N 03358 / B 812 *40*
Pencil, pen and watercolour 372 × 527
(14⅝ × 20¾)
Inscribed 'HELL Canto 22' in ink b.r. and, on
reverse in pencil, '81' t.l. turned through a
right-angle
Watermarked 'WE'
Purchased with the assistance of a special
grant from the National Gallery and
donations from the National Art-Collections
Fund, Lord Duveen and others, and presented
through the National Art-Collections Fund
1919

PROVENANCE
As for no. 131

EXHIBITED
Tate Gallery (41 ix), Manchester (48 ix),
Nottingham (42 xiv) and Edinburgh (63)
1913–14; Paris and Vienna 1937 (20)

LITERATURE
Rosseti 1863, p.219 no.101m[1], and 1880,
p.230 no.123m[1]; Roe 1953, pp.94–5 no.40,
repr.; Hagstrum 1964, pp.125–6, pl.70;
Klonsky 1980, p.147, pl.42; Butlin 1981,
pp.568–9 no.812 *40*; Gizzi 1983, p.120 repr.

This is an illustration to *Inferno* XXII, 1–30, a general impression of the trench of
corrupt politicians in the eighth circle, that of the fraudulent. On the right sellers of
public office are seen in a sea of boiling pitch. Virgil and Dante, with an escort of
devils, are shown on the left. The arched forms are the stone bridges that
characterise this part of Dante's Hell.

139(recto)

139 **The Hypocrites with Caiaphas** 1824–7 (recto)

Sketch of a Stooping Figure 1824–7 (verso)

N 03559/B 812 *44*
Recto: pencil, pen and watercolour; Verso:
pencil, approx. 140 × 55 ($5\frac{1}{2}$ × $2\frac{1}{4}$); on paper
373 × 527 ($14\frac{5}{8}$ × $20\frac{3}{4}$)
Inscribed 'HELL Canto 23' in ink b.r. and, on
reverse in pencil, '71' t.l., 'N38 next at p 72'
t.c. turned through a right-angle and again in
centre upside down, and 'Hell Canto 23 v 40'
upside down b.r.
Watermarked 'WELGAR 1796'
Purchased with the assistance of a special
grant from the National Gallery and
donations from the National Art-Collections
Fund, Lord Duveen and others, and presented
through the National Art-Collections Fund
1919

PROVENANCE
As for no. 131

EXHIBITED
Tate Gallery (41 x), Manchester (48 x),
Nottingham (42 xv) and Edinburgh (66)
1913–14; *John Flaxman*, Hamburg Kunsthalle
(207, recto repr.), Thorwaldsens Museum,
Copenhagen (no catalogue) and RA (198,
recto repr.) April–December 1979

LITERATURE
Rossetti 1863, p.219 no.101q[1], and 1880,
p.230 no.123q[1]; Blunt in *Warburg Journal*, VI,
1943, p.211, recto pl.62b; Roe 1953,
pp.98–100 no.44, recto repr.; Blunt 1959,
pp.40, 90, recto pl.61a; Klonsky 1977, p.117,
recto repr.; Klonsky 1980, pp.147–8, recto
repr. pl.46; Butlin 1981, pp.569–70 no.812 *44*;
Gizzi 1983, p.124 recto repr.; Fuller in *Art
History* 1988, p.358

The recto is an illustration to *Inferno* XXIII, 58–120. Virgil and Dante have just
escaped from the escort of demons shown in no.138 and who are shown flying off

above. Dante and Virgil are now in the sixth trench of the eighth circle, where the hypocrites, clad in leaden cloaks, file endlessly past Caiaphas who is staked to the ground in the shape of a cross. Caiaphas was the high priest who counselled that Christ should be put to death on the grounds that it was expedient that one man should die for the people rather than that the whole nation should perish. Each hypocrite steps on Caiaphas as they pass. For Blake Caiaphas embodied Natural, that is negative, religion; see *Jerusalem, c.*1804–18, plate 77 (Keynes *Writings* 1957, p.718).

The sketch on the reverse (at the bottom with the page held vertically) appears to show a figure similar to that in 'Death's Door', plate 15 of *Four Children: The Gates of Paradise*, 1793, reissued *c.*1818 (repr. Keynes *Writings* 1957, p.769). The motif was presumably taken up again by Blake for the pose of the stooping hypocrites, though there is no suggestion in this sketch of their hooded cloaks.

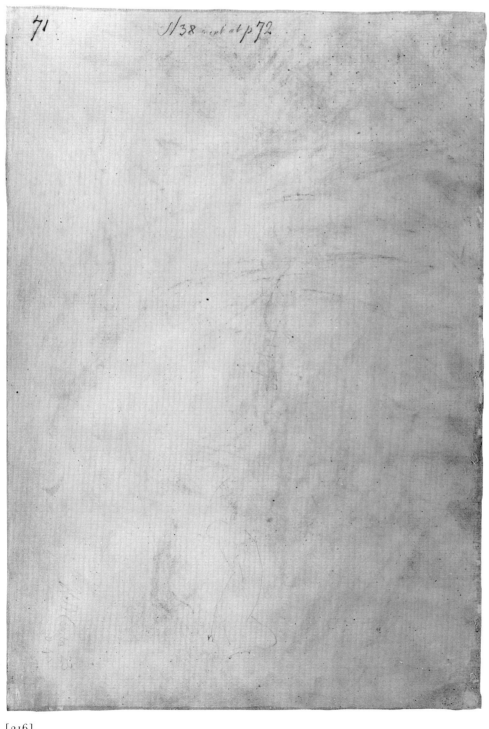

139(verso)

140

140   **The Laborious Passage along the Rocks** 1824–7

N 03360 / B 812 *46*
Pencil, pen and watercolour 373 × 527
($14\frac{11}{16}$ × $20\frac{3}{4}$)
Inscribed 'HELL Canto 24' in ink b.c. and
'Canto 24 v 30 [?]' in pencil b.r. and, on
reverse in pencil, 'N40 next at p 75' t.c., 'Hell
Canto 24 v 60' b.l. and '69' t.l., all turned
through a right-angle
Watermarked 'WELGAR 1796'
Purchased with the assistance of a special
grant from the National Gallery and
donations from the National Art-Collections
Fund, Lord Duveen and others, and presented
through the National Art-Collections Fund
1919

PROVENANCE
As for no. 131

EXHIBITED
Hamburg and Frankfurt 1975 (210, repr.)

LITERATURE
Rossetti 1863, p. 219 no. 101r[1] or s[1], and 1880,
p. 230 no. 123r[1] or s[1]; Roe 1953, pp. 100–1
no. 46, repr.; Klonsky 1980, p. 148, colour
pl. 48; Butlin 1981, p. 570 no. 812 *46*; Gizzi
1983, p. 126 repr.

This is an illustration to *Inferno* XXIV, 19–36: Virgil, having led Dante past a
shattered bridge, helps Dante up the series of massive boulders that separate the pit
of the hypocrites from the seventh pit in the eighth circle, that devoted to the
thieves. There is a second, upright treatment of this subject in the British Museum
(Butlin 1981, no. 812 *45*, repr. Roe 1953, pl. 45, Klonsky 1980, pl. 47 and Gizzi 1983,
p. 125). This may illustrate the slightly later passage, lines 37–63, where the cliff
becomes still steeper.

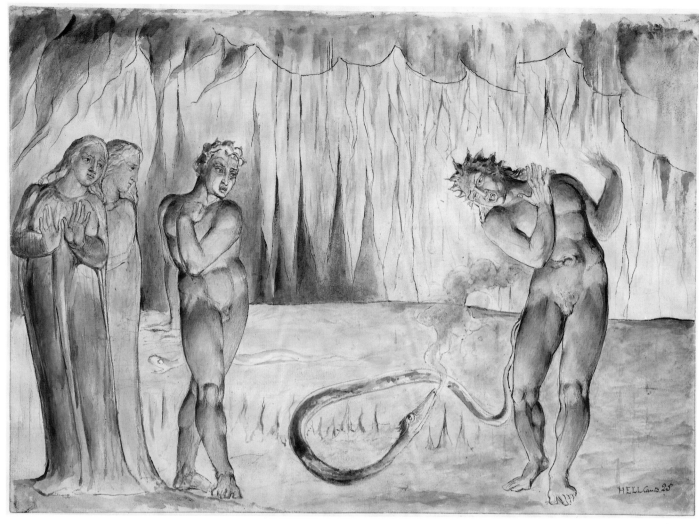

141 (recto)

141 **The Serpent Attacking Buoso Donati** 1824–7 (recto)

Sketch of a Man with a Transparent Hood (?) over his Head 1824–7 (verso)

N 03361 / B *812 *53*
Recto: pen and watercolour; verso: pencil, approx. 55 × 25 (2⅛ × 1); on paper 372 × 527 (14¹¹⁄₁₆ × 20¾)
Inscribed 'HELL Canto 25' in ink b.r. and, on reverse in pencil, '72' t.l., 'N39 next at p.69' t.c. turned through a right-angle and again in centre, and 'HELL Canto 23' b.r.
Watermarked 'WE'
Purchased with the assistance of a special grant from the National Gallery and donations from the National Art-Collections Fund, Lord Duveen and others, and presented through the National Art-Collections Fund 1919

PROVENANCE
As for no. 131

EXHIBITED
RA 1893 (14); Tate Gallery (41 xi), Manchester (48 xi), Nottingham (42 xvi) and Edinburgh (65) 1913–14; Paris and Vienna 1937 (22); Tate Gallery 1947 (58)

LITERATURE
Rossetti 1863, p.219 no.101z[1], and 1880, p.231 no.123z[1]; Roe 1953, pp.109–10 no.53, recto repr.; Klonsky 1980, p.149, recto repr. pl.56, verso p.21; Butlin 1981, p.572 no.812 *53*, verso pl.105b; Gizzi 1983, p.134 recto repr., and repr. in colour p.63; Fuller in *Art History* 1988, pp.369–70. *Also repr.: Mizue,* no.882, 1978, 9, p.36, recto only in colour

141 (verso)

This is an illustration to *Inferno* XXV, 79–93, a scene in the seventh trench, that of the thieves, of the eighth circle. Francesco de' Cavalcanti, in the guise of a serpent, bites Buoso Donati with the result that Buoso turns into a serpent while Cavalcanti reverts to his human form; Puccio Sciancato looks on. The completion of the process of transformation shown in this watercolour is shown in the next work in this series, 'Buoso Donati Transformed into a Serpent; Francesco de' Cavalcanti Retransformed from a Serpent into a Man', now in the Fogg Art Museum (Butlin 1981, no.812 *54*, repr. Roe 1953, pl.54, Klonsky 1980, pl.57 and Gizzi 1983, p.135).

This is one of the designs engraved by Blake (repr. Roe 1953, pl.53 E, Bindman 1978, pl.651 and Klonsky 1980, pl.107); see also no.156.

The small but clearly defined drawing on the back (lower right with the page held horizontally) shows the head and shoulders of a man in profile, his head in some kind of transparent hood or bubble, possibly in the process of being transformed into a serpent though no exact parallels can be found among the Dante drawings. There is no similarity to the hooded hypocrites of Canto XXIII as might be supposed from the reference to that Canto on the verso (see no.139).

142

142   **The Pit of Disease: the Falsifiers** 1824–7

N 03362 / B 812 *58*
Pen and watercolour 372 × 527 (14⅝ × 20¾)
Signed 'WB' and inscribed 'HELL Canto 29 &
30' in ink b.r. and, on reverse in pencil, 'For
this see P 62' t.c. and '28' t.r., both turned
through a right-angle
Watermarked 'WE'
Purchased with the assistance of a special
grant from the National Gallery and
donations from the National Art-Collections
Fund, Lord Duveen and others, and presented
through the National Art-Collections Fund
1919

PROVENANCE
As for no. 131

EXHIBITED
RA 1893 (16); Paris and Vienna 1937 (23)

LITERATURE
Rossetti 1863, p.220 no.101e[2], and 1880,
p.231 no.123e[2]; Roe 1953, pp.115–17 no.58,
repr.; Klonsky 1980, p.150, colour pl.61;
Butlin 1981, p.574 no.812 *58*; Gizzi 1983,
p.139 repr.

This is an illustration to *Inferno* XXIX, 46–84, and XXX, 49–99, a scene in the tenth
trench of the eighth circle, that devoted to the falsifiers who are punished with
innumerable diseases. The two figures scratching themselves are Griffolino of
Arezzo and Capocchio of Florence. The three figures on the left may be Adam of
Brescia, described by Dante as being lute-shaped (see especially the engraving),
with Potiphar's wife and Sinon the Greek, who persuaded the Trojans to admit the
Trojan Horse.

This is one of the subjects engraved by Blake (repr. Roe 1953, pl.58 E, Bindman
1978, pl.652 and Klonsky 1980, pl.108); see also no.157.

143

The bridge of petrified figures is similar to those that appear in 'The Devils under the Bridge' and 'Dante Striking against Bocca degli Abati' (National Gallery of Victoria and City Museum and Art Gallery, Birmingham respectively; Butlin 1981, nos. 812 *34* and *65*, repr. Roe 1953, pls. 34 and 64, Klonsky 1980, pls. 39 and 68 and Gizzi 1983, pp. 117 and 146). They seem to represent Fallen Man at his furthest remove from Divine Energy and are a suitable setting for these scenes of physical suffering.

143   **The Primaeval Giants Sunk in the Soil** 1824–7

N 03363 / B 812 *60*
Pencil, black chalk, pen and watercolour
372×527 ($14\frac{5}{8} \times 20\frac{3}{4}$)
Inscribed 'HELL Canto 31' in ink over pencil
b.r. and, on reverse in pencil, 'N 52 next at
p 25' centre, 'Hell Canto 29' b.l. and '27' t.r.,
the last turned through a right-angle

Watermarked 'WELGAR 1796'
Purchased with the assistance of a special
grant from the National Gallery and
donations from the National Art-Collections
Fund, Lord Duveen and others, and presented
through the National Art-Collections Fund,
1919

PROVENANCE
As for no.131

EXHIBITED
RA 1893 (17); Tate Gallery (41 xii),
Manchester (48 xii), Nottingham (42 xviii)
and Edinburgh (68) 1913–14; Paris, Antwerp,
Zurich and Tate Gallery 1947 (29 iii)

LITERATURE
Rossetti 1863, p.220 no.101g², and 1880,
p.232 no.123g²; Damon 1924, p.219; Roe
1953, pp.112–20 no.60, repr.; Klonsky 1977,
p.120, repr.; Klonsky 1980, pp.17, 151, pl.63;
Butlin 1981, pp.574–5 no.812 60; Gizzi 1983,
p.141 repr.

This is an illustration to *Inferno* XXXI, 19–45: Dante and Virgil, leaving the last trench of the eighth circle, come across the primaeval giants set waist deep in the bank. For Blake they symbolise the five senses bogged down in materialism. Blake devoted three futher designs to the giants, 'The Complaint of the Giant Nimrod' in the Fogg Art Museum, and 'Ephialtes and Two other Titans' and 'Antaeus Setting Down Dante and Virgil in the Last Circle of Hell', both in the National Gallery of Victoria (Butlin 1981, nos.812 *61*, *62* and *63*; all repr. Roe 1953 pls. 61, 62 and 63, Klonsky 1980, pls. 64, 65 and 66, and Gizzi 1983, pp.142, 143 and 144, the last two also in colour pp.65–66); Dante does not name the other two giants.

144   **Virgil Girding Dante's Brow with a Rush** 1824–7

N 03365/B 812 *70*
Pencil and watercolour 527 × 371 (20¾ × 14⅝)
Inscribed 'P–g Canto I' in ink b.l. and, on
reverse in pencil, '61' t.l. and 'Pg Canto 2'
b.r., the last turned through a right-angle
Watermarked 'WELGAR 1796'
Purchased with the assistance of a special
grant from the National Gallery and
donations from the National Art-Collections
Fund, Lord Duveen and others, and presented
through the National Art-Collections Fund,
1919

PROVENANCE
As for no.131

EXHIBITED
Tate Gallery (41 xv), Manchester (48 xv),
Nottingham (42 i) and Ediburgh (51)
1913–14

LITERATURE
Rossetti 1863, p.221 no.102a, and 1880, p.232
no.124a; Roe 1953, pp.137–8 no.70, repr.;
Klonsky 1980, p.154, colour pl.73; Butlin
1981, p.578 no.812 *70*; Gizzi 1983, p.151 repr.

This is an illustration to *Purgatorio* I, 130–6. It was formerly catalogued as 'Dante and Virgil again Beholding the Sun as they Issue from Hell' but in fact the events shown in this watercolour occur after the poets' meeting with Cato, the subject of 'Dante, Virgil and Cato', now in the Fogg Art Museum (Butlin 1981, no.812 *71*, repr. Roe 1953, pl.71, Klonsky 1981, pl.74 and Gizzi 1983, p.152). In the Tate watercolour Cato has told Virgil to bathe Dante's face and to gird his brow with one of the rushes growing by the shore, during which time the sun will have risen enough to show them their route up the Mountain of Purgatory.

For Blake the rising sun may well have symbolised the Poetic Imagination, plyaing its part as the link between Fallen Man, in Hell, and Paradise, or as Blake would term it, Eden.

144

145 The Ascent of the Mountain of Purgatory 1824–7

N 03366/B 812 *74*
Pencil, pen and watercolour 528 × 372
(20¾ × 14⅝)
Inscribed 'P-g-Canto 4' in ink b.c. and, on
reverse in pencil, 'Pg Canto 8' turned through
a right-angle b.r.
Watermarked 'WELGAR 1796'
Purchased with the assistance of a special
grant from the National Gallery and
donations from the National Art-Collections
Fund, Lord Duveen and others, and presented
through the National Art-Collections Fund
1919

PROVENANCE
As for no.131

EXHIBITED
RA 1893 (19); Tate Gallery (41 xvi),
Manchester (48 xvi), Nottingham (42 ii) and
Edinburgh (52) 1913–14; *English Painting*
Paris 1938 (164); Tate Gallery 1947 (59)

LITERATURE
Rossetti 1863, p.221 no.102e, and 1880, p.233
no.124e; Roe 1953, pp.142–3 no.74, repr.;
Bindman 1977, p.218; Klonsky 1980, p.154,
colour pl.76; Butlin 1981, p.579 no.812 *74*;
Gizzi 1983, p.154 repr. *Also repr: Savoy*, no.4,
August 1896, p.35

This is an illustration to *Purgatorio* IV, 31–45, like the previous work an event before
the poets have arrived at Purgatory itself; Dante calls to Virgil in his weariness on
the long climb up the Mountain of Purgatory. The sun is partly covered by cloud,
as in all the scenes in Purgatory, and was originally drawn emerging over the
horizon. The version of 'The Laborious Passage along the Rocks' in the British
Museum may have originally been designed as an illustration to this scene in a
horizontal format (Butlin 1981, no.812 *45*, repr. Roe 1953, pl.45, Klonsky 1980,
pl.47 and Gizzi 1983, p.125).

The graceful, echoing poses of Dante and Virgil recall those of the two brothers
plucking grapes in the illustrations to Milton's *Comus* of *c.*1801 and *c.*1815 (Butlin
nos.527 *3* and 528 *3*, colour pls.618 and 626).

146 Dante and Virgil Approaching the Angel who Guards the Entrance of Purgatory 1824–7

N 03367/B 812 *78*
Pencil, pen and watercolour 527 × 373
(20¾ × 14¹¹⁄₁₆)
Inscribed 'P-g-Canto 9' in ink b.l. and 'Pg
Canto 9 v [?]…[?] 'b.r., and, on reverse in
pencil, 'Pg Canto 9' b.r. and '35' t.r. turned
through a right-angle
Watermarked 'WE'
Purchased with the assistance of a special
grant from the National Gallery and
donations from the National Art-Collections
Fund, Lord Duveen and others, and presented
through the National Art-Collections Fund
1919

PROVENANCE
As for no.131

EXHIBITED
Tate Gallery 1947 (65)

LITERATURE
Rossetti 1863, p.221 no.102i, and 1880, p.233
no.124i; Roe 1953, pp.148–50 no.78, repr.;
Paley 1978, p.73; Klonsky 1980, pp.17,
155–6, colour pl.81; Butlin 1981, pp.580–1
no.812 *78*; Gizzi 1983, p.159 repr; Warner
1984, p.120; Fuller in *Art History* 1988, p.372
n.17

This is an illustration to *Purgatorio* IX, 73–105. Still ascending the Mountain of
Purgatory, Dante and Virgil approach the angel who guards the gate to Purgatory
itself; the three steps, in white polished marble, a dark rough stone and a flaming
porphyry, represent sincerity, contrition and love.

Roe suggests that the resemblance of the angel to Urizen, who represents for

Blake the materialism of pure reason, and the increased clouding over of the sun reflect Blake's disapproval of Dante's conception of Purgatory and Paradise. Fuller, however, disputes the identification with Urizen, citing this as a typical example of Roe's overinterpretation and pointing out that the symbolic use of the veiled sun derives from Dante's own imagery.

146

147

147 **The Rock Sculptured with the Recovery of the Ark and the Annunciation** 1824–7

N 03368/B 812 *80*
Pencil, pen and watercolour 528 × 374
$\left(20\frac{3}{4} \times 14\frac{11}{16}\right)$
Inscribed 'Pg Canto 10' in pencil b.r. and, on
reverse in pencil, 'Pg Canto 12' b.r. and '38'
t.r. turned through a right-angle.
Watermarked 'WE'
Purchased with the assistance of a special

grant from the National Gallery and
donations from the National Art-Collections
Fund, Lord Duveen and others, and presented
through the Natonal Art-Collection Fund
1919

PROVENANCE
As for no. 131

EXHIBITED
Paris and Vienna 1937 (24); Tate Gallery
1947 (64)

LITERATURE
Rossetti 1863, pp.221 no.102k, and 1880,
p.233 no.124k; Damon 1924, p.219; Frye

1947, p.368; Roe 1953, pp.150–2 no.80,
repr.; Paley 1978, p.73, pl.113; Paley in Essick
and Pearce 1978, pp.172–3; Klonsky 1980,
p.156, pl.83; Butlin 1981, p.581 no.812 *80*;
Gizzi 1983, p.161 repr.; Fuller in *Art History*
1988, pp.357, 362

This is an illustration to *Purgatorio* x, 17–69; the poets have reached the first terrace
on the Mountain of Purgatory and are shown looking at two of the three examples
of humility described by Dante as being carved along the ledge around the
Mountain. The scene of the return of the ark to Jerusalem combines two episodes,
the smiting of Uzzah and Michal's scorn for her husband David (II Samuel vi, 7
and 16).

Blake adds the two angels hovering over the ark; according to Roe they probably
represent the Daughters of Beulah while David represents the visionary imagination, Uzzah a narrow reliance on the law, and Michal the fallen Female Will.
Beulah is Blake's half-way house, equivalent to Purgatory. Roe suggests that Blake
probably picked these two particular scenes of the three to contrast two aspects of
female love, the Annunciation being placed, contrary to the text, on the right-
hand, divine, side. The third scene, omitted by Blake, showed Trajan and the poor
widow.

Fuller on the other hand denies that Blake goes beyond illustrating Dante's text
even though, in his more personal works, he found negative elements in the
Covering Cherub that guards the ark and appears in the Annunciation story.

148 **Beatrice Addressing Dante from the Car** 1824–7

N 03369/B *88*
Pen and watercolour 372 × 527 (14 $\frac{5}{8}$ × 20 $\frac{3}{4}$)
Inscribed 'P-g Canto 29 & 30' in ink b.r. and,
on reverse in pencil, 'Pg Canto 29' b.r. upside
down and '24' turned through a right-angle
Watermarked 'WELGAR 1796'
Purchased with the assistance of a special
grant from the National Gallery and
donations from the National Art-Collections
Fund, Lord Duveen and others, and presented
through the National Art-Collections Fund
1919.

PROVENANCE
As for no.131

EXHIBITED
RA 1893 (27); Paris and Vienna 1937 (27);
Paris, Antwerp, Zurich and Tate Gallery 1947
(29v, repr.); Hamburg and Frankfurt 1975

(215, colour pl.15); Tate Gallery 1978 (334,
repr.); Pescara 1983 (18, repr.in colour).

LITERATURE
Rossetti 1863, p.222 no.102s, and 1880, p.234
no.124s; Keynes *Faber Gallery* 1946, p.22,
colour pl.10; Roe 1953, pp.164–71 no.88,
repr.; Blunt 1959, p.91, pl.63; Roe in
Rosenfeld 1969, p.183, pl.20; Gage in *Warburg
Journal*, XXXIV, 1971, p.375 n.26e; Bindman
1977, pp.218–19, pl.179; Klonsky 1977,
p.111, repr.in colour; Paley 1978, p.73, colour
pl.112; Paley in Essick and Pearce 1978,
p.177; Klonsky 1980, pp.17, 158–9, colour
pl.91; Butlin 1981, p.584 no.812 *88*, colour
pl.973; Gizzi 1983, p.169 repr., and in colour
pp.70–1; Hilton 1983, pp.216, 228, pl.69;
Baine 1986, p.109, pl.47; Fuller in *Art History*
1988, pp.354–7, pl.42. *Also repr: Savoy*, no.5,
September 1896, p.29; *Mizue*, no.882, 1978, 9,
pp.34–5 in colour

This is an illustration to *Purgatorio* XIX, 92–129, XXX, 31–3 and 64–81, and XXXI,
113–14 and 130–45; the scene takes place in the Terrestial Paradise. For Dante the
gryphon and Beatrice symbolised Christ and the Church, and the three girls (in
white, green and red) Faith, Hope and Charity; the figures at the four corners of
the car are the four Evangelists. The previous illustration, now in the British
Museum (Butlin 1981, no.812 *87*, repr. Roe 1953, pl.87, Klonsky 1980, pl.90 in

148

colour, and Gizzi 1983, p.168) shows the poet's first view of Beatrice on the car (or chariot) seen across the river Lethe; Virgil has now left Dante at the borders of Purgatory itself and Dante is escorted by Matilda, probably the Grancomtessa of Tuscany (1046–1115), a great benefactor of the Holy See and Church.

This is one of the key works in Roe's interpretation of the series as in part a criticism of Dante. The divergences from Dante's text, such as the vortex that acts as the wheel of the car, the gold crown substitued for Beatrice's olive wreath, the book towards which Faith is pointing, the child-like forms surrounding Charity, and the fact that Dante is shown having now crossed the river Lethe, are taken to suggest that Blake is depicting the subjection of the Poetic Genius (Dante) to the Female Will (Beatrice); the latter is equated with Rahab, the fallen state of Vala, Blake's goddess of nature, the three attendant figures with the Daughters of Memory, and the Evangelists with the four Zoas. Dante is thus shown as choosing the wrong way out of Beulah, Blake's equivalent for Purgatory. Fuller however disputes this, suggesting that, despite Blake's inscription, the scene is actually that described in Canto XXXI of *Purgatorio* with elements taken from the previous two Cantos. In Canto XXXI Dante has crossed Lethe and Beatrice is shown at the moment when she draws aside her veil. The reason she wears a crown rather than a wreath is that Blake disliked Dante's association of Beatrice with Minerva; Dante describes Beatrice as wearing the 'fronde di Minerva' (XXX, 68). Charity is usually shown surrounded by children, as indeed in Blake's tempera painting of the subject (Butlin 1981, no.428, pl.494). The book at which Faith is pointing is the scriptures. Hope, though usually shown with an anchor, is twice mentioned by Dante as dancing. The reason for the colourful vortex that replaces the wheel of the car, Fuller suggests, is that Blake wanted to convey the intense light by which Dante is dazzled; in the text this comes from the candelabrum borne ahead of the car, and indeed its rays are suggested flooding across the composition from the right. The source for Blake's imagery is Ezekiel's vision (Ezekiel, I, 15–21) of great wheels full of eyes and turned by the spirits of living creatures. Ezekiel also provides the source of the animal heads shown each side of Beatrice which are merely hinted at by Dante; they are of course the traditional symbols of the Evangelists. Fuller suggests that Blake avoids the identification of Beatrice with the Church but sees her as Divine Wisdom. The great advantage of Fuller's interpretation is that, unlike Roe's, it does not run counter to the generally joyous effect of this glowing watercolour, which has always been a problem to at least some Blake scholars.

A newly discovered pencil sketch of a standing woman of the Huntington Library is related to the figure of Charity, in red and standing second from the left, and also, in the turn of the head and the piling up of the hair, to that of Faith, in white in the centre of the composition. This drawing was found on the back of a sketch for the engraving of another of the Dante compositions, 'The Six-footed Serpent Attacking Agnolo Brunelleschi' (Butlin no.822; for the new drawing see Jenijoy La Belle, 'A Pencil Sketch for Blake's Dante Illustrations', *Blake*, XIX, 1985–6, pp.73–4, repr.pl.1, and Essick *Huntington* 1985, pp.128–31).

149   **Dante in the Empyrean, Drinking at the River of Light** 1824–7

N 03370 / B 812 *98*
Pencil and watercolour 528 × 371 (20¾ × 14⅝)
Inscribed 'Par.Canto 30' in ink over 'Paradiso Canto 30' in pencil b.r. and, on reverse in pencil, 'N49 next at p16' t.c., '37' t.r. and 'Hell Canto 26' b.r., the last with the page turned through a right-angle
Watermarked 'WE'
Purchased with the assistance of a special grant from the National Gallery and donations from the National Art-Collections Fund, Lord Duveen and others, and presented through the National Art-Collections Fund 1919

PROVENANCE
As for no.131

EXHIBITED
Tate Gallery 1947 (63); *British Painting* Hamburg, Oslo, Stockholm and Copenhagen 1949–50 (3)

LITERATURE
Rossetti 1863, p.223 no.103i, and 1880, p.234 no.125i; Roe 1953, pp.189–93 no.98, repr.; Klonsky 1980, pp.161–2, pl.101; Butlin 1981, p.587 no.812 *98*; Gizzi 1983, p.179 repr.

This is the only illustration in the Tate Gallery to *Paradiso*: XXX, 61–96. This does in fact reflect the relative paucity of illustrations to Dante's third book, ten as opposed to twenty illustrations to *Purgatorio* and seventy-two to *Inferno*, though Blake might well have rectified this inbalance had he lived to complete the series. Dante, with Beatrice, has now left the heaven of space to enter the infinite heaven of light, love and joy, through which runs a stream of light in the form of a river. The poet kneels drinking on the left, while Beatrice is on the right.

The other figures do not appear in Dante's text. Those on the left, above Dante, symbolise the arts, represented by an aged poet (identified by Roe as the regenerate Urizen) together with a scene of painting and engraving. On the other side, according to Roe, is the realm of Nature, represented by Enion, Blake's 'Earth-Mother', while Beatrice is equated with Vala, the Female Will. The sparkles in the water are shown as tiny figures, 'infant joys'. The whole scene thus represents, according to Roe's interpretation, Art and Nature raised to the Eternal World through the agency of the River of Divine Imagination; even the figures normally condemned in Blake's mythology, Urizen, Enion and Vala, are here shown in their positive aspects.

149

150　**The Punishment of the Thieves**　1824–7

N 03364 / B 812 *102*
Black chalk, pen and watercolour 372 × 527
($14\frac{5}{8} \times 20\frac{3}{4}$)
Inscribed 'Hell' in pencil t.r. running
vertically and, on reverse in pencil, 'N20 next
at p79' t.c. and '80' t.l., turned through a
right-angle
Watermarked 'WE'
Purchased with the assistance of a special
grant from the National Gallery and
donations from the National Art-Collections
Fund, Lord Duveen and others, and presented
through the National Art-Collections Fund
1919

PROVENANCE
As for no. 131

EXHIBITED
Tate Gallery (42), Manchester (47),
Nottingham (41) and Edinburgh (70)
1913–14, all as 'Unidentified Subject of
Dantesque Character'; *English Painting* Paris
1938 (165); Paris (repr.), Antwerp, Zurich
(repr.) and Tate Gallery 1947 (29 vi)

LITERATURE
?Rossetti 1863, p.216 under no.101, and 1880,
p.227 under no.123; Collins Baker in
Huntington Library Quarterly, IV, 1940–1, p.365,
repr.p.361 (reprinted in Essick 1973,
pp.121–2, pl.44); Roe 1953, pp.101–4, 200–1
no.102, repr.; Klonsky 1977, p.119, repr.;
Klonsky 1980, pp.148–9, pl.50; Butlin 1981,
p.589 no.812 *102*; Gizzi 1983, p.128 repr.;
Fuller in *Art History* 1988, pp.369–70

This watercolour is almost certainly a general view of the pit of thieves, the seventh
pit of the eighth circle, as described in *Inferno* XXIV, 77–95, though no specific
incident is depicted; another watercolour from the series, in the National Gallery of
Victoria (Butlin 1981, no.812 *47* recto, repr. Roe 1953, pl.47, Klonsky 1980, pl.49
and Gizzi 1983, p.127) gives a similarly generalized impression. There are seven
further drawings from the two Cantos dealing with the thieves, who seem to have
had a particular interest for Blake.

　Roe, on the erroneous assumption that all the figures shown are female, suggests that the drawing is an allegory of Woman after the Fall with only a general reference to the *Inferno*: Woman, having accepted the help of the Serpent of Materialism to dominate Man, has here become its victim. Fuller sees a sexual suggestion in the serpents in Blake's designs showing the punishment of the thieves (see also no.141), and sees the rape by serpents as a negation of the victims' identities, which is of course the theme of these designs in which human beings turn into serpents and vice versa.

The figures in this watercolour are particularly Michelangelo-esque in the style and Collins Baker suggests that the figure of the standing woman leaning over in the centre is derived from an engraving after Michelangelo's 'Last Judgement' (a detail repr. 1940–1, p.361; 1973, pl.45).

151 (recto)

151 **Composition Sketch, Possibly a Subject from Dante** 1824–7(?) (recto)

A Man Standing over a Figure Reclining on a Bed *c.*1800–1810(?) (verso)

A 00047 / B 826
Pencil 454 × 339 ($17\frac{7}{8}$ × $13\frac{3}{8}$), the verso horizontal in format, on paper watermarked 'JWHATMAN'
Presented by Mrs John Richmond 1922

PROVENANCE
Mrs Blake; Frederick Tatham; his brother-in-

law George Richmond, sold Christie's 29 April 1897 (in 147 with 22 other items; see no.2) £2.10.0 bt Dr Richard Sisley; his daughter Mrs John Richmond

LITERATURE
Butlin 1981, p.594, no.826, pls.1077 and 1078

The recto, which appears to show two figures in a sailing boat with three further figures in the water, is similar in style to the drawing for 'The Vestibule of Hell and the Souls mustering to Cross the Acheron' in the British Museum (Butlin 1981, no.815, pl.1076). It may show another scene to do with the souls crossing the Acheron in Charon's bark or an incident on the Stygian Lake, *Inferno* Cantos VII and VIII, but it is not recognizably related to any of the finished watercolours.

The drawing on the verso appears to show a man threatening a figure lying on a bed. The sun appears in the top right-hand corner and there is a crescent moon low down on the left. The style suggests an earlier date than the recto, possibly *c.*1800–10.

Rossetti lists a drawing of a similar subject then in the possession of the dealer Francis Harvey, 'A Man approaching a recumbent Woman...Slovenly, with no point of merit save the freedom of action' (1863, p.253 list 2 no.152, and 1880, p.272 list 2 no.181). This is otherwise untraced (see Butlin no.858) but could be this drawing, though if so the provenance for the group of drawings in the Tate Gallery from the Richmond collection would have to be altered, with Harvey buying them at the Tatham sale on 29 April 1862 and George Richmond acquiring them either directly from him or later.

This work was formerly inventoried as no.3694 xx.

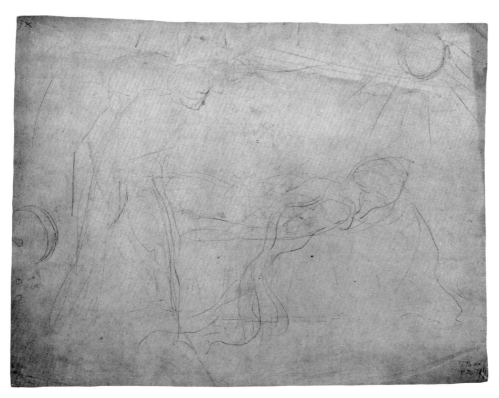

151 (verso)

152–8 Illustrations to Dante's *Divine Comedy*: Engravings 1826–7/1892

A 00005–11

Seven line engravings on india paper laid on
drawing paper, each approx. 240 × 335
(9½ × 13¼)
Purchased with the assistance of a special
grant from the National Gallery and
donations from the National Art-Collections
Fund, Lord Duveen and others, and presented
through the National Art-Collections Fund
1919

PROVENANCE

John Linnell; his heirs, sold Christie's 15
March 1918 (in 148, with the 102 watercolour
illustrations to Dante) £7,665 bt Martin for
the donors

LITERATURE

Russell *Engravings* 1912, pp.115–8 no.34;
Keynes *Bibliography* 1921, pp.182–5 no.56;
Keynes *Engravings* 1950, pp.16–17; Roe 1953,
pp.4–6, 41–2, 65, 96, 97, 108, 110, 116–7,
127–8, series repr. pls.10E, 41E, 42E, 51E, 53E,
58E and 65E; Keynes *Writings* 1957, pp.873,
876–7, 879; Ruthven Todd, *Blake's Dante
Plates*, 1968 (reprinted with additions from
Book Collecting & Library Monthly, VI, 1968,
pp.164–71, itself based on a letter to *The Times
Literary Supplement* 29 August 1968, p.928);
Bentley *Blake Records* 1969, pp.315–6; Bentley
Blake Books 1977, pp.544–6 no.448; Bindman
Graphic Works 1978, p.487 nos.647–53, series
repr. plus full-size details; Essick *Printmaker*
1981, pp.78–9, 250–4

This is the first of two sets in the Tate Gallery of prints taken from the original
plates. Altogether four printings have been done, two while the plates belonged to
the Linnell family and two while they belonged to Lessing J. Rosenwald. In a 'List
of John Linnell Senior's Letters and Papers' (in the Ivimy Collection) Linnell's son
John Linnell Jr wrote that, following a few proofs taken by Blake himself, his father
had 'had India proofs taken (all disposed of)'; the accounts and day books of
Dickson & Ross show that this was in 1838. John Linnell Jr goes on to say that after
his father's death fifty further copies, in 'india on drawing paper', were printed by
Holdgate; the draft of a letter from the same writer to Bernard Quaritch of 6 May
1892 (also in the Ivimy Collection) implies that this second printing was about to
be made. As all of the 1838 printing was 'disposed of' it was presumably one of the
later series that was acquired for the Tate Gallery in the Linnell sale of 1918. Of
what seem to be Blake's original proofs there is a complete set of one proof for each
composition in the British Museum and individual proofs elsewhere. The plates
have passed, with the Rosenwald Collection, to the National Gallery of Art,
Washington.

The subject of each engraving was identified on a label pasted to the cover of the
1838 issue that reads as follows:

> BLAKE'S ILLUSTRATIONS OF DANTE. | *Seven Plates, designed and
> engraved by* W. BLAKE, *Author of* 'Illustrations of | the Book of Job,' *&c. &c.* | Price
> £2. 2s. India Paper. | — | PLATE I. | ... and like a corse fell to the ground. |
> HELL; Canto v. line 137. | PLATE II. | .... seiz'd on his arm, | And mangled
> bore away the sinewy part. | HELL; Canto xxii. line 70. | PLATE III. | .... so
> turn'd | His talons on his comrade. | HELL; Canto xxii. line 135. | PLATE IV.
> | ... lo! a serpent with six feet | Springs forth on one, | HELL; Canto xxv. line
> 45. | PLATE V. | He ey'd the serpent and the serpent him. | HELL; Canto xxv.
> line 82. | PLATE VI. | ... Then two I mark'd, that sat Propp'd 'gainst each
> other, | HELL; Canto xxix, line 71. | PLATE VII. | 'Wherefore dost bruise
> me?' weeping he | exclaim'd. | HELL; Canto xxxii. line 79. | CARY'S DANTE.

The first record of Blake working on the engravings comes in a letter by him to
Linnell of 2 July 1826, in which he wrote that he was coming to stay with him in
Hampstead bringing, 'besides our necessary change of apparel, Only My Book of
Drawings from Dante & one Plate shut up in the Book'. On 25 April 1827 Blake
wrote to Linnell to say that 'I have Proved the Six Plates, & reduced the Fighting
devils for the Copper'. Blake's death on 12 August 1827 prevented any further work

on the engravings, and 'The Baffled Devils Fighting' is noticeably incomplete; Blake might, of course, have intended to work further on the other plates as well.

These engravings were formerly inventoried as nos. 3371 i–viii.

152

152 **The Circle of the Lustful: Francesca da Rimini ('The Whirlwind of Lovers')**

Inscribed 'The Whirlwind of Lovers from Dantes Inferno Canto V' in mirror-writing, b.r.
Engraving 243 × 335 ($9\frac{9}{16}$ × $13\frac{3}{16}$); platemark 276 × 353 ($10\frac{7}{8}$ × $13\frac{7}{8}$)

Inferno v, 25–45, 127–142. Dante swoons at Virgil's feet on seeing the ill-starred lovers Paolo and Francesca da Rimini. They also appear, reunited, above Virgil in a glory of light. The original watercolour is in the City Museum and Art Gallery, Birmingham (Butlin 1981, no.812 *10*, repr. Roe 1953, Klonsky 1980 and Gizzi 1983, all as pl. 10).

153 **Ciampolo the Barrator Tormented by the Devils**

Engraving 240 × 338 ($9\frac{7}{16}$ × $13\frac{5}{16}$); platemark 380 × 356 (11 × 14)

Inferno XXII, 31–42, 70–72. Ciampolo was a servant of King Thibaut II of Navarre. Blake illustrates the particular moment when the

devil Libicocco tears at his arm; the devil behind on the right is Ciriatto. The original watercolour is in the Fogg Art Museum, Harvard University (Butlin 1981, no.812 *41*, repr. Roe 1953, pl.41, Klonsky 1980, pl.43 and Gizzi 1983, pl.43).

153

154

154   **The Baffled Devils Fighting**

Engraving 242 × 334 (9$\frac{1}{2}$ × 13$\frac{3}{16}$); platemark
280 × 357 (11 × 14)

EXHIBITED
Tate Gallery 1978 (326, repr.)

Inferno XXII, 133–140. After Ciampolo's escape
the devils Alichino and Calabrina fall to
fighting each other while their companions
watch from the shore; Dante and Virgil retire
in the distance. The original watercolour is in
the City Museum and Art Gallery,
Birmingham (Butlin 1981, no.812 *42*,
repr.Roe 1953, pl.42, Klonsky 1980, pl.44 in
colour and Gizzi 1983, pl.44).

155

155 **The Six-footed Serpent Attacking Agnolo Brunelleschi**

Engraving 246 × 340 ($9\frac{11}{16}$ × $13\frac{3}{8}$); platemark 280 × 356 (11 × 14)

Inferno xxv, 49–78. Cianfa de' Donati, in the guise of a six-footed serpent, attacks Agnolo Brunelleschi and their two bodies merge into one; their fellow Florentines Puccio Scanciato and Buoso degli Abati or de' Donati stand on the right. The finished watercolur is in the National Gallery of Victoria, Melbourne (Butlin 1981, no.812 51, repr. Roe 1953, pl.51, Klonsky 1980, pl.54 and Gizzi 1983, p.62 in colour).

156

156   **The Serpent Attacking Buoso Donati**

Engraving 241 × 335 ($9\frac{1}{2}$ × $13\frac{3}{16}$); platemark
280 × 354 (11 × $13\frac{15}{16}$)

EXHIBITED
Tate Gallery 1978 (327, repr.)

Inferno XXV, 79–93. For the finished
watercolour in the Tate Gallery see no. 141.

157

157   **The Pit of Disease: The Falsifiers**

Engravings 243 × 340 ($9\frac{9}{16}$ × $13\frac{3}{8}$); platemark
276 × 353 ($10\frac{7}{8}$ × $13\frac{7}{8}$)

Inferno XXIX, 46–84 and XXX, 49–99. For the
finished watercolour in the Tate Gallery see
no. 142.

158 **Dante Striking Against Bocca degli Abati**

Engraving 236 × 340 ($9\frac{5}{16}$ × $13\frac{3}{8}$); platemark 277 × 353 ($10\frac{7}{8}$ × $13\frac{7}{8}$)

Inferno XXXII, 70–96. Dante stumbles against Bocca degli Abati, who betrayed the Guelfs at the battle of Montaperti, among the figures frozen in the Circle of Traitors. The finished watercolour is in the City Museum and Art Gallery, Birmingham (Butlin 1981, no.812 *65*, repr. Roe 1953, pl.65, Klonsky 1980, pl.68 in colour and Gizzi 1983, pl.68).

159–165   Illustrations to Dante's 'Divine Comedy': Restrikes 1826–7/1968

T 01950–6/–
Seven line-engravings on Japanese paper
383 × 459 ($15\frac{1}{16} \times 18\frac{1}{16}$)
Inscribed in pencil below each print, 'A
restrike from the copper plate in my collection.
August 1968 Lessing J. Rosenwald' b.r. within
platemark, and 2/25 hoehn imp 68' b.r.
outside platemark.
Presented by Lessing J. Rosenwald 1975

PROVENANCE
Commissioned by Lessing J. Rosenwald 1968

LITERATURE
As for nos. 152–8; Bentley *Blake Books* 1977,
p.545, no.448D

Nos. 159–165 are restrikes made in 1968 from Blake's original plates in the
Rosenwald collection, now in the National Gallery of Art, Washington. They were
printed by Harry Hoehn for Lessing J. Rosenwald at the suggestion of Ruthven
Todd. The edition was of twenty-five sets. In 1955 Mr Rosenwald had had
another, less successful set of restrikes pulled, also in an edition of twenty-five.

159   **The Circle of the Lustful; Francesca
da Rimini ('The Whirlwind of Lovers')**

Engraving, 243 × 335 ($9\frac{9}{16} \times 13\frac{3}{16}$);
platemark 276 × 353 ($10\frac{7}{8} \times 13\frac{7}{8}$)

Inscribed 'The Whirlwind of Lovers from
Dantes Inferno Canto V' in mirror-
writing, b.r.; see also above

Inferno V, 25–45, 127–142.

160   **Ciampolo the Barrator Tormented by
the Devils**

Engraving, 238 × 335 ($9\frac{3}{8} \times 13\frac{3}{16}$);
platemark 278 × 354 ($10\frac{15}{16} \times 13\frac{15}{16}$)

Inferno XXII, 31–42, 70–72.

161   **The Baffled Devils Fighting**

Engraving, 241 × 332 ($9\frac{1}{2} \times 13\frac{1}{16}$);
platemark 278 × 354 ($10\frac{15}{16} \times 13\frac{15}{16}$)

Inferno XXII, 133–140.

162   **The Six-footed Serpent Attacking
Agnolo Brunelleschi**

Engraving 245 × 337 ($9\frac{5}{8} \times 13\frac{1}{4}$); platemark
280 × 353 ($11 \times 13\frac{7}{8}$)

Inferno XXV, 49–78.

163   **The Serpent Attacking Buoso Donati**

Engraving 241 × 335 ($9\frac{1}{2} \times 13\frac{3}{16}$);
platemark 280 × 354 ($11 \times 13\frac{15}{16}$)

Inferno XXV, 79–93.

164   **The Pit of Disease: The Falsifiers**

Engraving 240 × 335 ($9\frac{7}{16} \times 13\frac{3}{16}$);
platemark 276 × 351 ($10\frac{7}{8} \times 13\frac{13}{16}$)

Inferno XXIX, 46–84 and XXX, 49–99.

165   **Dante Striking Against Bocca delgi
Abati**

Engraving 235 × 337 ($9\frac{1}{4} \times 13\frac{1}{4}$); platemark
275 × 353 ($10\frac{13}{16} \times 13\frac{7}{8}$)

Inferno XXXII, 70–96.

DRAWINGS ATTRIBUTED TO ROBERT BLAKE 1767–1787

Robert Blake, William's youngest and favourite brother, was admitted to the Royal Academy Schools at the age of fourteen on 2 April 1782, when he was said to have been born on 4 August 1767. A sketchbook in the Huntington Library, entitled on the cover 'Robert Blake's Book 1777' seems to show Robert learning to draw by copying figure drawings by his brother, or from bird and animal illustrations (see Butlin 1981, p.617, no.R1, pls.1126–77; the attribution of these drawings has however been contested). He died in 1787, being buried on 11 February. Blake held his memory in particular reverence, and even claimed that it was Robert who, posthumously, revealed to him in a vision his special process of relief etching.

Gilchrist saw a group of Robert's drawings that had passed from William to his widow, and then presumably to Frederick Tatham, the source of those catalogued below. He described them as 'naif and archaic-looking; rude, faltering, often puerile or absurd in drawing; but...characterized by Blake-like feeling and intention...True imaginative *animus* is often made manifest by very imperfect means.' Two of the works he mentions are the basis for further attributions, 'The Approach of Doom' in the British Museum and 'A Druid Ceremony' in the Geoffrey Keynes collection (Butlin nos.R2 and R3, pls.1181 and 1182). Some of Robert's drawings were done in a notebook later used by Blake and now generally known as the Rossetti Manuscript or Blake's Notebook (Butlin no.201, the complete book repr. David V. Erdman and Donald K. Moore, *The Notebook of William Blake, A Photographic and Typographic Facsimile*, 1973, second ed.1977).

LITERATURE
Gilchrist 1863, I, pp.57–8; Collins Baker and Wark 1957, pp.50–1; Bentley *Blake Records* 1969, pp.6–8, 20, 29–32; Keynes *Blake Studies* 1971, pp.1–9; Butlin 1981, pp.617–24; Essick *Huntington* 1985, 235–6

166(recto)

166(verso)

ROBERT BLAKE

166 **The Preaching of Warning** (recto)

Possibly by William Blake: **An Old Man Enthroned between Two Groups of Figures** (verso)

A 00003 / B R6
Pencil 342 × 466 ($13\frac{1}{2}$ × $18\frac{3}{8}$)
Inscribed on recto by Frederick Tatham
'These sublime lines by William Blake – The
preaching of warning – vouched by Fred^k
Tatham' b.r.
Presented by Mrs John Richmond 1922

PROVENANCE
Mrs Blake; Frederick Tatham; his brother-in-
law George Richmond, sold Christie's
29 April 1897 (in 147 with 22 other items; see
no. 2) £2.10.0 bt Dr Richard Sisley; his
daughter Mrs John Richmond

LITERATURE
Butlin 1981, p.622 no.R6, pls.1179 and 1180

Despite Tatham's attribution to William Blake, Sir Geoffrey Keynes suggested that the drawing might be by Robert in a letter of 23 October 1926. The recto is close in style and apparent subject to the 'Druid Grove' in the Keynes collection (Butlin 1981, no.R4, colour pl.176).

The drawing on the verso seems to depict a ruler enthroned with two seated counsellors on the left while four other figures converse in a huddle on the right. The style of the right-hand group of figures is much more relaxed than in most works thought to be by Robert, though those on the left are close to nos.168 and 169.

This work was formerly inventoried by the Tate Gallery as no.3694 x.

ROBERT BLAKE

167 **A Figure Bowing Before a Seated Old Man with his Arm Outstretched in Benediction** (recto)

Indecipherable Sketch (verso)

A 00001 / B R9
Recto: pen, wash, black chalk and pencil;
Verso: pencil; on paper 393 × 422 (15½ × 16⅝);
the paper has been cut irregularly at the left,
narrowing to 220 (8¾) and, before starting the
drawing, the artist added 90 (3½) at the right
Presented by Mrs John Richmond 1922

PROVENANCE
Mrs Blake; Frederick Tatham; his brother-in-
law George Richmond, sold Christie's 29 April
1897 (in 147 with 22 other items; see no.2)
£2.10.0. bt Dr Richard Sisley; his daughter
Mrs John Richmond

LITERATURE
Butlin 1981, p.623 no.R9, pls.1189 and 1190

The attribution to Robert Blake was made by Sir Geofrey Keynes in a letter of 23
October 1926. The fragment on the recto is close in style and general arrangement
to 'A Druid Ceremony' in the Keynes collection (Butlin 1981, no.R3, pl.1182).
The paper has been cut roughly to follow the back of the stooping figure on the left,
then diagonally up towards the upper edge; there was originally at least one
standing figure behind the stooping one.

This work was formerly inventoried by the Tate Gallery as no.3694 ii.

168

[245]

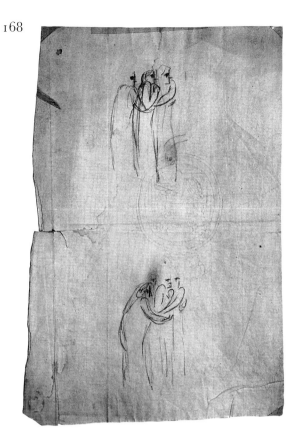

ROBERT BLAKE

168 **Two Groups of Frightened Figures, Probably for 'The Approach of Doom'**

A 00002 / B R7
Pencil, each approx. 95 × 55 ($3\frac{3}{4} \times 2\frac{1}{4}$), on
paper, cut irregularly, 311 × 212 ($12\frac{1}{4} \times 8\frac{5}{16}$);
the paper has been folded horizontally
between the two drawings
Presented by Mrs John Richmond 1922

PROVENANCE
Mrs Blake; Frederick Tatham; his brother-in-
law George Richmond, sold Christie's 29 April
1897 (in 147 with 22 other items; see no.2)
£2.10.0. bt Dr Richard Sisley; his daughter
Mrs John Richmond

LITERATURE
Butlin 1981, pp.622–3 no.R7, pl.1178

Two drawings of a group of three frightened figures. In the lower drawing the
position of the head of the left-hand figure has been altered or an additional head
added to enlarge the group to four.

A similar group, though more extended, appears in the more finished pen and
wash drawing known as 'The Approach of Doom' (Butlin 1981, no.R2, pl.1181).
The Tate's drawing is presumably the first stage in the evolution of the
composition.

This work was formerly inventoried by the Tate Gallery as no.3694 ix.

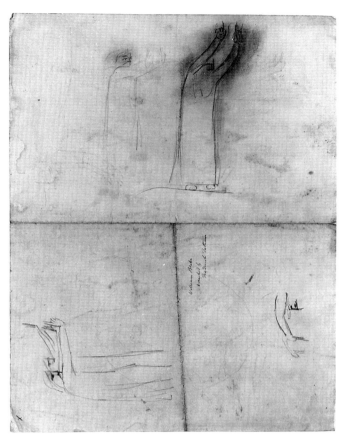

169(recto)

169(verso)

ROBERT BLAKE

169 **Six Drawings of Figures with Outstretched Arms** (recto and verso)

A 00004 / B R8
Pencil, each approx. 150 × 95 (6 × 3¾), on
paper 395 × 319 (15 9/16 × 12 9/16); the paper has
been folded twice, once in each direction
Watermarked 'PRO PATRIA' and 'GR'
Inscribed on recto by Frederick Tatham
'William Blake vouched by Frederick
Tatham' b.r.
Presented by Mrs John Richmond 1922

PROVENANCE
Mrs Blake; Frederick Tatham; his brother-in-
law George Richmond, sold Christie's 29 April
1897 (in 147 with 22 other items; see no. 2)
£2.10.0. bt Dr Richard Sisley; his daughter
Mrs John Richmond

LITERATURE
Butlin 1981, p.623 no. R8, pls. 1187 and 1188

Similar to no. 168 above. The upper half of the recto contains a single drawing of
two figures. At first both held their arms out before them but the artist subsequently
raised the arms of the right-hand figure to a more upright position.

The paper was then folded vertically as well as horizontally, dividing each side
into four sections. The two new sections on the recto and three of those on the verso
(excluding the lower right-hand section which is blank) were then filled with
separate drawings, all facing in different directions but showing similar figures,
singly or in pairs, full-length or head-and-shoulders only, raising or holding out
their arms. In each case the gesture is stressed by the figures' exaggeratedly long
index fingers.

This work was formerly inventoried by the Tate Gallery as no. 3694 xiv.

WORKS FORMERLY ATTRIBUTED TO WILLIAM BLAKE

ATTRIBUTED TO GEORGE RICHMOND (1809–1896)

170   **A Fettered Nude Figure Reclining by a Rock**   *c*.1825

A 00838
Pen and wash 235 × 343 ($9\frac{1}{4}$ × $13\frac{1}{2}$)
Inscribed by George Richmond, 'Drawn by
W. Blake, GR' b.r.
Presented by Mrs George Richmond 1922

PROVENANCE
George Richmond, sold Christie's 29 April
1897 (in 147, with 22 other items, see no.2)
£2.10.0 bt Dr. Richard Sisley; his daughter
Mrs John Richmond.

Despite the inscription in George Richmond's own hand this drawing is stylistically unlike anything known to be by Blake. The similarity of the figure in this drawing to that in Richmond's tempera painting of 1825, 'Abel the Shepherd' in the Tate Gallery (N 05858) suggests some confusion in Richmond's mind arising from the fact that, according to Mrs Gilchrist, Blake 'made a careful correction-drawing of the shepherd's arm in his pupil's [Richmond's] sketchbook' (H.H. Gilchrist, *Anne Gilchrist: Her Life and Writings*, 1887, p.261; Bentley *Blake Records* 1969, pp.293 n.1). A number of Richmond's early drawings bear inscriptions and dates that seem to have been added by him very much later; in some cases alternative dates are given, demonstrating that he was working from memory, and this would seem to have been so, mistakenly, in this case.

This work was formerly inventoried as no.3694 iii.

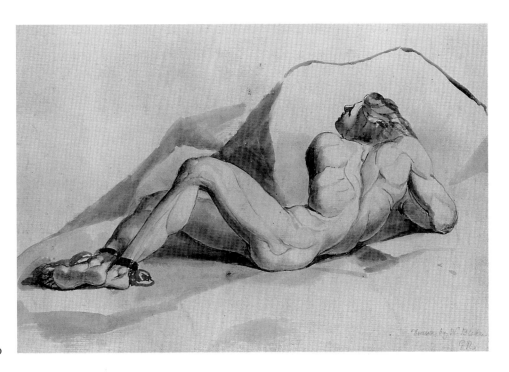

170

ATTRIBUTED TO GEORGE RICHMOND OR HIS CIRCLE

171 **Tracing of Title-Page to *Illustrations of the Book of Job***

171

A 00050
Pencil on tracing paper, stuck on card
193 × 146 (7⅝ × 5¼) on paper
214 × 157 (8⁷⁄₁₆ × 6³⁄₁₆)
Presented by Mrs George Richmond 1922

PROVENANCE
George Richmond, sold Christie's 29 April
1897 (in 147, with 22 other items, see no.2)
£2.10.0 bt Dr. Richard Sisley; his daughter
Mrs John Richmond.

This is a straightforward copy of the engraved title page to *Illustrations of the Book of Job*, no.109.

This work was formerly inventoried as no.3694 xvii.

THOMAS STOTHARD (1755–1834)

172 **Religion Teaching her Children**

N 05194
Pen and watercolour 255 × 355 (10 × 14)

Inscribed 'w.b.' b.r.
Bequeathed by Miss A.G.E. Carthew 1940

The so-called signature is not particularly close to any known form of Blake's own autograph, and for stylistic reasons the work can be attributed convincingly to Thomas Stothard.

172

APPENDIX

Paolo and Francesca

Archive 7714.5
Colour print, approx. 490 × 375 ($19\frac{1}{4} \times 14\frac{3}{4}$) on
wove paper, irregular 600 × 403 ($23\frac{5}{8} \times 15\frac{7}{8}$)
Purchased 1976

W. Graham Robertson, bequeathed to
Kerrison Preston, sold Sotheby's 10–12 March
1975, 1st day (in 125 with another) bt Abbott
and Holder, sold 1976 to the Tate Gallery and
transferred to the Archive 1977

EXHIBITED
*Paintings, drawings and colour prints of W. Graham
Robertson*, Carfax & Co., February 1906 (59);
Abbott and Holder September-October 1976
(unnumbered)

LITERATURE
Gilchrist 1907, pp.404–6

W. Graham Robertson (1866–1948) was a professional artist of independent
means. He was also actively involved in the theatre, his play *Pinkie and the Fairies*
being produced in 1908 by Beerbohm Tree with a cast including Ellen Terry; his
other writings included further plays, books of poems and stories for children and
other works, many illustrated by himself. A pupil of Albert Moore, he was a keen

collector of works by the Pre-Raphaelites, including Moore and also Rossetti and Burne-Jones, and above all of William Blake; works by all these artists were given or bequeathed by him to the Tate Gallery (for the works by Blake see nos.14, 25–34, 37, 38, 44, 47–9, 51, 52, 64 and 69). He is also the subject of the Tate Gallery's full-length portrait of 1894 by Sargent (N 05066). (For further information on W. Graham Robertson see his autobiographical *Time Was*, 1931, and Kerrison Preston, ed., *Letters from Graham Robertson*, 1953.)

This copy after a drawing by William Blake was exhibited by Graham Robertson in his one-man show of 1906 as one of a group of 'Colour Prints: Experiments in Search of the Lost Method of William Blake'. He was particularly interested in recreating the technique of Blake's colour prints, whether in his illuminated books, his 'Small' and 'Large' Books of Designs, or his large prints, of which ten examples from Graham Robertson's collection are now in the Tate Gallery (nos.25–34). Graham Robertson also discussed this technique in his 1907 edition of Alexander Gilchrist's *Life of William Blake*, in a supplementary chapter on 'The Colour Prints'. In this he describes the technique as he envisaged it and as he experimented in works such as this. After correcting Frederick Tatham's account by pointing out that Blake used a medium probably based on yolk of egg rather than oil paint he went on to say, 'The drawing being made upon thick millboard, the main lines were traced over in a paint thus mixed (usually a warm brown or Indian red), and an impression from this was stamped upon paper while the paint was still wet. Thus a delicate outline of the whole composition was obtained. Then, still with the same medium, the shadows and dark masses were filled in on the millboard and transferred to the paper, the result having much the appearance of an uncoloured page of one of the Prophetic Books. This impression was allowed to dry thoroughly. Then came the stamping of the local colours. For these later printings water-colour was probably used, though a very similar effect can be obtained by the use of diluted carpenter's glue and varnish, well mixed together, and of course applied when warm'. As has been set out on pp.82–3, this account is no longer fully accepted. In particular Blake seems to have used metal plates rather than millboard, and, at least in the large colour prints, he soon seems to have dispensed with making a separate printed outline before applying the areas of colour. The technique was, however, that used by Graham Robertson in his own experiments. In this case the outline seems to have been painted in brown, after which two different browns, a brick red, and a blueish grey were added in a second printing.

The composition of this work is based on a pencil drawing by Blake (Butlin 1981, no.816, pl.1060), thought to be for the figures of Paolo and Francesca in the watercolour of that subject from the series of illustrations to Dante's *Divine Comedy* (Butlin no.812 *10*), one of the compositions engraved by Blake and known as 'The Whirlwind of Lovers' (see nos.152 and 159). This drawing belonged to Graham Robertson and was also exhibited at Carfax & Co. in 1906 (62). Graham Robertson's print is, as a result of his process, in reverse to the original Blake drawing.

The following work was acquired after this catalogue went to press. It should be associated with the 'Visionary Heads', numbers 61–67 in this catalogue.

A Vision: The Inspiration of the Poet *c.*1819–20 (?)

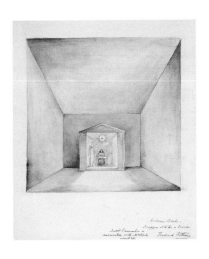

T 05716/B756
Watercolour over pencil 171 × 178 (6¾ × 7) on wove paper 244 × 210 (9 9/16 × 8¼)
Inscribed in ink by Frederick Tatham, 'William Blake./I suppose it to be a Vision/Frederick Tatham' and 'Indeed I remember a/conversation with Mʳˢ Blake/about it' b.r.
Watermarked 'RUSE & TURNERS'
Acquired through the generosity of Mr Edwin Cohen and The General Atlantic Partners Foundation 1989

PROVENANCE
Mrs Blake; Frederick Tatham; . . . ; Quaritch, offered *catalogue* November 1882 (in 346 with 44 others) £36 and *catalogue 350* 10 August 1883 (in 13843) £36, sold 30 June 1886 to W. Graham Robertson, sold Christie's 22 July 1949 (62) £115.10.0 Kerrison Preston; Sotheby's 21 March 1974 (17, repr.) £2,800 bt in A. Chambers for the executors of Kerrison Preston; his son David C. Preston by whom sold through Christie's to the Tate Gallery

EXHIBITED
Bournemouth, Southampton and Brighton 1949 (47); Port Sunlight 1950 (18); Hamburg and Frankfurt 1975 (66, repr.); Tate Gallery 1978 (286, repr.)

LITERATURE
Robertson in Gilchrist 1907, p.494 no.4; Preston 1952, pp.180–2 no.72, pl.58; Rosenblum 1967, pp.189–91, pl.212; Butlin 1981, pp.527–8 no.756, pl.984

The drawing shows a small pedimented shrine in a large bare room seen in steep perspective; an angel stands dictating to a seated figure writing, over whose head hangs a lamp looking much like the Holy Ghost in old master paintings of the Trinity. The title was suggested by W. Graham Robertson who once owned the drawing and who wrote on a label formerly on the back of the frame and now separately preserved, 'A Vision. Probably representing the Poet, in the/innermost shrine of the imagination,/writing from angelic dictation'.

Although different in character from the other Visionary Heads this drawing probably dates from about the same time. The paper is watermarked 'RUSE & TURNERS' vertically along the right hand edge of the sheet. In other cases when Blake used the same make of paper the watermark includes the dates 1810, 1812 and 1815 (see G. E. Bentley Jr, *Blake Books*, Oxford 1977, p.72). The second part of Tatham's inscription was clearly added as an afterthought; the original ink inscription has been slightly strengthened with pencil by a different hand at a later date.

R. H.